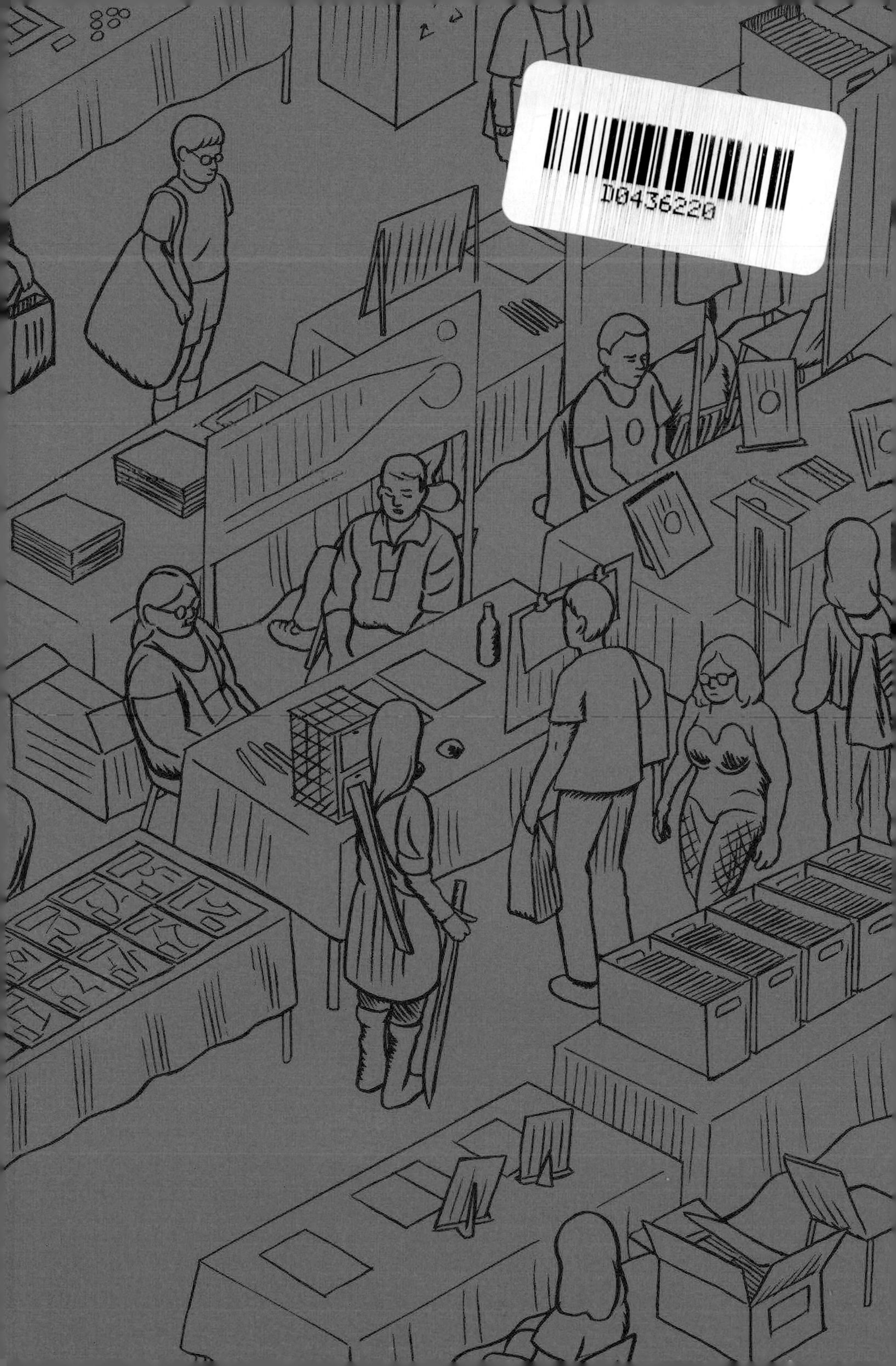

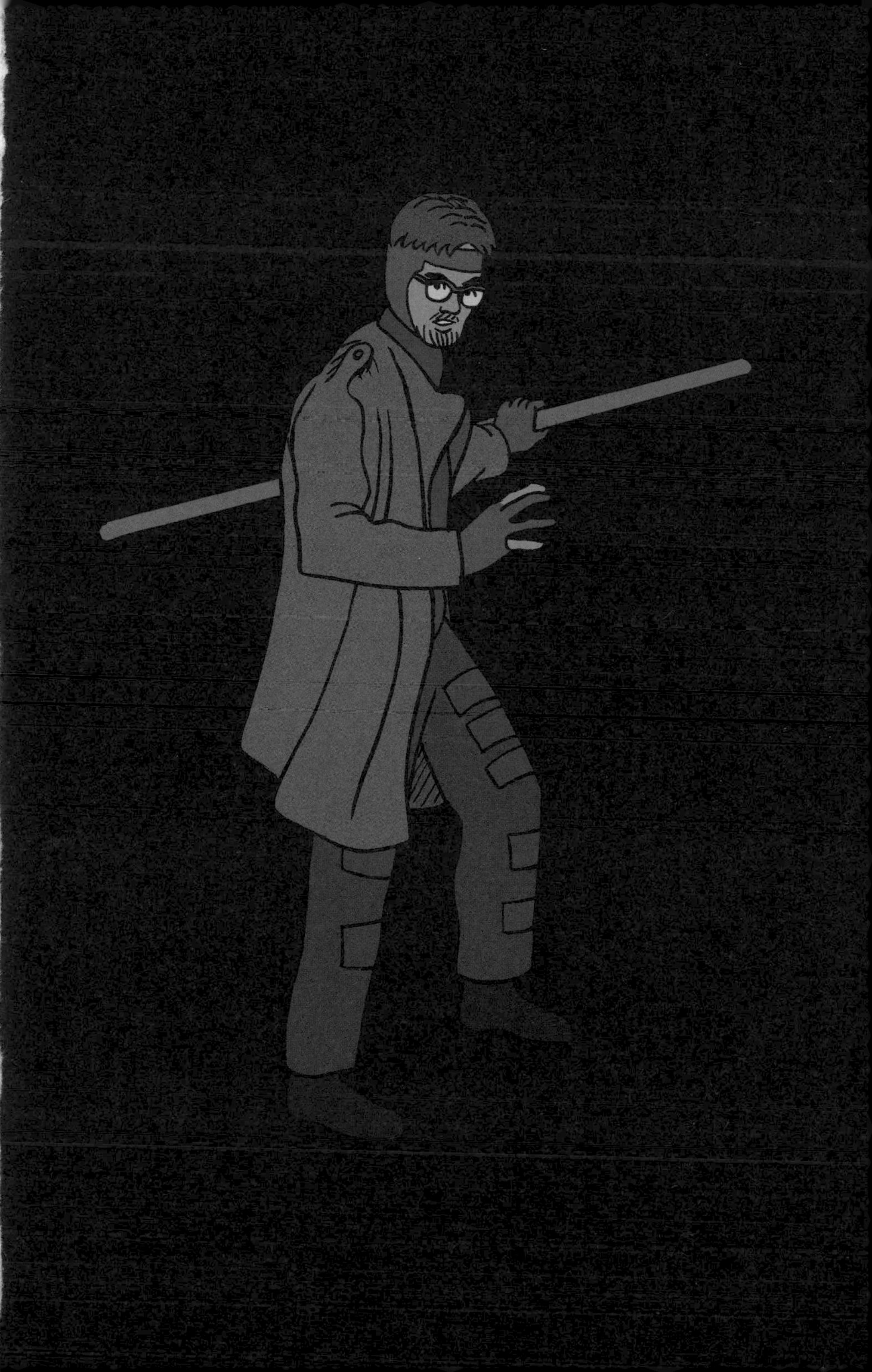

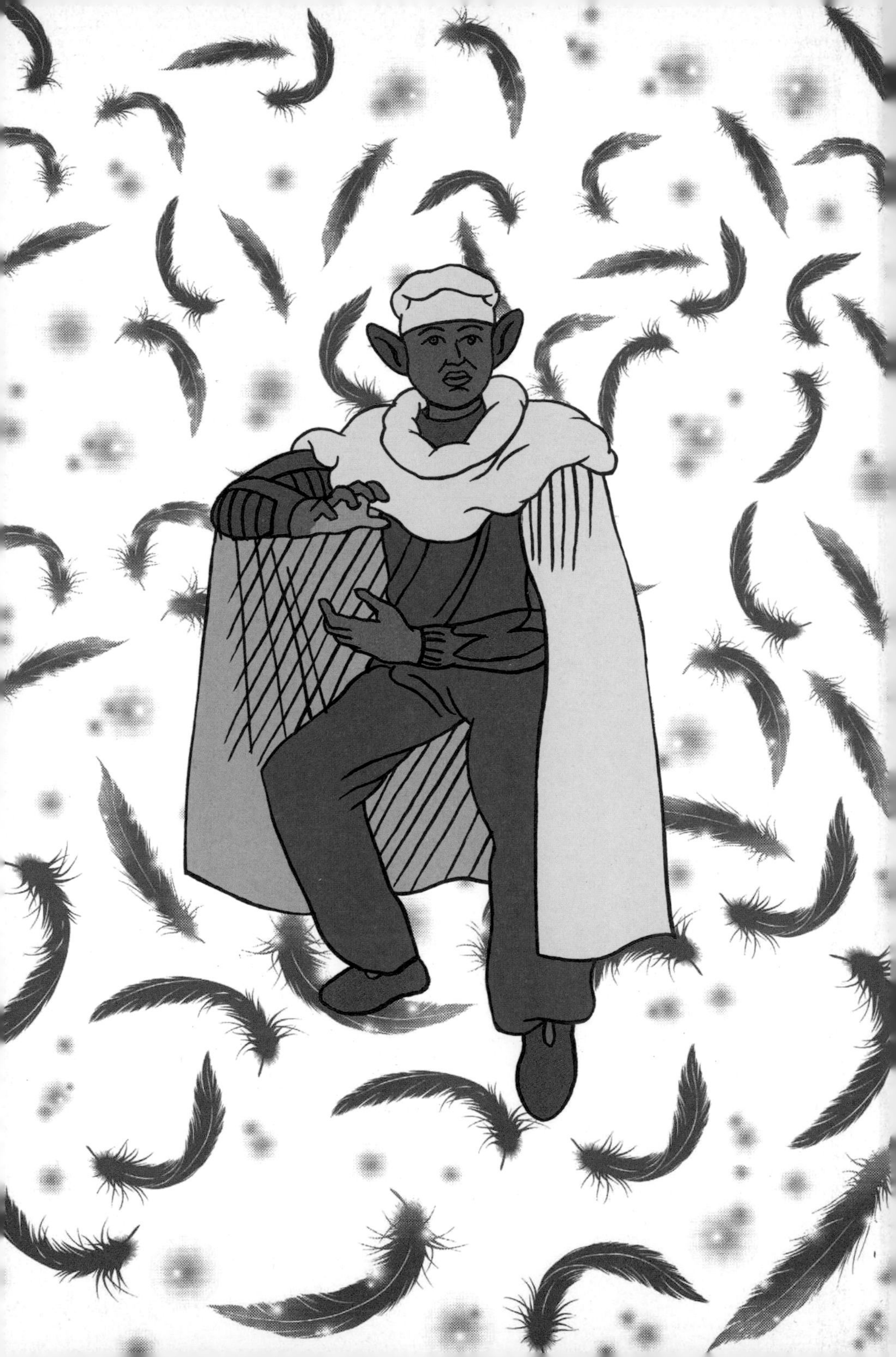

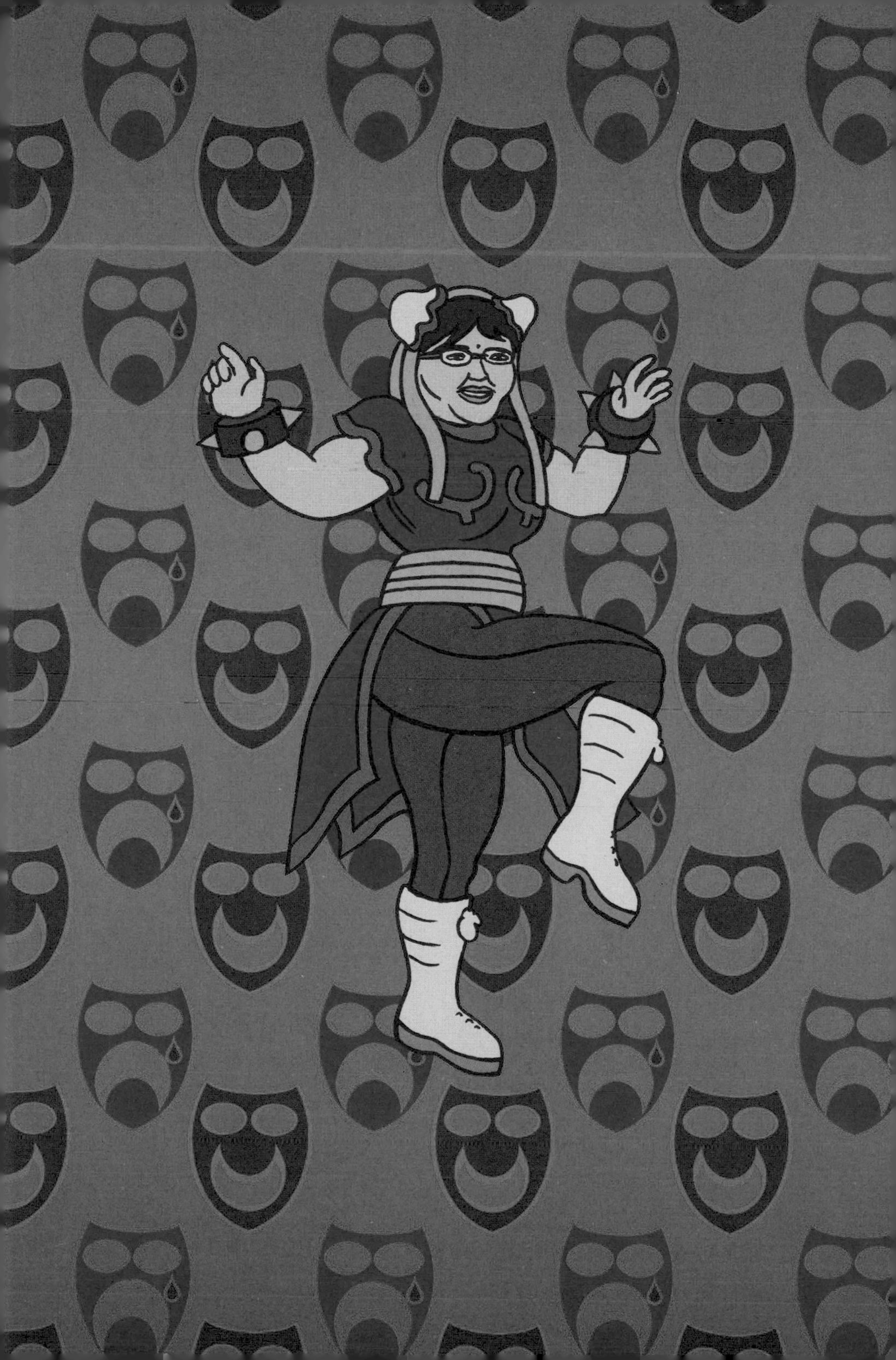

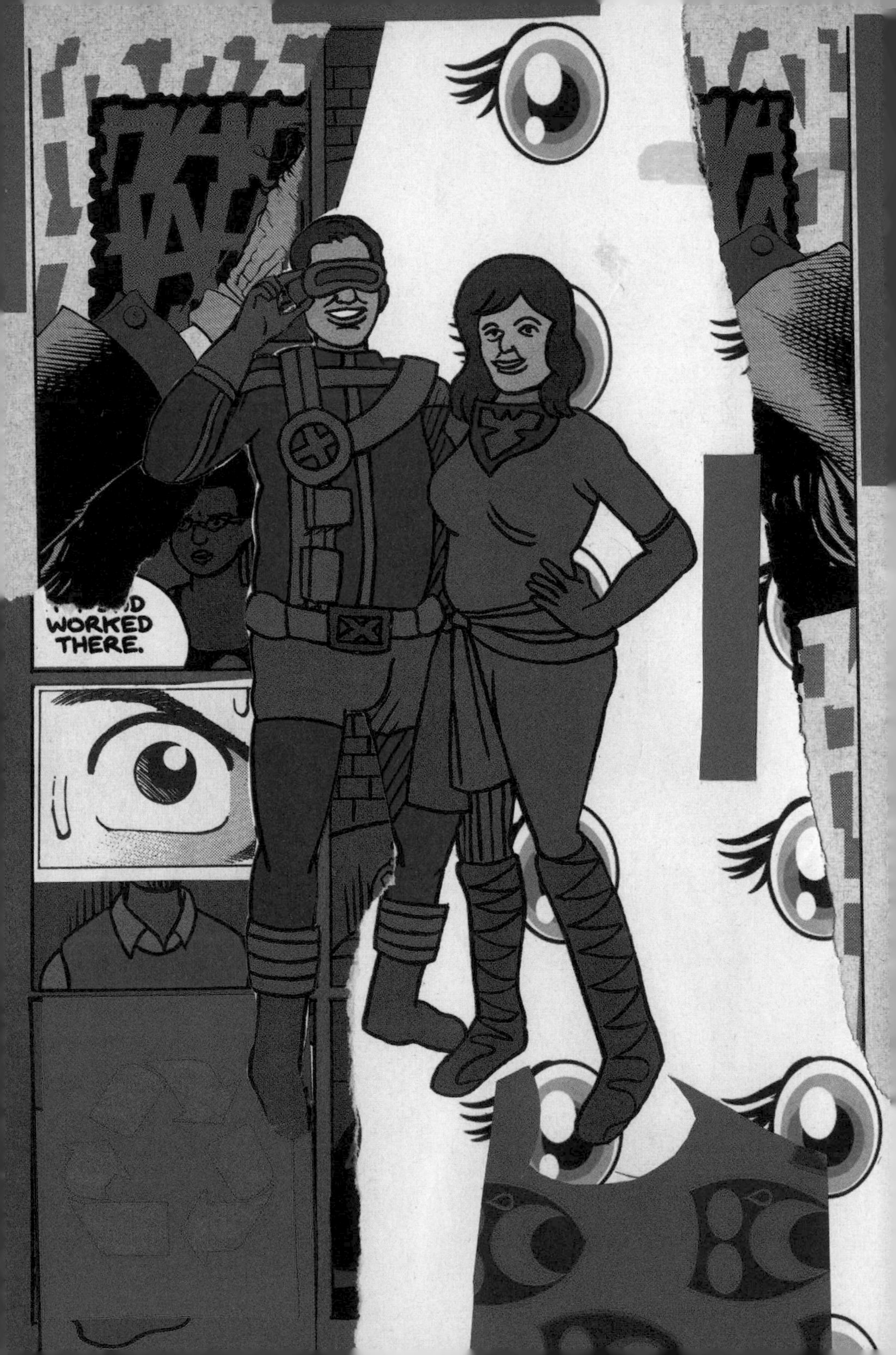
WORKED THERE.

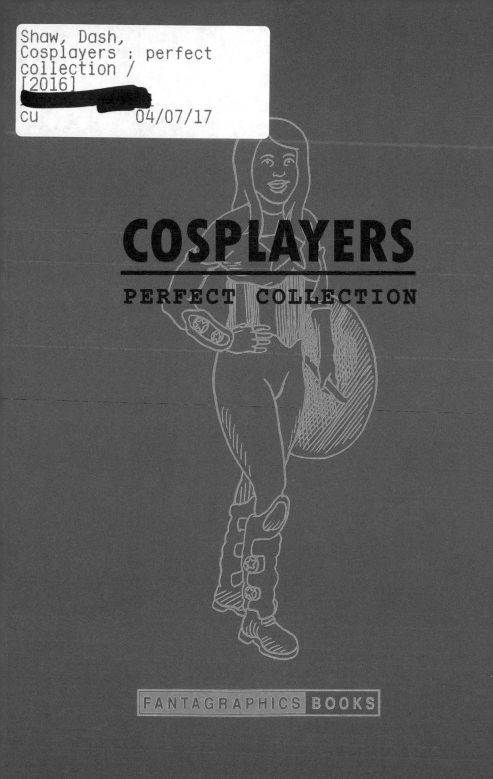

COSPLAYERS

PERFECT COLLECTION

FANTAGRAPHICS BOOKS

FANTAGRAPHICS BOOKS INC.
7563 Lake City Way NE
Seattle, Washington, 98115

Editor and associate publisher: Eric Reynolds
Book Design: Dash Shaw and Michael Heck
Production: Paul Baresh
Publisher: Gary Groth

ISBN 978-1-60699-948-6
Library of Congress Control Number: 2016934405

First printing: September 2016
Printed in China

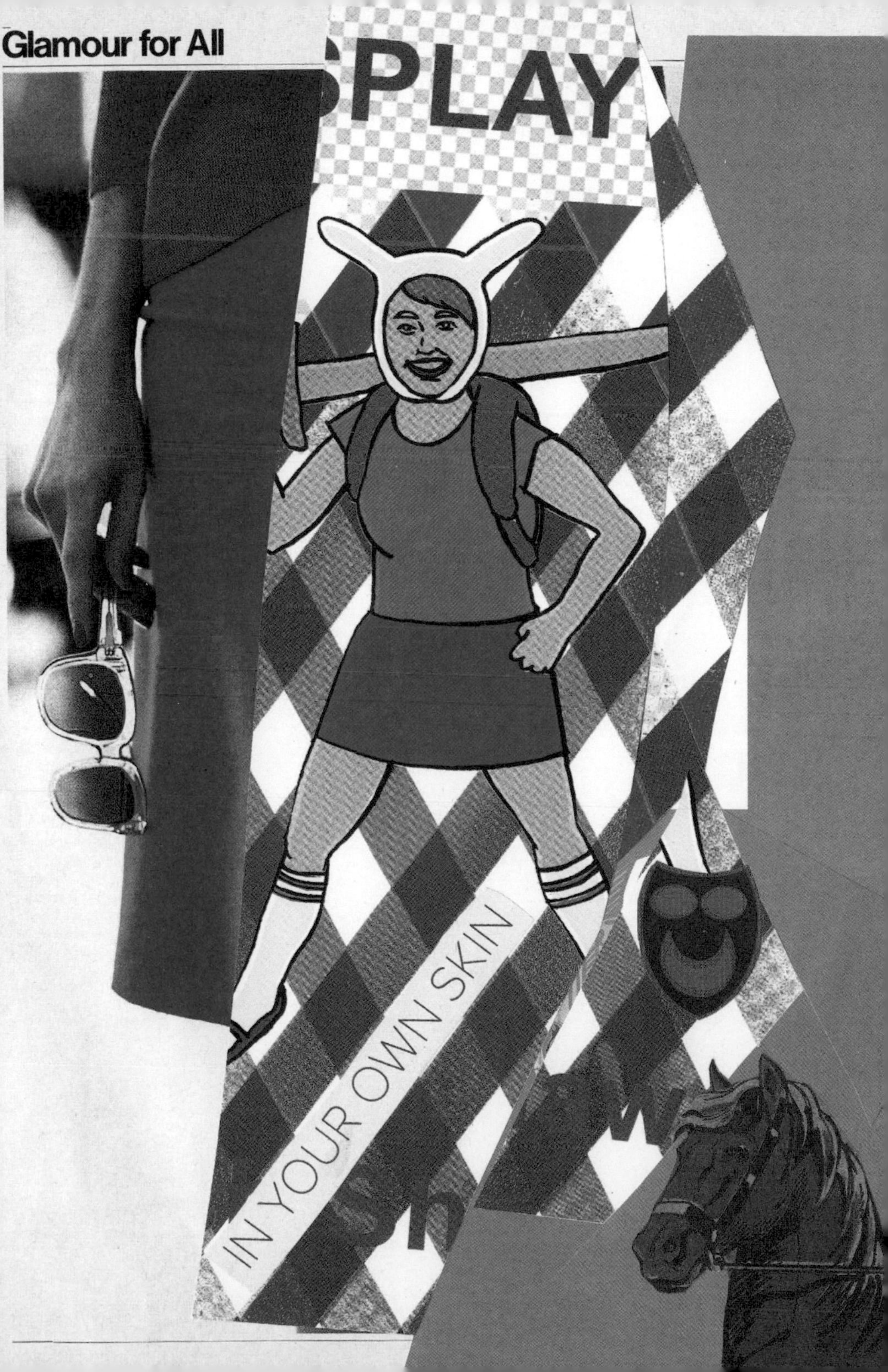
PLAY
IN YOUR OWN SKIN

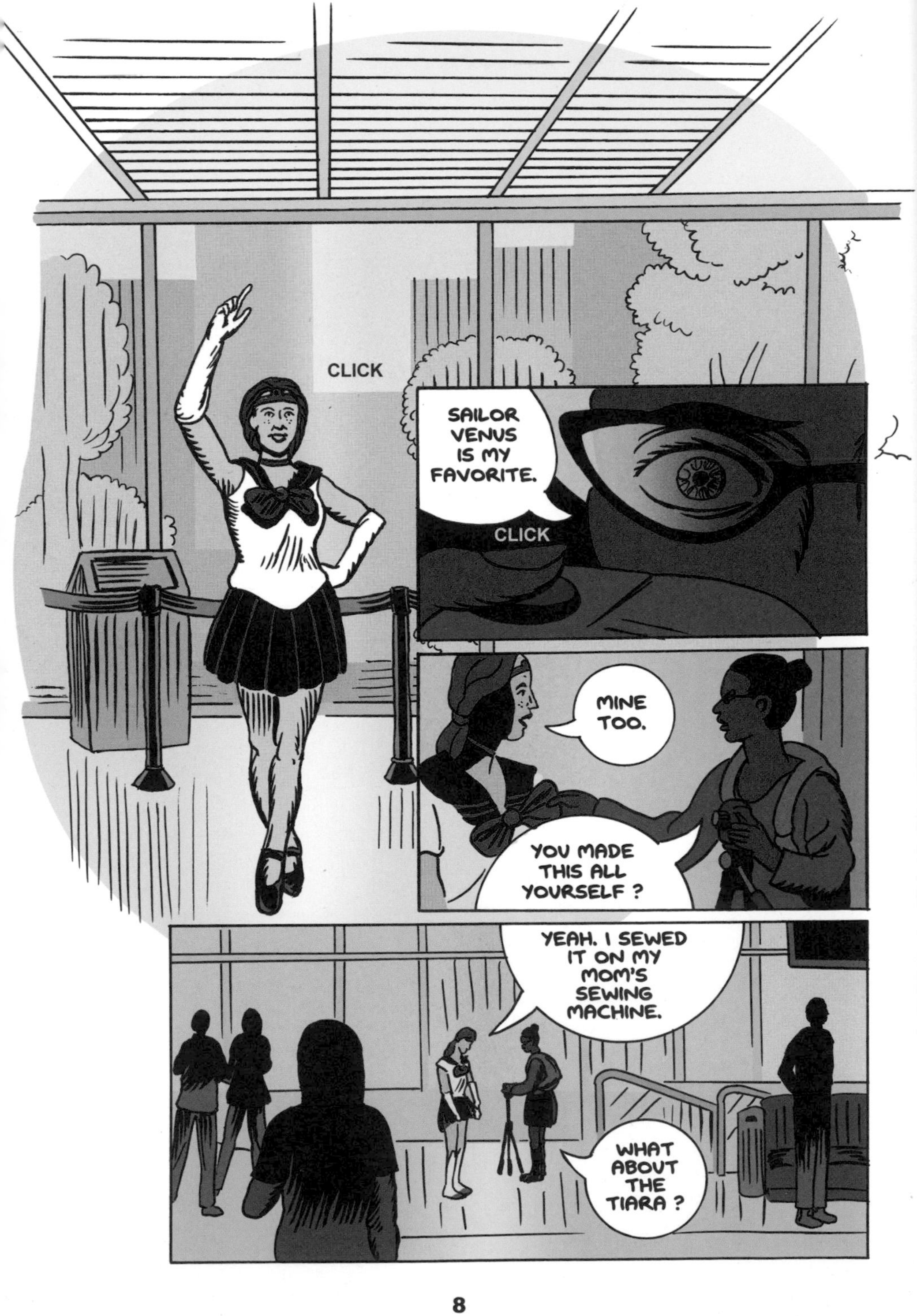
CLICK
SAILOR VENUS IS MY FAVORITE.
CLICK
MINE TOO.
YOU MADE THIS ALL YOURSELF ?
YEAH. I SEWED IT ON MY MOM'S SEWING MACHINE.
WHAT ABOUT THE TIARA ?

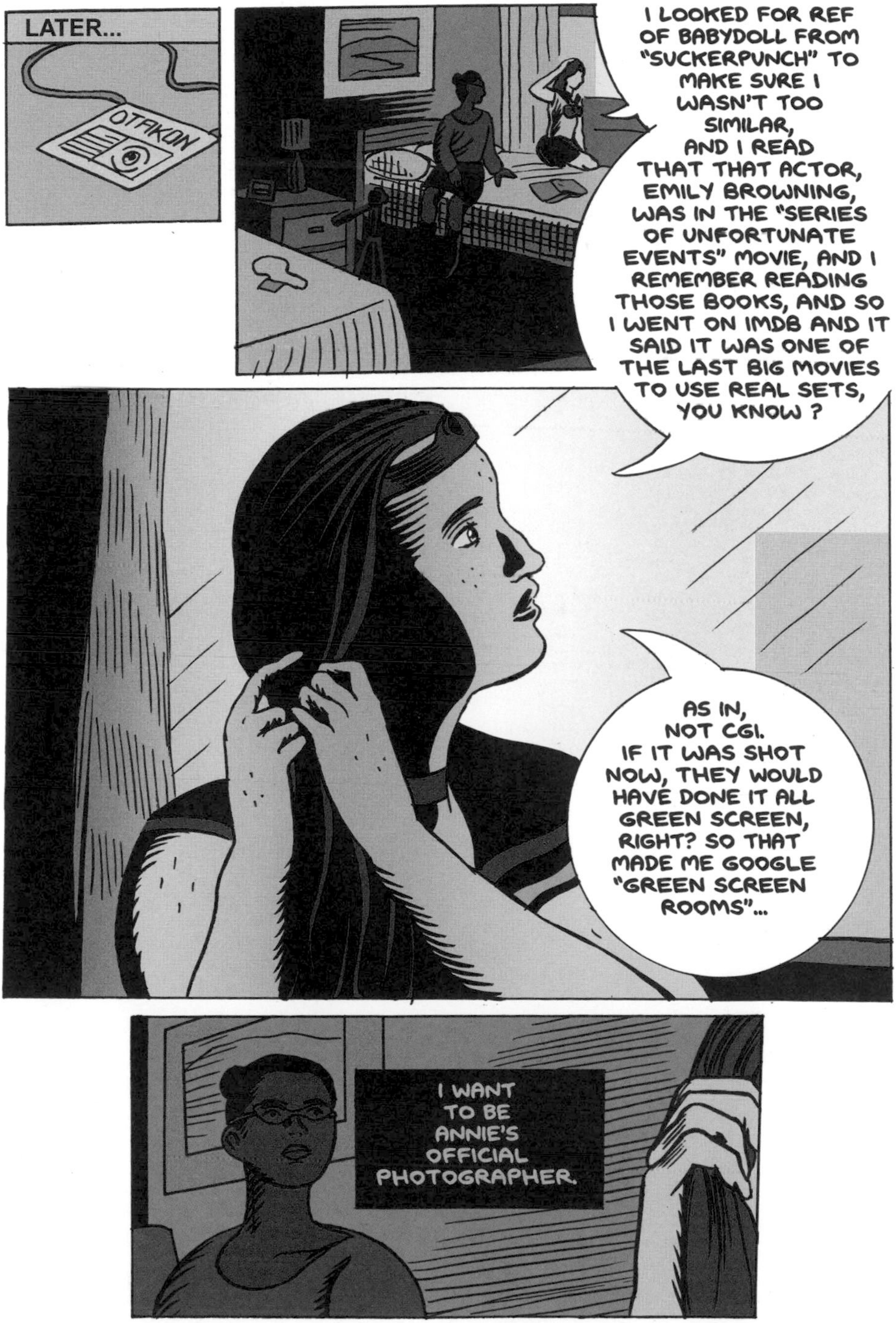

LATER...
OTAKON
I LOOKED FOR REF OF BABYDOLL FROM "SUCKERPUNCH" TO MAKE SURE I WASN'T TOO SIMILAR, AND I READ THAT THAT ACTOR, EMILY BROWNING, WAS IN THE "SERIES OF UNFORTUNATE EVENTS" MOVIE, AND I REMEMBER READING THOSE BOOKS, AND SO I WENT ON IMDB AND IT SAID IT WAS ONE OF THE LAST BIG MOVIES TO USE REAL SETS, YOU KNOW ?
AS IN, NOT CGI. IF IT WAS SHOT NOW, THEY WOULD HAVE DONE IT ALL GREEN SCREEN, RIGHT? SO THAT MADE ME GOOGLE "GREEN SCREEN ROOMS"...
I WANT TO BE ANNIE'S OFFICIAL PHOTOGRAPHER.

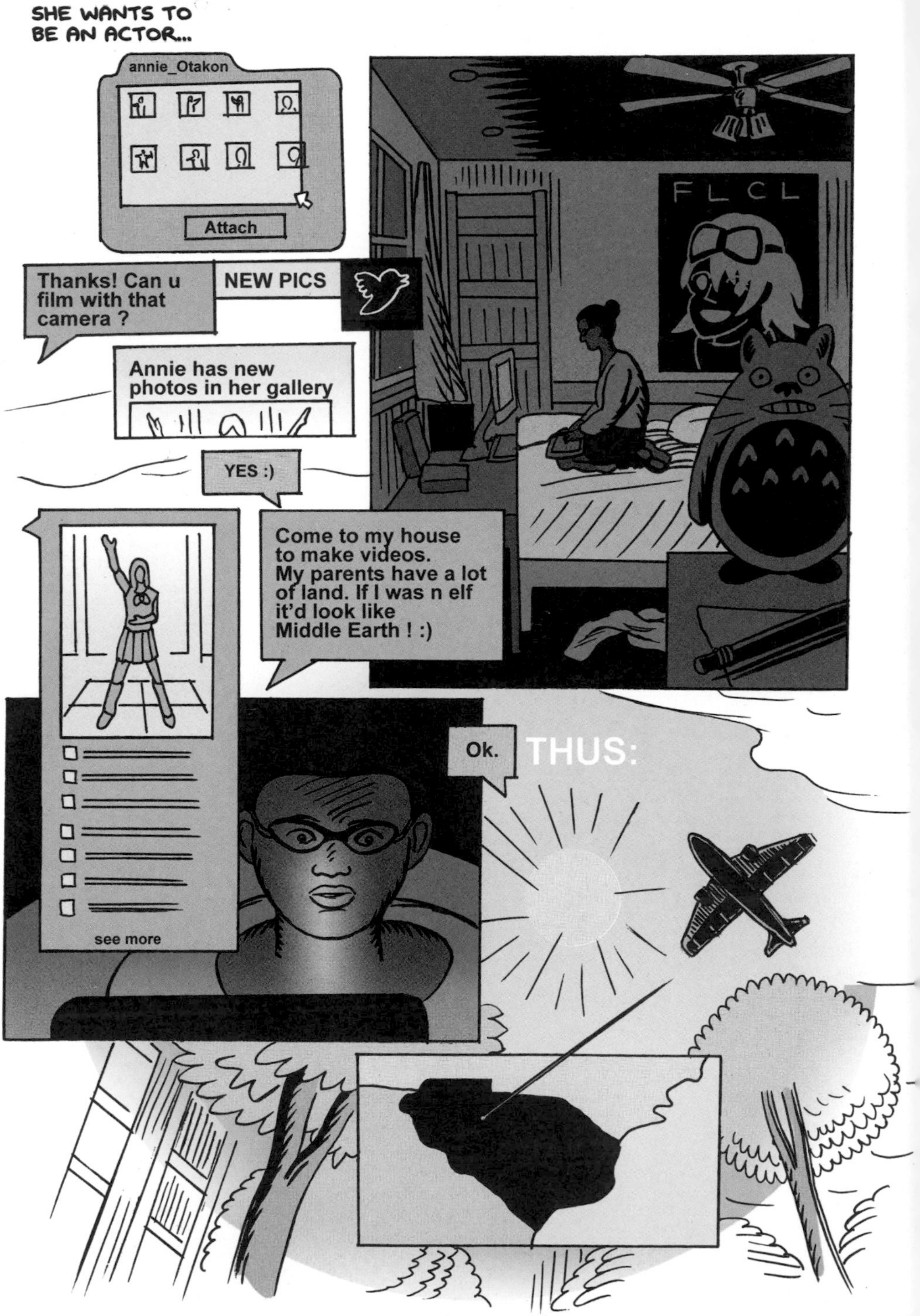
SHE WANTS TO BE AN ACTOR...
annie_Otakon
Attach
Thanks! Can u film with that camera ?
NEW PICS
Annie has new photos in her gallery
YES :)
F L C L
Come to my house to make videos. My parents have a lot of land. If I was n elf it'd look like Middle Earth ! :)
see more
Ok.
THUS:

WE'RE BOTH TAKING A YEAR OFF BETWEEN HIGH SCHOOL AND COLLEGE.

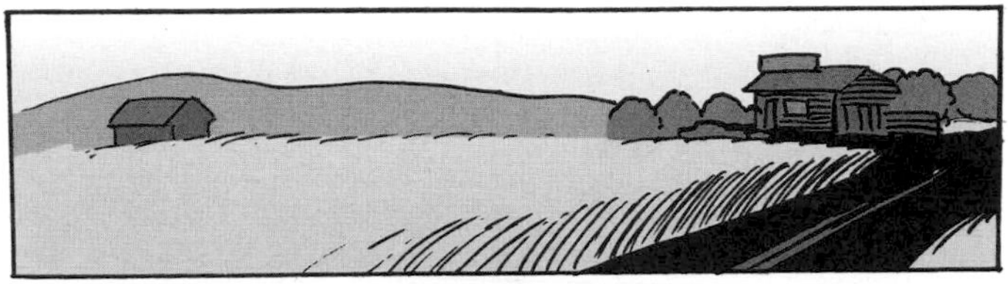

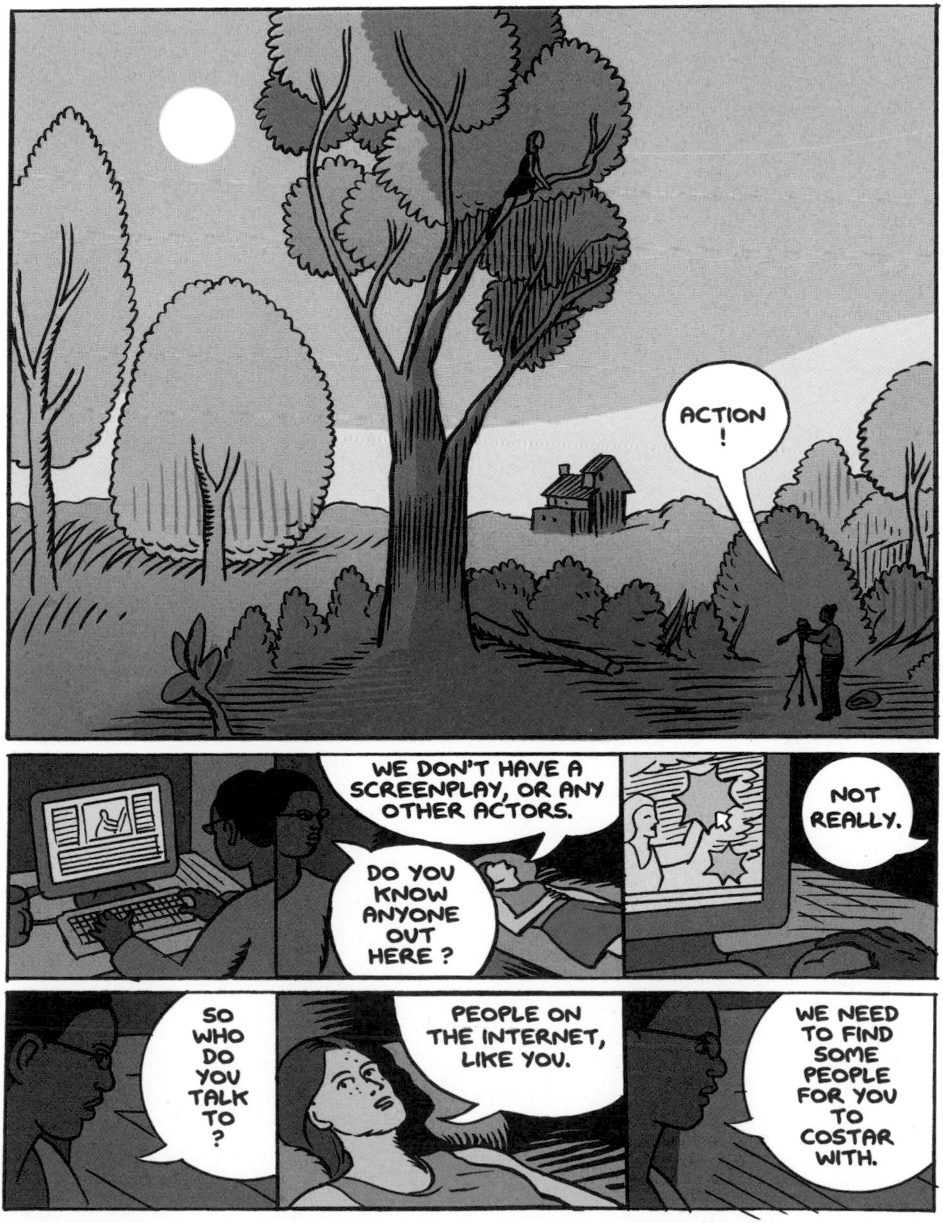
ACTION !
WE DON'T HAVE A SCREENPLAY, OR ANY OTHER ACTORS.
DO YOU KNOW ANYONE OUT HERE ?
NOT REALLY.
SO WHO DO YOU TALK TO ?
PEOPLE ON THE INTERNET, LIKE YOU.
WE NEED TO FIND SOME PEOPLE FOR YOU TO COSTAR WITH.

SO...

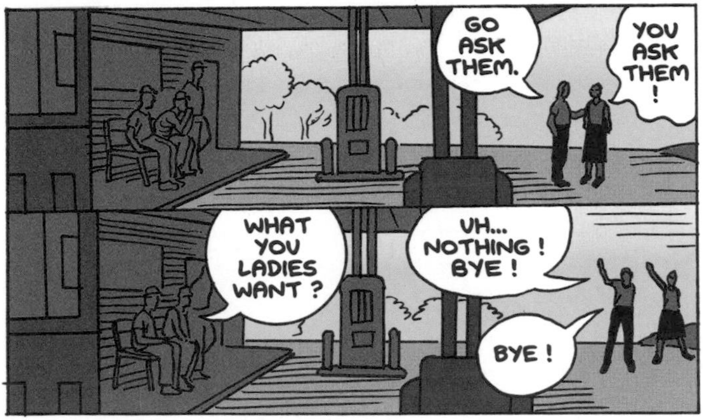
GO ASK THEM.
YOU ASK THEM !
WHAT YOU LADIES WANT ?
UH... NOTHING ! BYE !
BYE !

LATER...

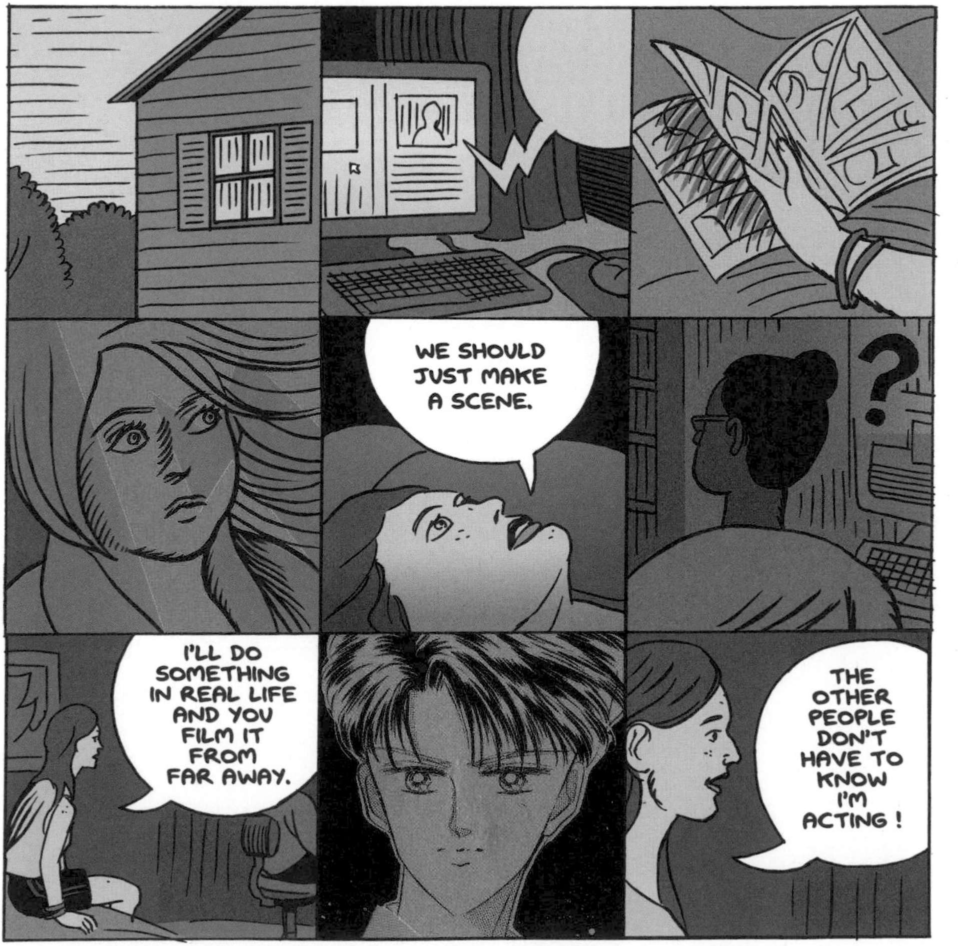
WE SHOULD JUST MAKE A SCENE.
?
I'LL DO SOMETHING IN REAL LIFE AND YOU FILM IT FROM FAR AWAY.
THE OTHER PEOPLE DON'T HAVE TO KNOW I'M ACTING !

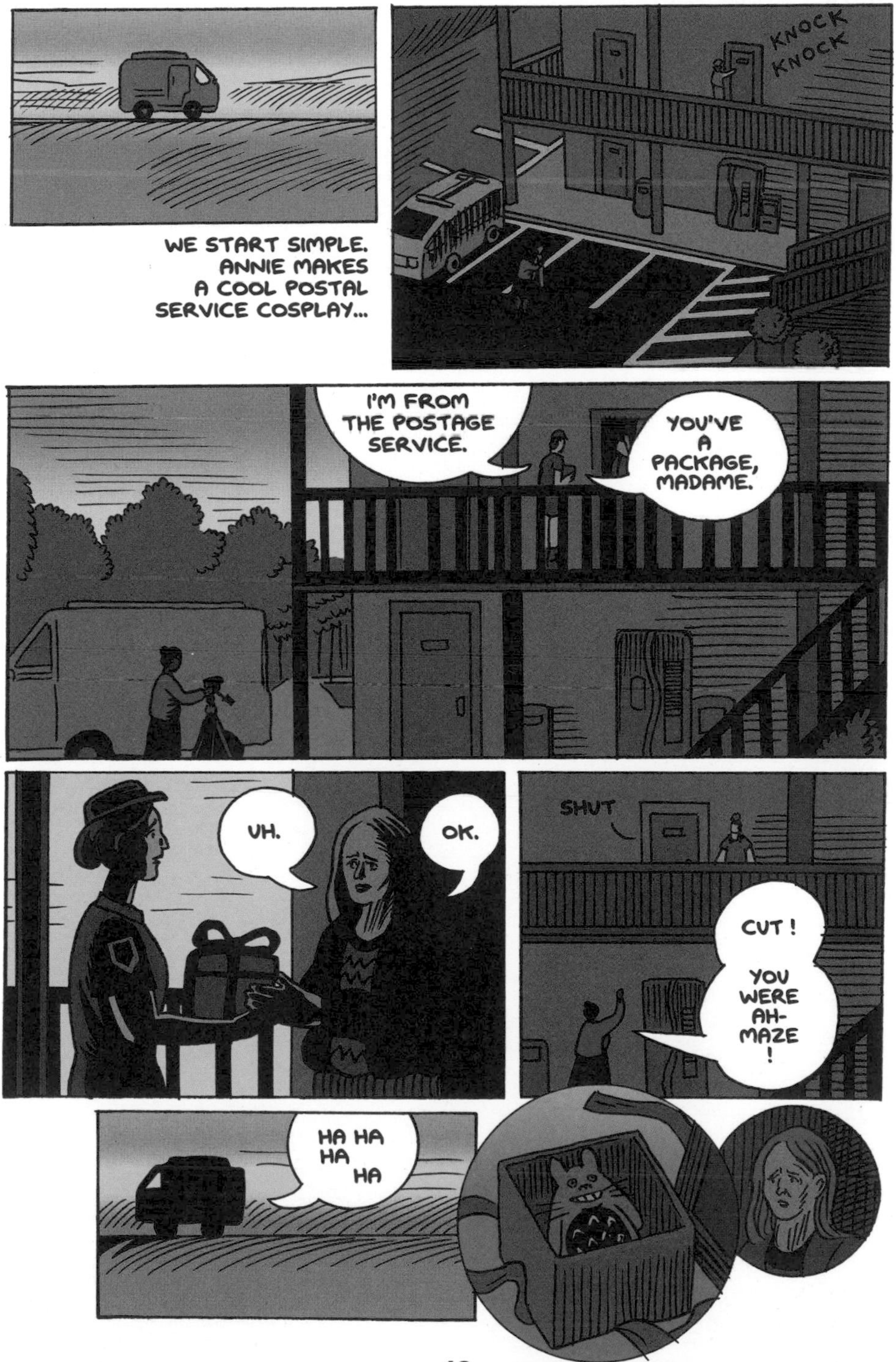
WE START SIMPLE. ANNIE MAKES A COOL POSTAL SERVICE COSPLAY...
KNOCK KNOCK
I'M FROM THE POSTAGE SERVICE.
YOU'VE A PACKAGE, MADAME.
UH.
OK.
SHUT
CUT!
YOU WERE AH-MAZE!
HA HA HA HA

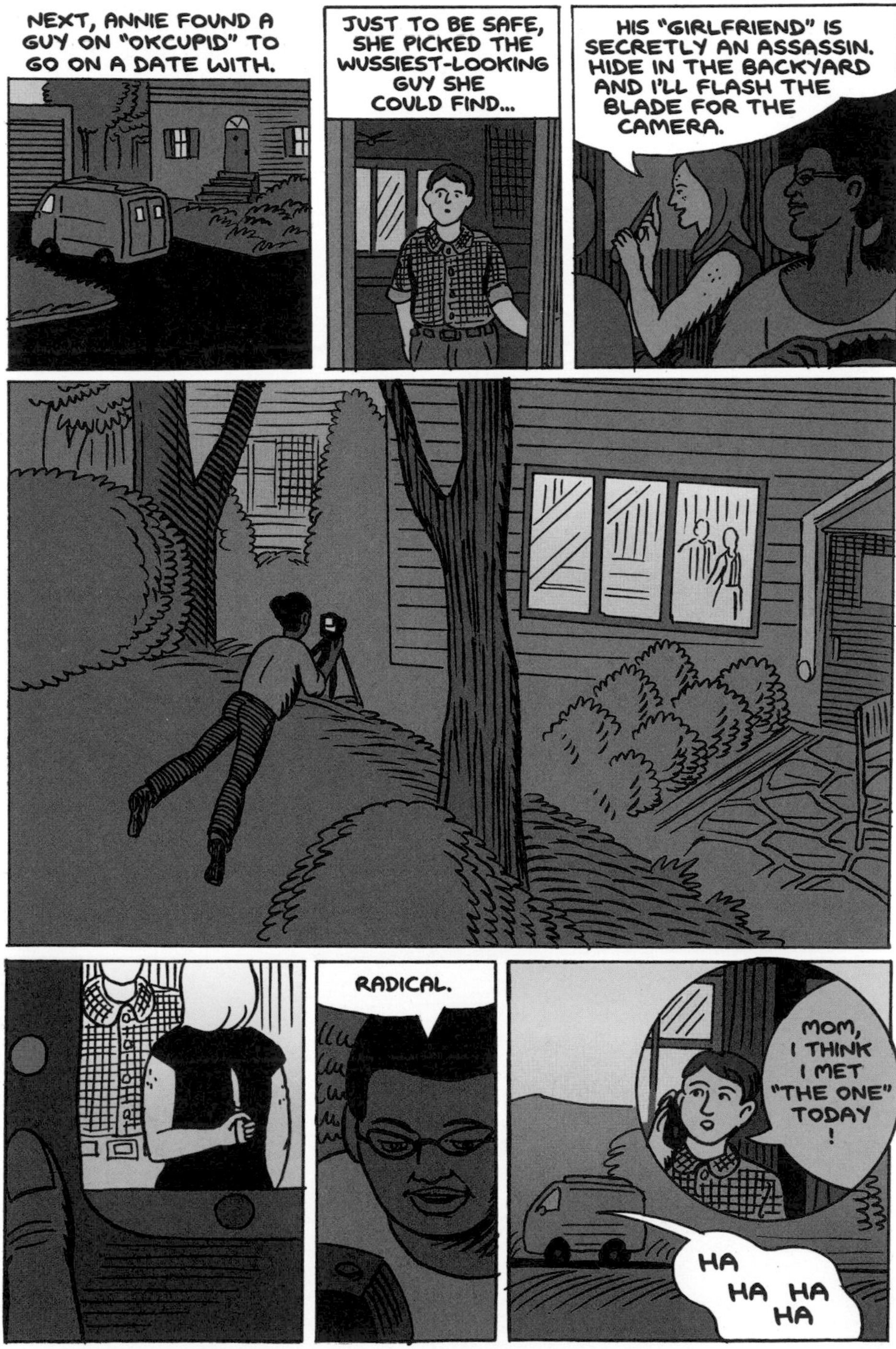
NEXT, ANNIE FOUND A GUY ON "OKCUPID" TO GO ON A DATE WITH.
JUST TO BE SAFE, SHE PICKED THE WUSSIEST-LOOKING GUY SHE COULD FIND...
HIS "GIRLFRIEND" IS SECRETLY AN ASSASSIN. HIDE IN THE BACKYARD AND I'LL FLASH THE BLADE FOR THE CAMERA.
RADICAL.
MOM, I THINK I MET "THE ONE" TODAY !
HA HA HA HA

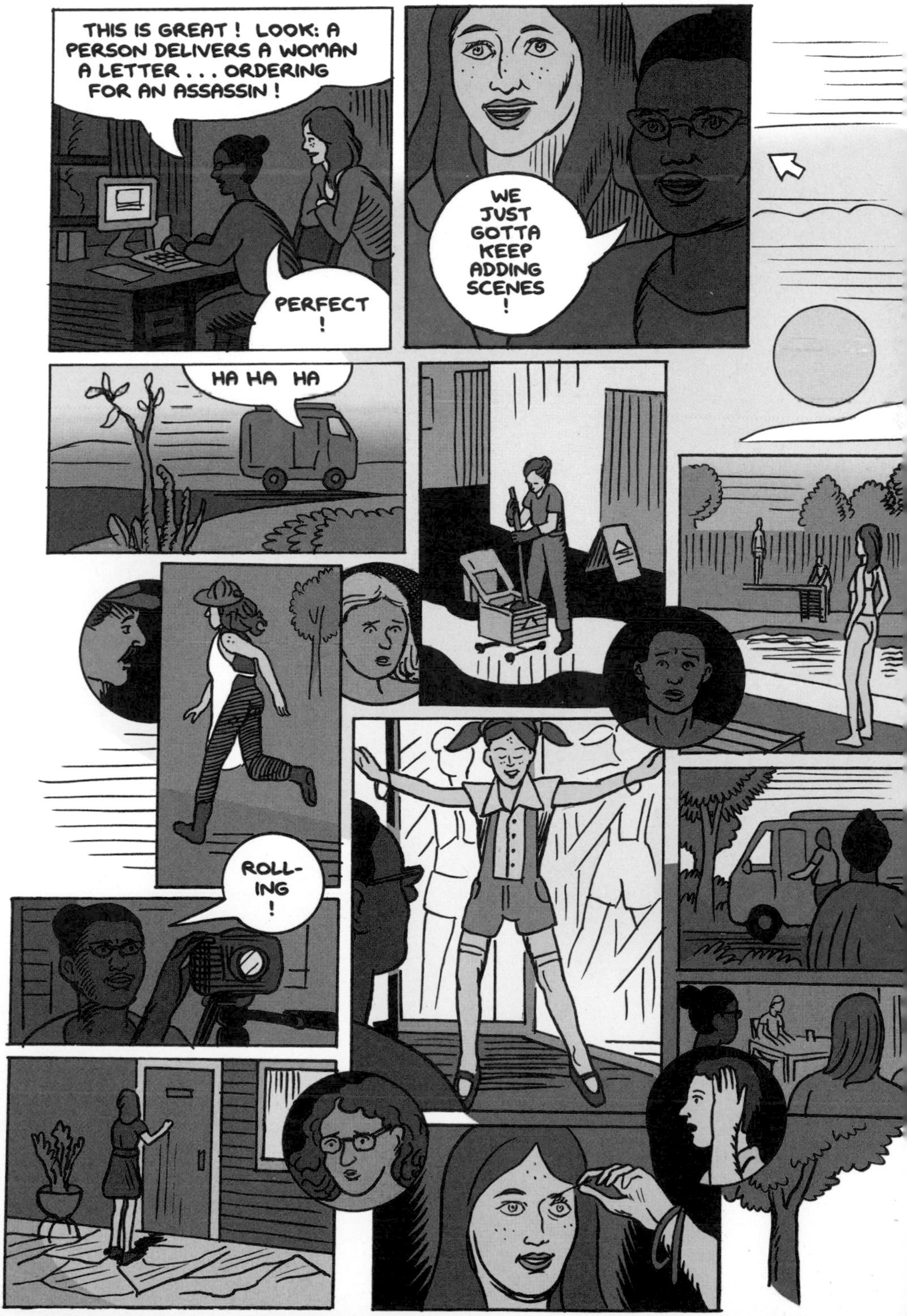
THIS IS GREAT ! LOOK: A PERSON DELIVERS A WOMAN A LETTER . . . ORDERING FOR AN ASSASSIN !
PERFECT !
WE JUST GOTTA KEEP ADDING SCENES !
HA HA HA
ROLL-ING !

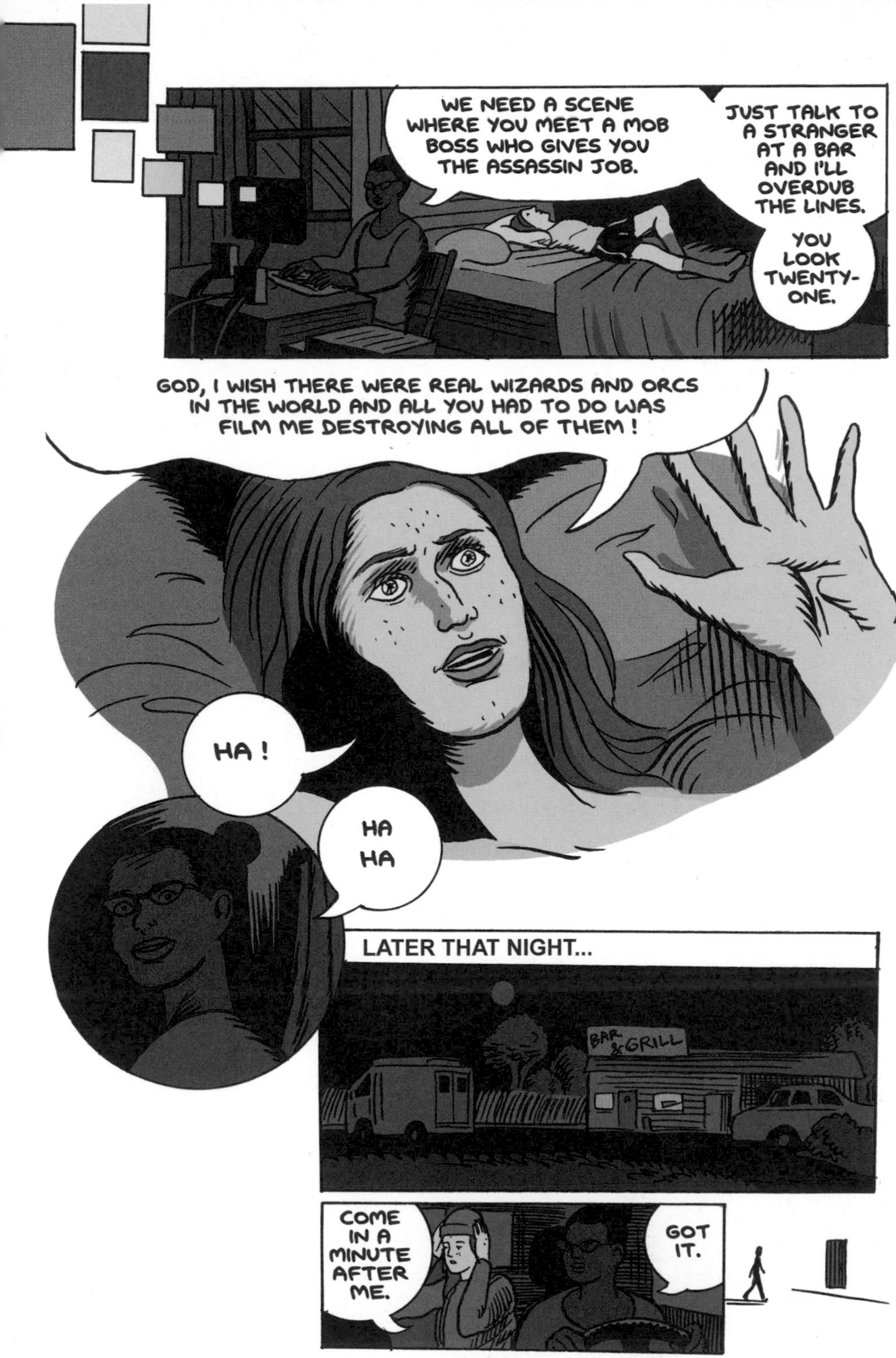
WE NEED A SCENE WHERE YOU MEET A MOB BOSS WHO GIVES YOU THE ASSASSIN JOB.
JUST TALK TO A STRANGER AT A BAR AND I'LL OVERDUB THE LINES.
YOU LOOK TWENTY-ONE.
GOD, I WISH THERE WERE REAL WIZARDS AND ORCS IN THE WORLD AND ALL YOU HAD TO DO WAS FILM ME DESTROYING ALL OF THEM!
HA!
HA HA
LATER THAT NIGHT...
BAR & GRILL
COME IN A MINUTE AFTER ME.
GOT IT.

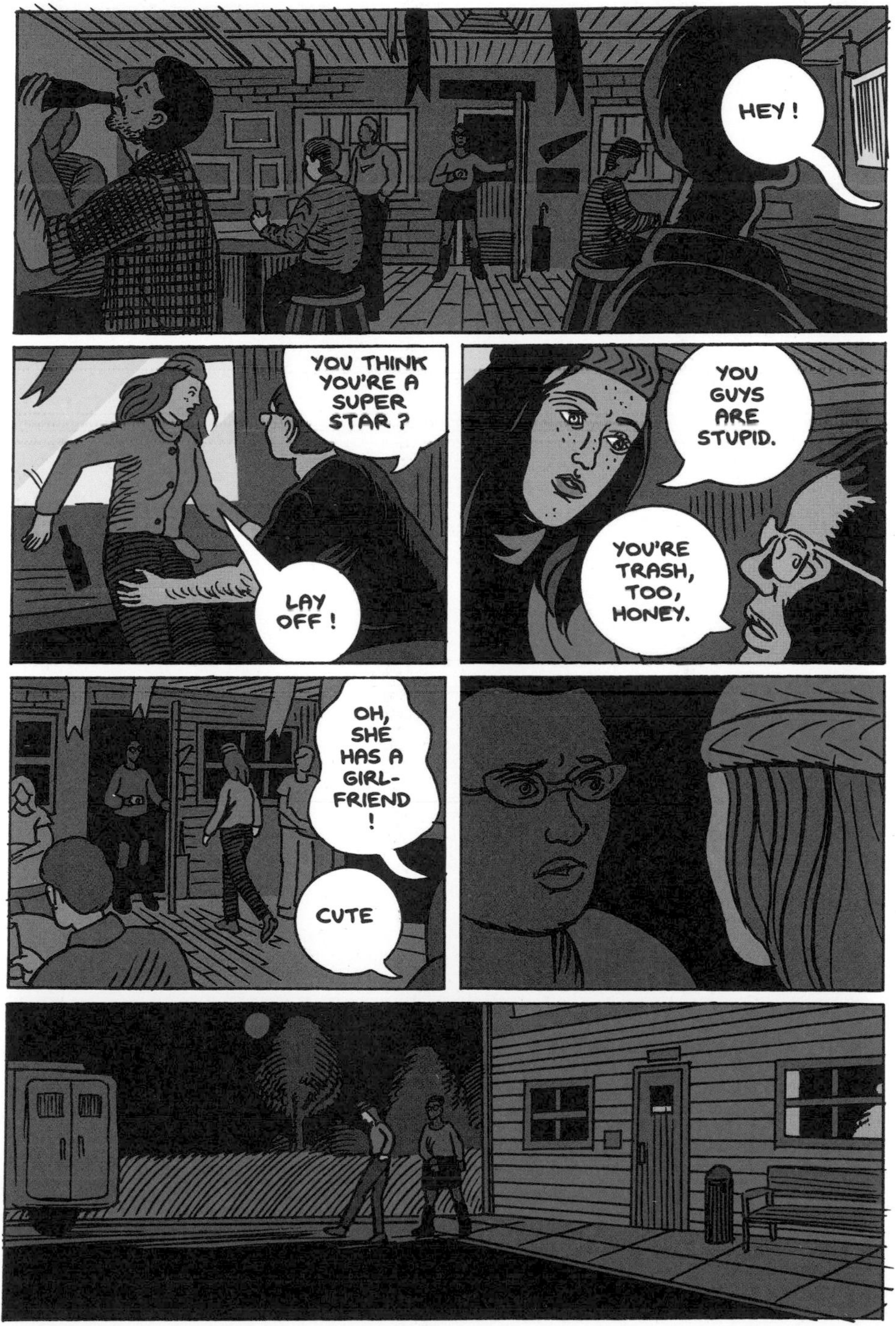
HEY!
YOU THINK YOU'RE A SUPER STAR?
LAY OFF!
YOU GUYS ARE STUPID.
YOU'RE TRASH, TOO, HONEY.
OH, SHE HAS A GIRL-FRIEND!
CUTE

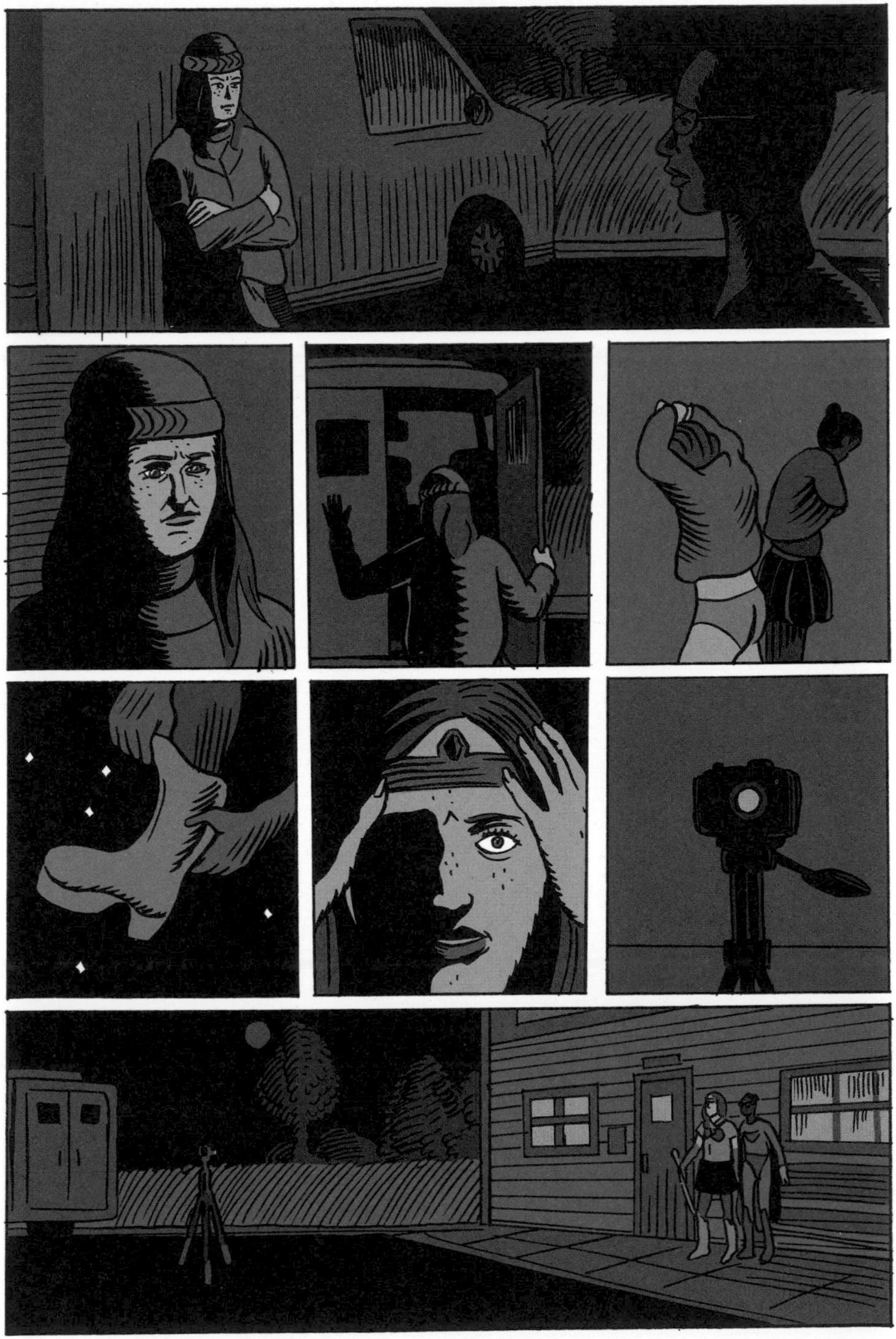

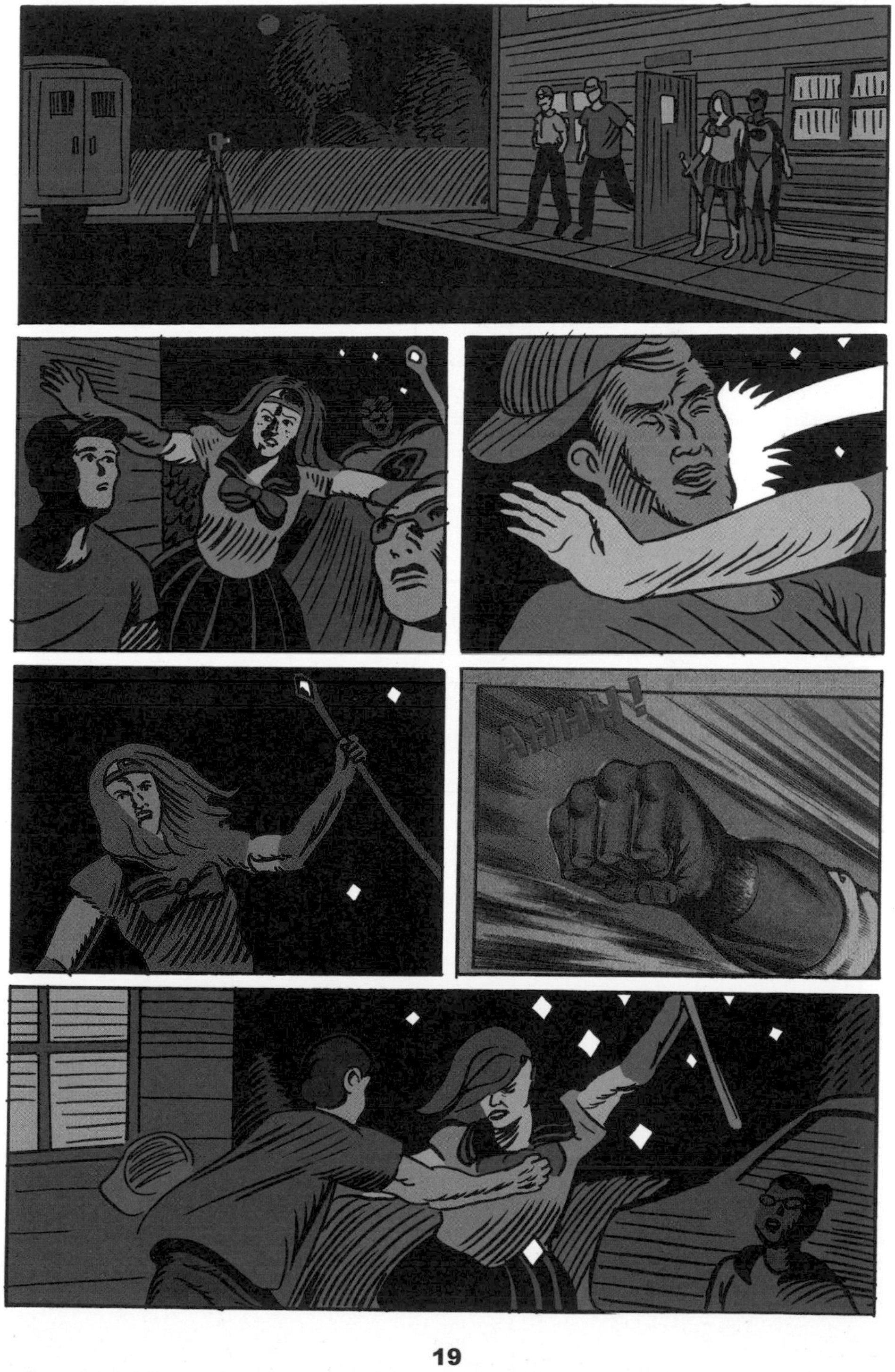
AHHH!

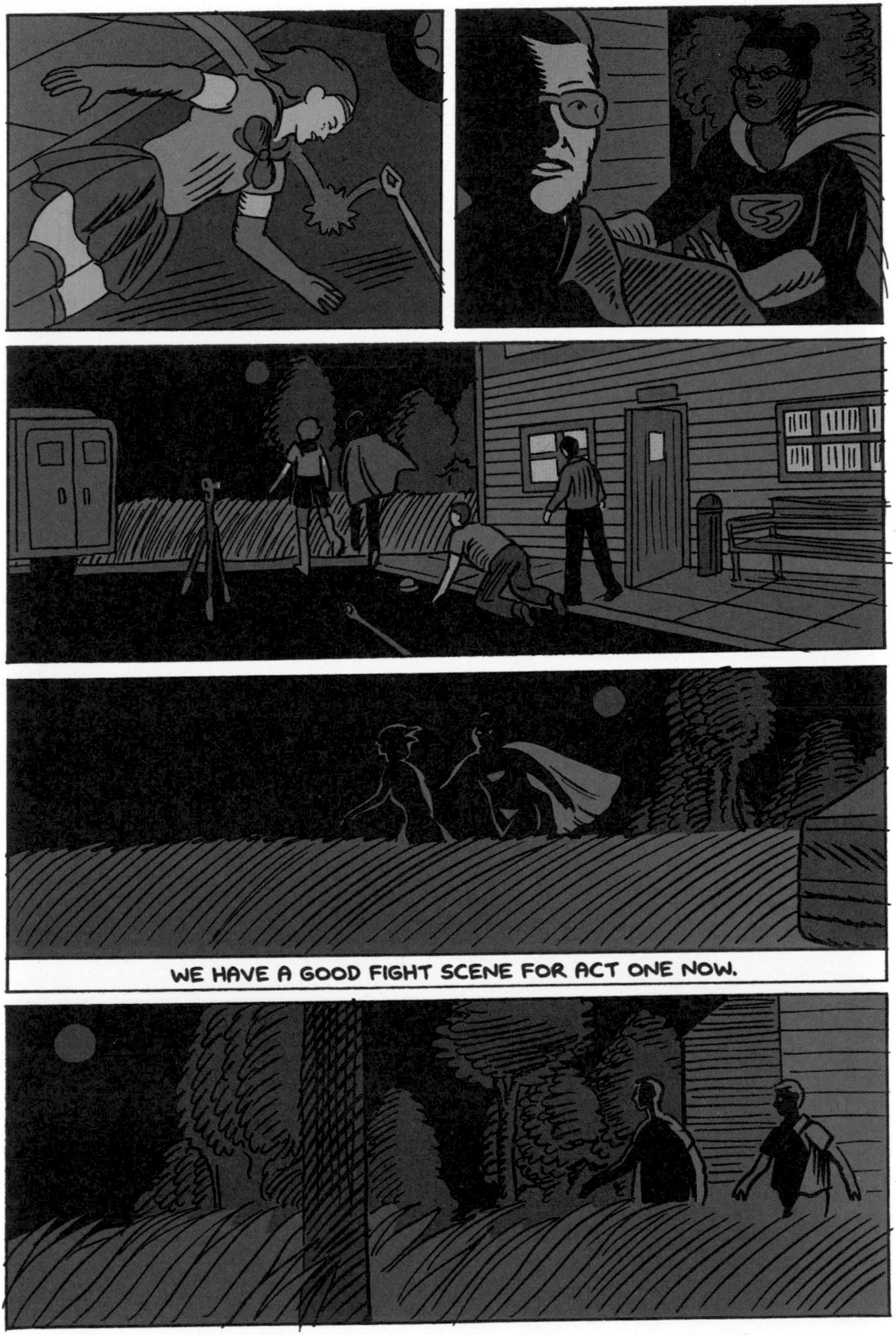
WE HAVE A GOOD FIGHT SCENE FOR ACT ONE NOW.

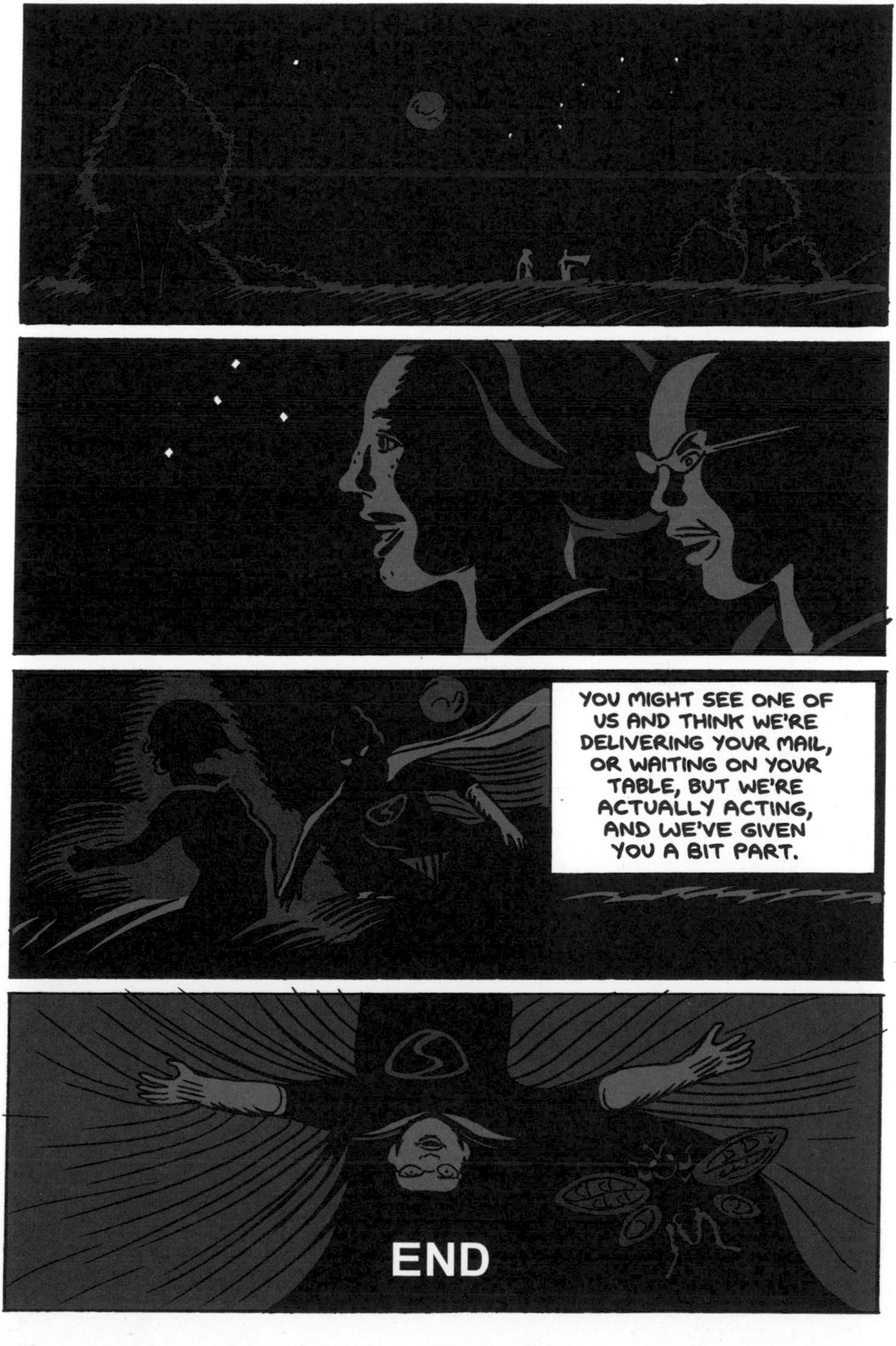
YOU MIGHT SEE ONE OF US AND THINK WE'RE DELIVERING YOUR MAIL, OR WAITING ON YOUR TABLE, BUT WE'RE ACTUALLY ACTING, AND WE'VE GIVEN YOU A BIT PART.
END

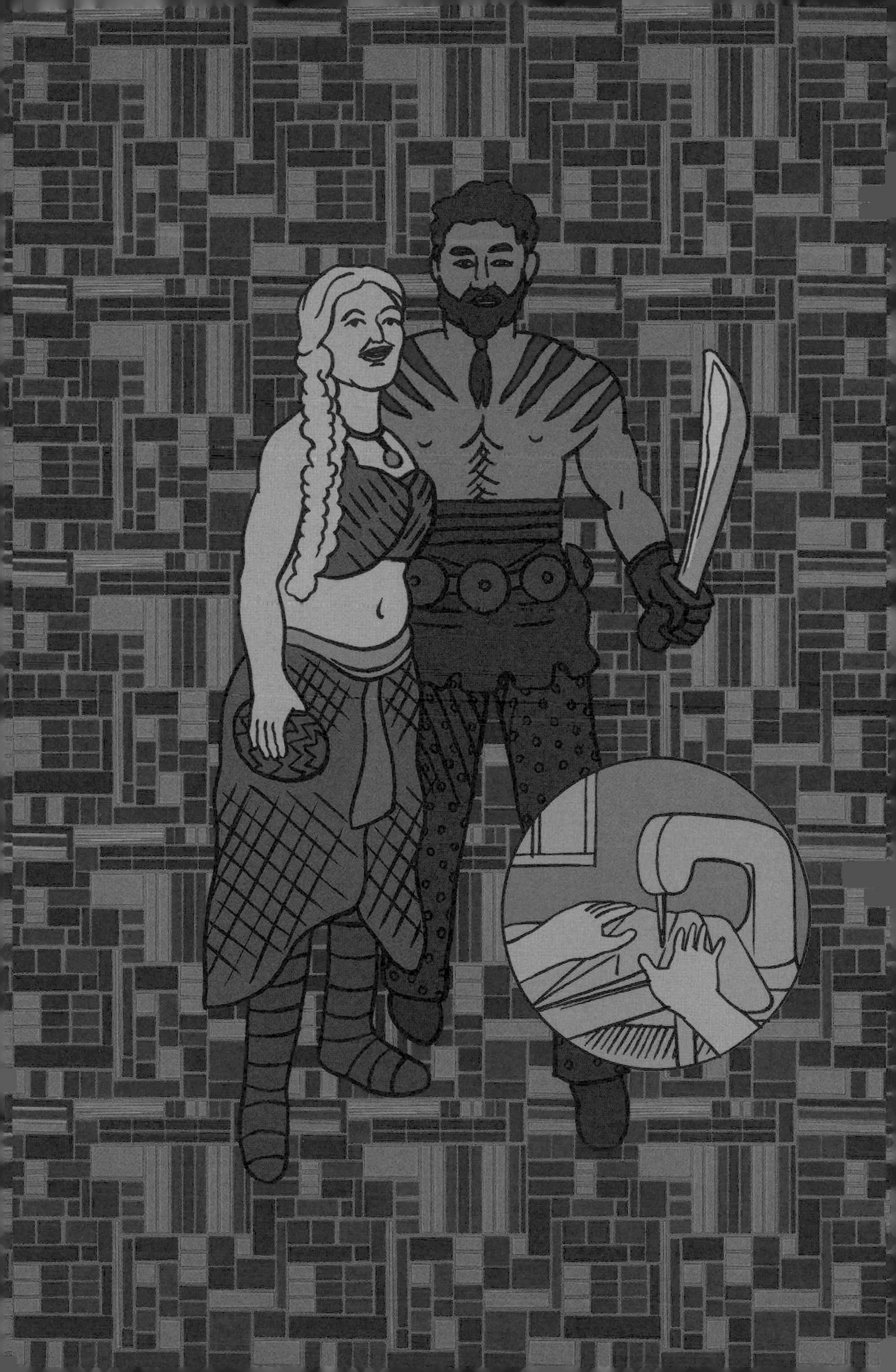

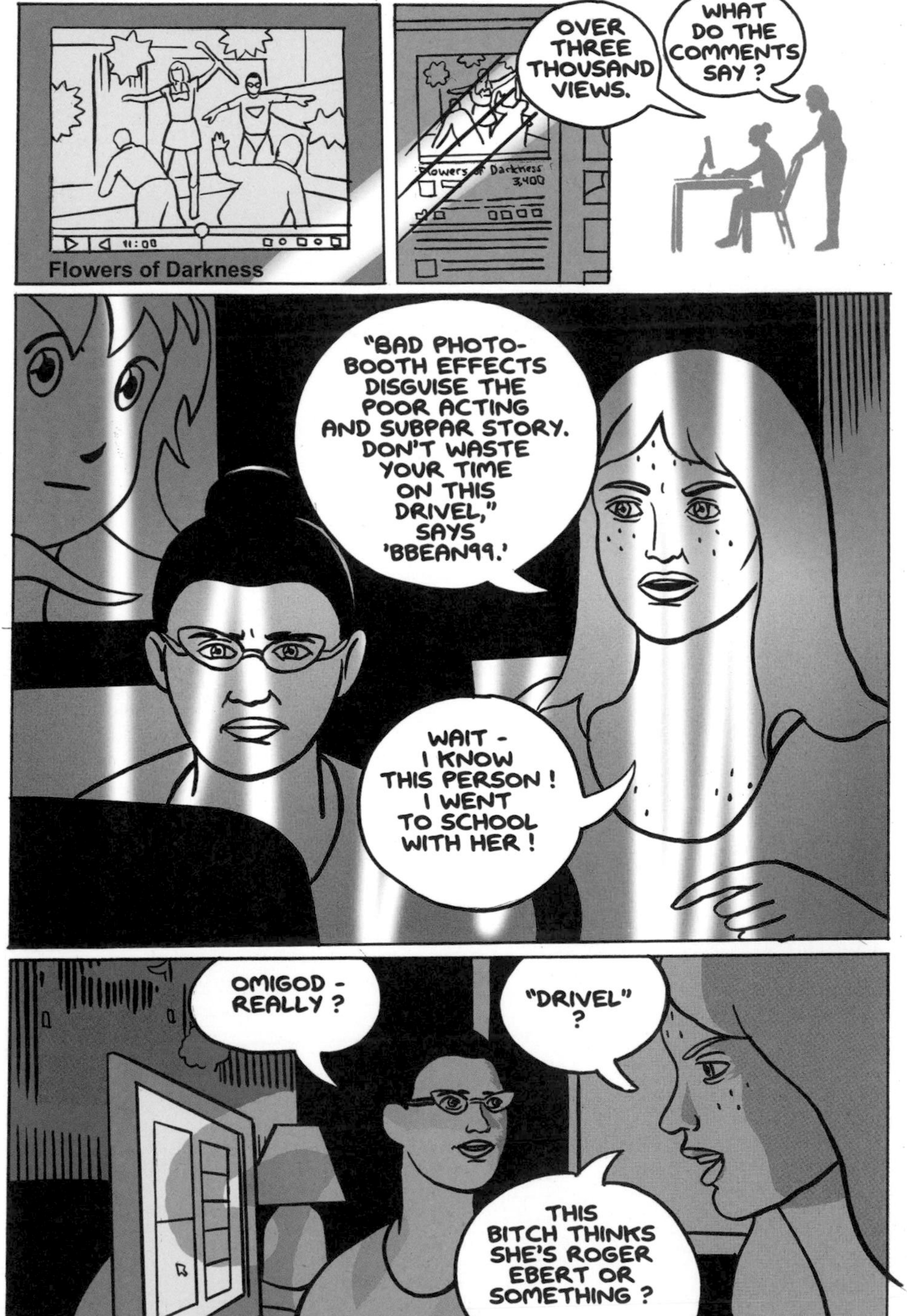
Flowers of Darkness
Flowers of Darkness 3,400
OVER THREE THOUSAND VIEWS.
WHAT DO THE COMMENTS SAY ?
"BAD PHOTO-BOOTH EFFECTS DISGUISE THE POOR ACTING AND SUBPAR STORY. DON'T WASTE YOUR TIME ON THIS DRIVEL," SAYS 'BBEAN99.'
WAIT - I KNOW THIS PERSON ! I WENT TO SCHOOL WITH HER !
OMIGOD - REALLY ?
"DRIVEL" ?
THIS BITCH THINKS SHE'S ROGER EBERT OR SOMETHING ?

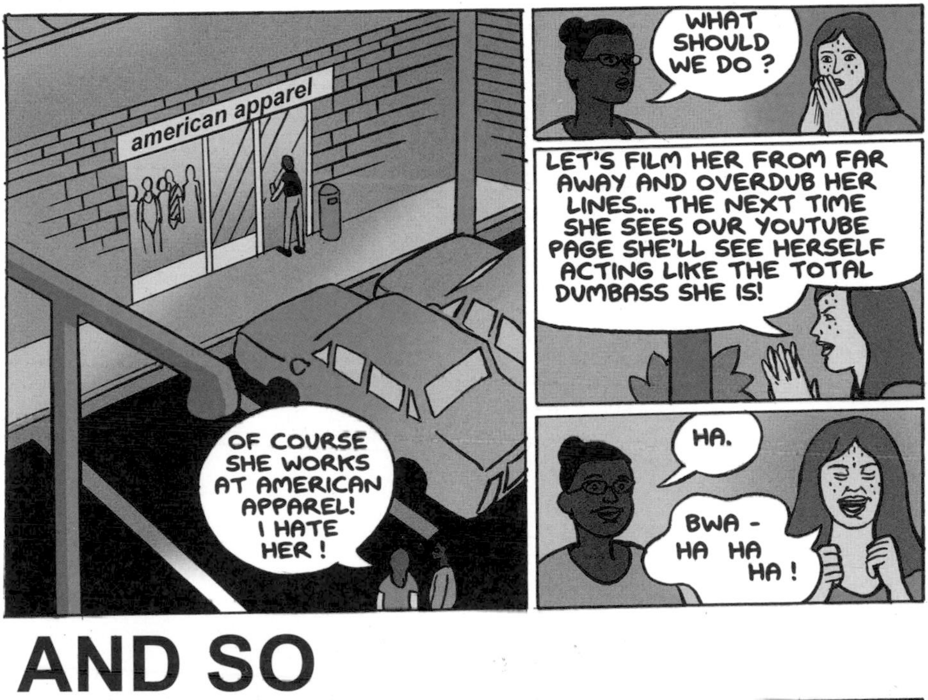
american apparel
OF COURSE SHE WORKS AT AMERICAN APPAREL! I HATE HER!
WHAT SHOULD WE DO ?
LET'S FILM HER FROM FAR AWAY AND OVERDUB HER LINES... THE NEXT TIME SHE SEES OUR YOUTUBE PAGE SHE'LL SEE HERSELF ACTING LIKE THE TOTAL DUMBASS SHE IS!
HA.
BWA - HA HA HA !

AND SO

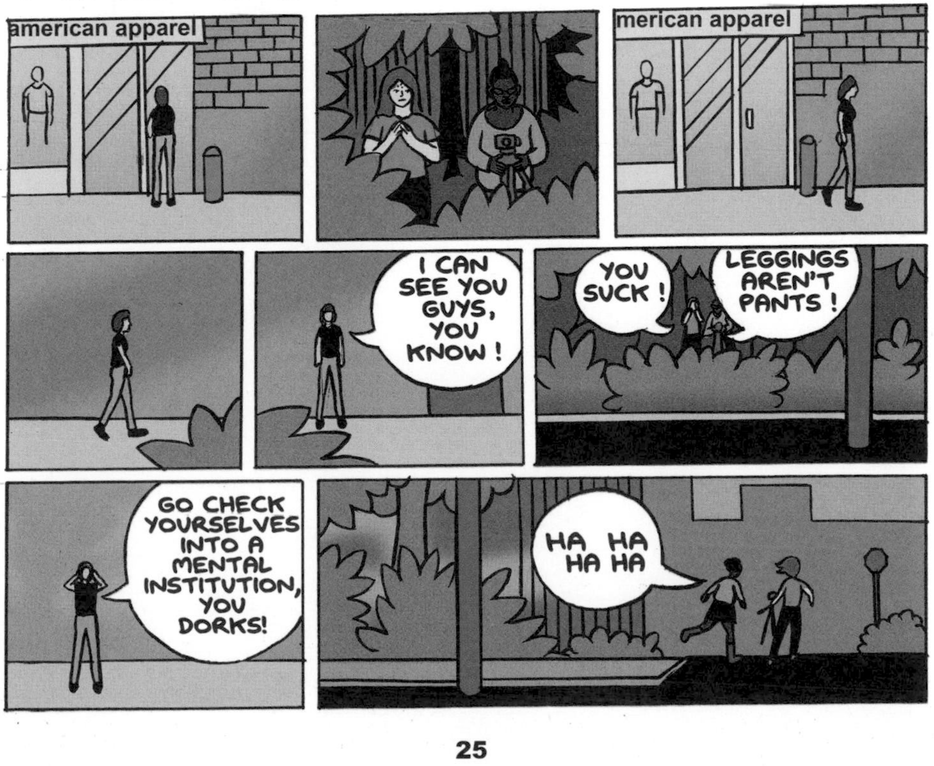
american apparel
merican apparel
I CAN SEE YOU GUYS, YOU KNOW !
YOU SUCK !
LEGGINGS AREN'T PANTS !
GO CHECK YOURSELVES INTO A MENTAL INSTITUTION, YOU DORKS!
HA HA HA HA

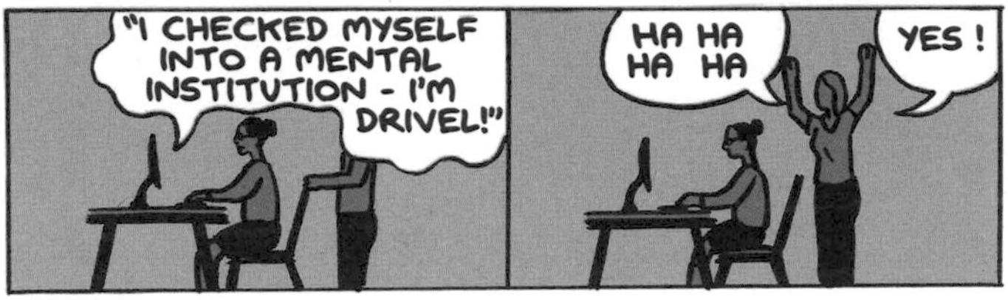
"I CHECKED MYSELF INTO A MENTAL INSTITUTION - I'M DRIVEL!"
HA HA HA HA
YES !

AND THEN

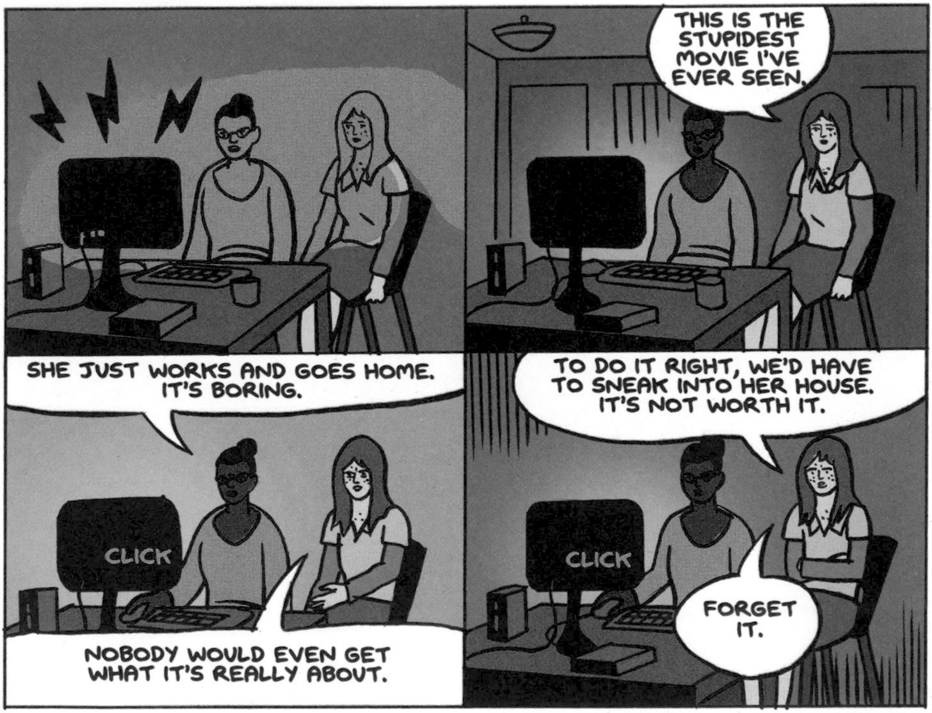
THIS IS THE STUPIDEST MOVIE I'VE EVER SEEN.
SHE JUST WORKS AND GOES HOME. IT'S BORING.
TO DO IT RIGHT, WE'D HAVE TO SNEAK INTO HER HOUSE. IT'S NOT WORTH IT.
CLICK
NOBODY WOULD EVEN GET WHAT IT'S REALLY ABOUT.
CLICK
FORGET IT.

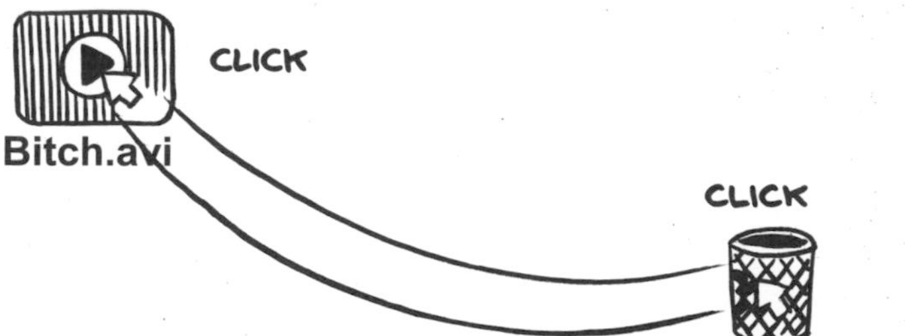
CLICK
Bitch.avi
CLICK
Recycle Bin

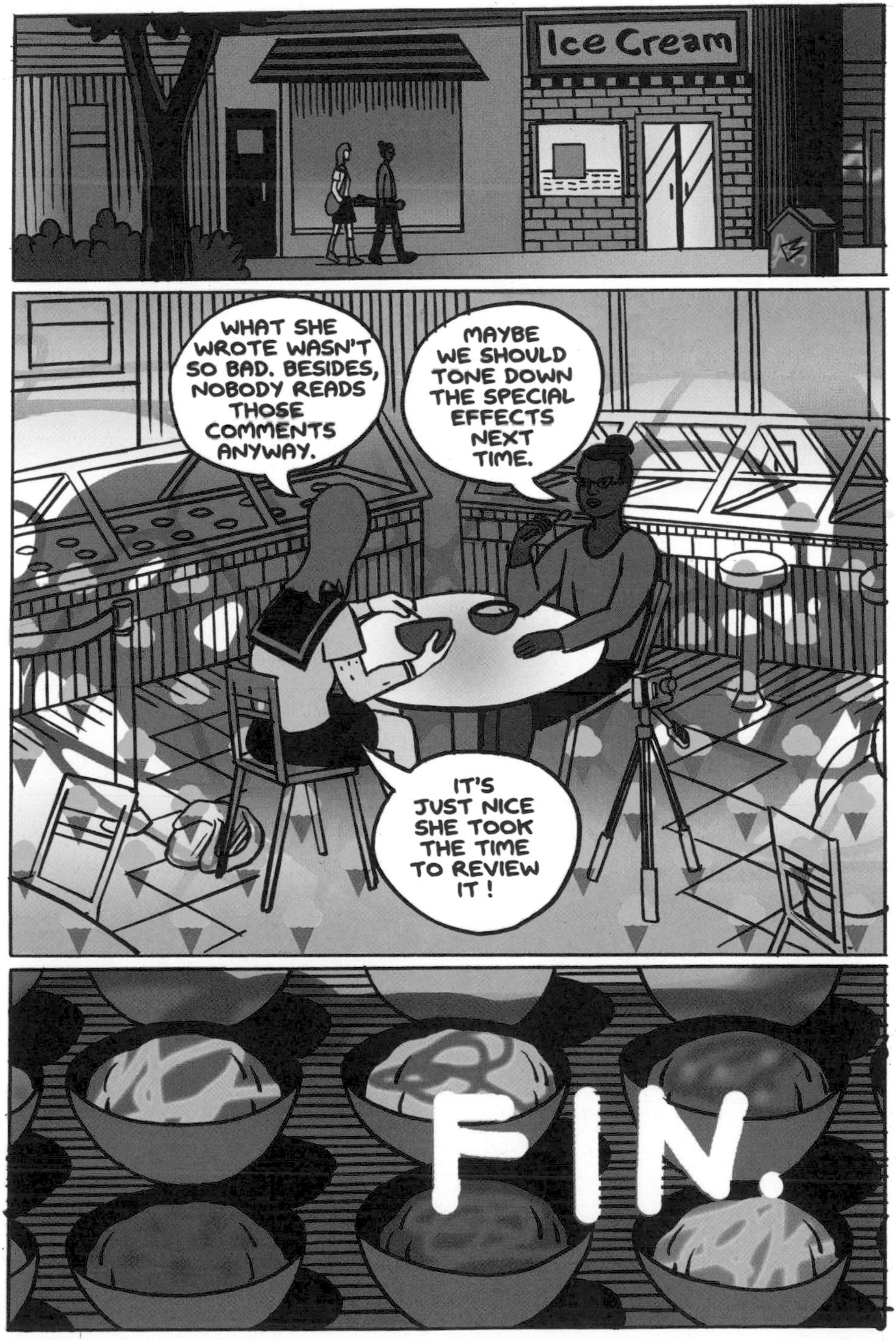
Ice Cream
WHAT SHE WROTE WASN'T SO BAD. BESIDES, NOBODY READS THOSE COMMENTS ANYWAY.
MAYBE WE SHOULD TONE DOWN THE SPECIAL EFFECTS NEXT TIME.
IT'S JUST NICE SHE TOOK THE TIME TO REVIEW IT !
FIN.

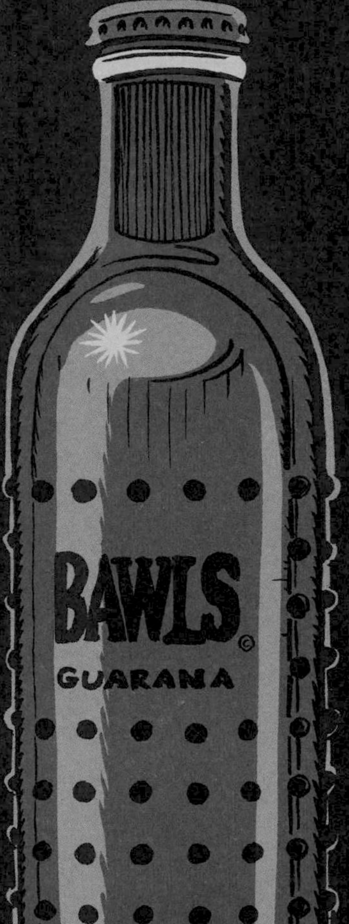
BAWLS©
GUARANA

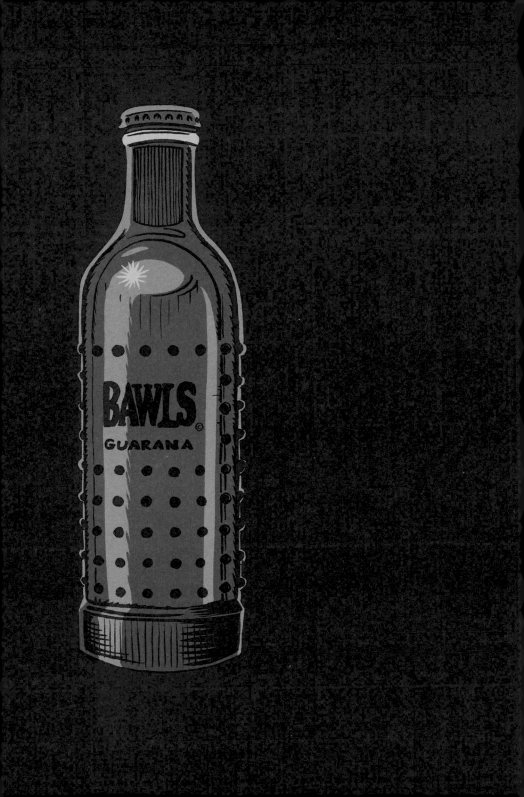

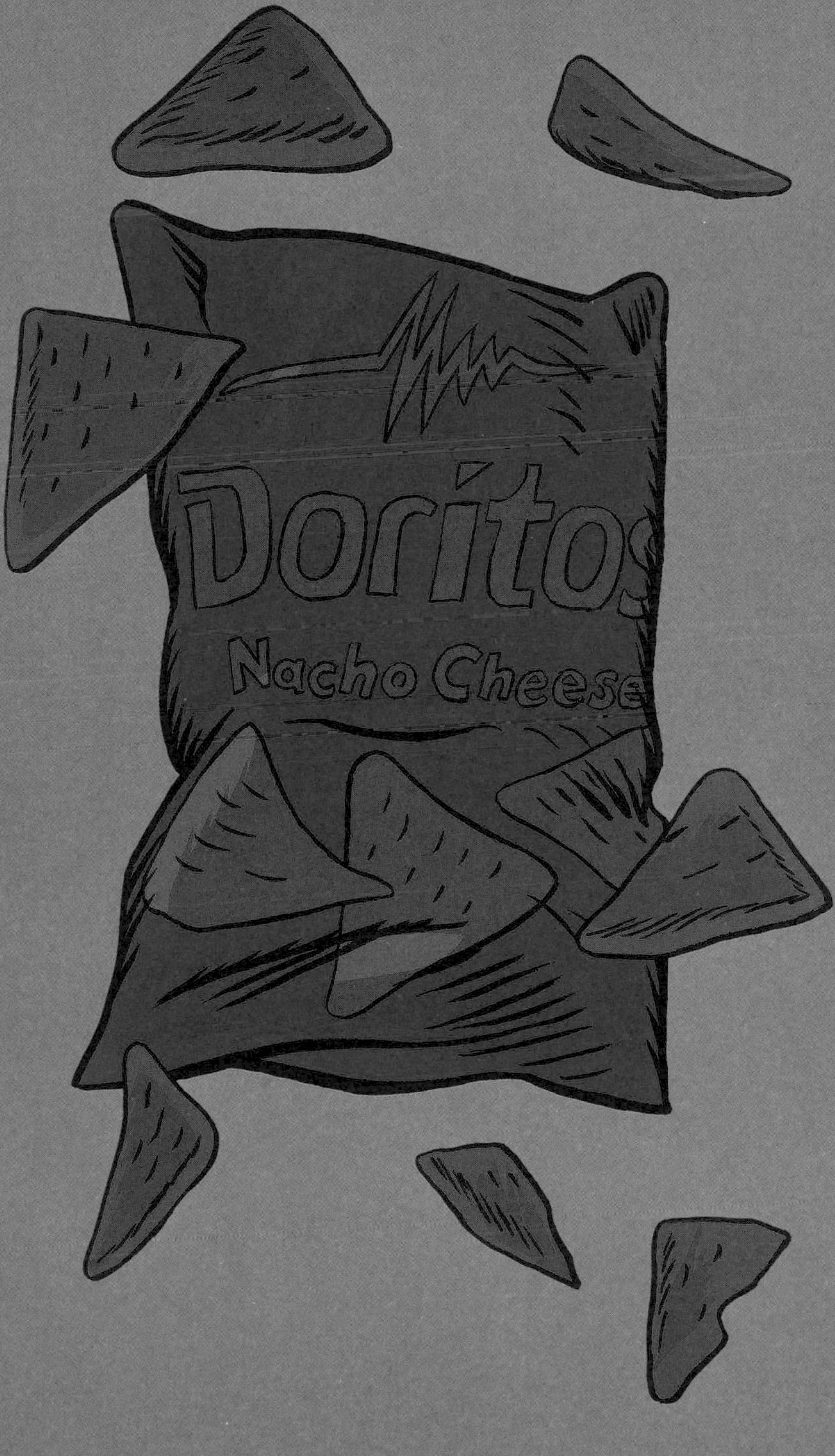
Doritos
Nacho Cheese

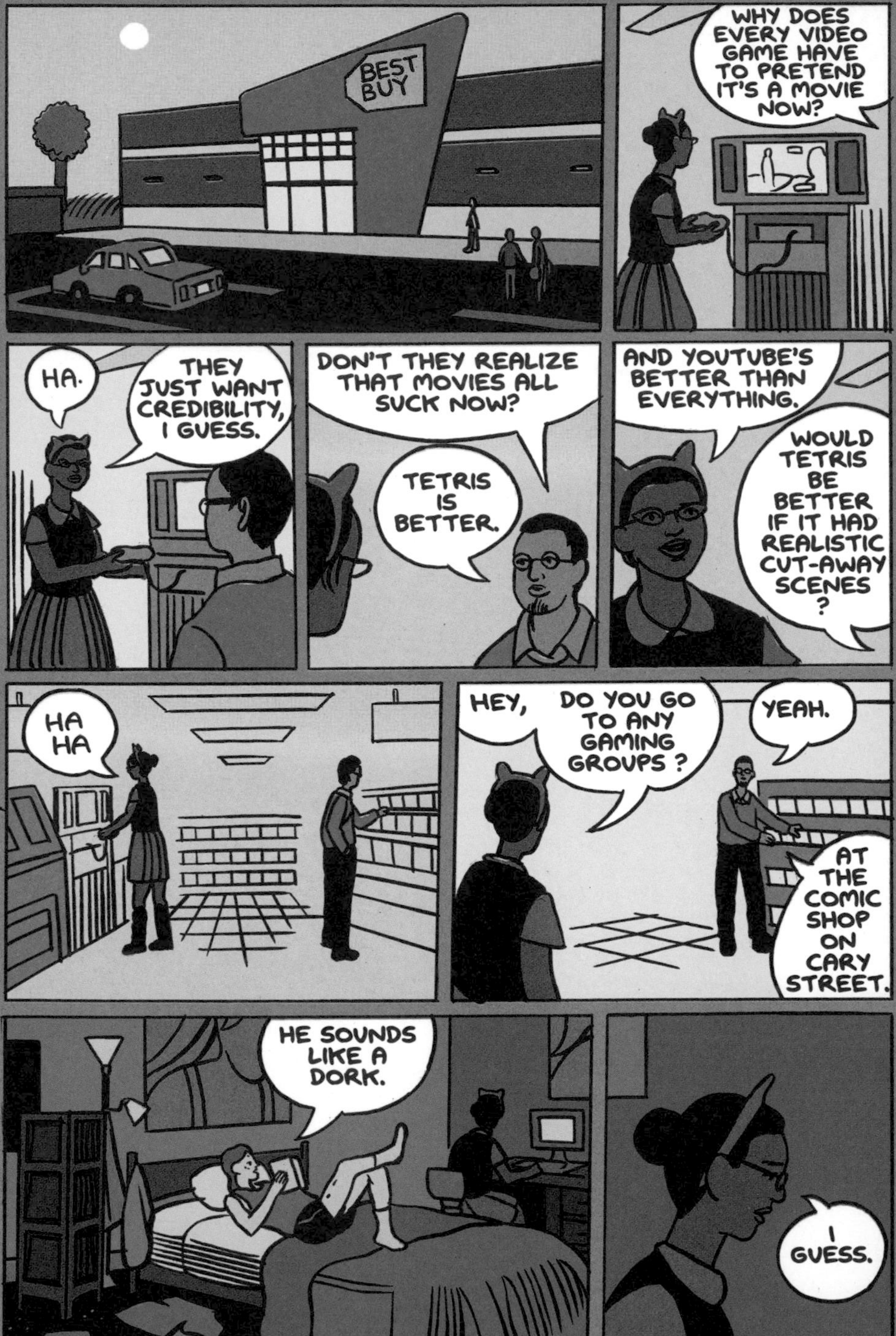
BEST BUY
WHY DOES EVERY VIDEO GAME HAVE TO PRETEND IT'S A MOVIE NOW?
HA.
THEY JUST WANT CREDIBILITY, I GUESS.
DON'T THEY REALIZE THAT MOVIES ALL SUCK NOW?
TETRIS IS BETTER.
AND YOUTUBE'S BETTER THAN EVERYTHING.
WOULD TETRIS BE BETTER IF IT HAD REALISTIC CUT-AWAY SCENES ?
HA HA
HEY,
DO YOU GO TO ANY GAMING GROUPS ?
YEAH.
AT THE COMIC SHOP ON CARY STREET.
HE SOUNDS LIKE A DORK.
I GUESS.

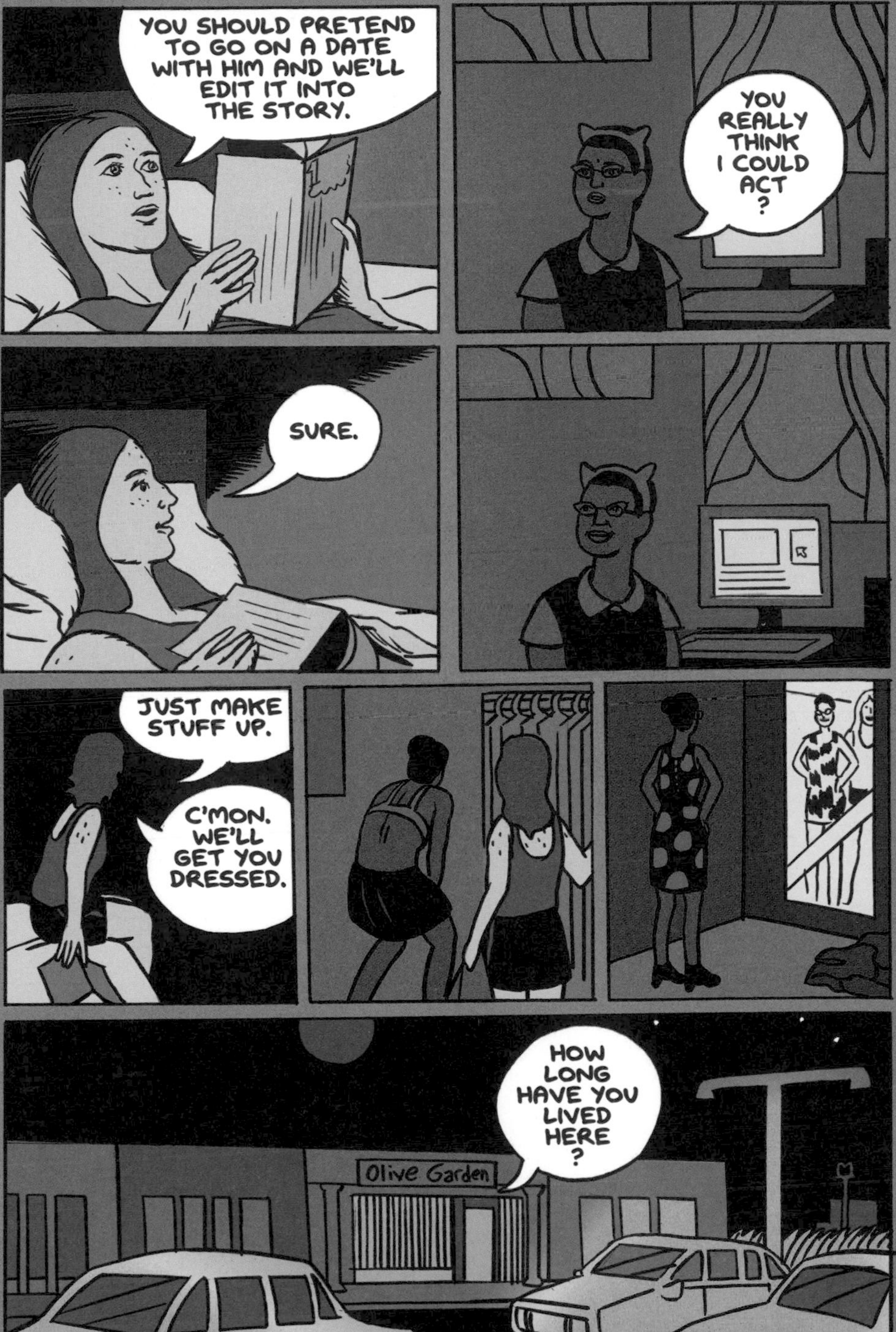
YOU SHOULD PRETEND TO GO ON A DATE WITH HIM AND WE'LL EDIT IT INTO THE STORY.
YOU REALLY THINK I COULD ACT?
SURE.
JUST MAKE STUFF UP.
C'MON. WE'LL GET YOU DRESSED.
HOW LONG HAVE YOU LIVED HERE?
Olive Garden

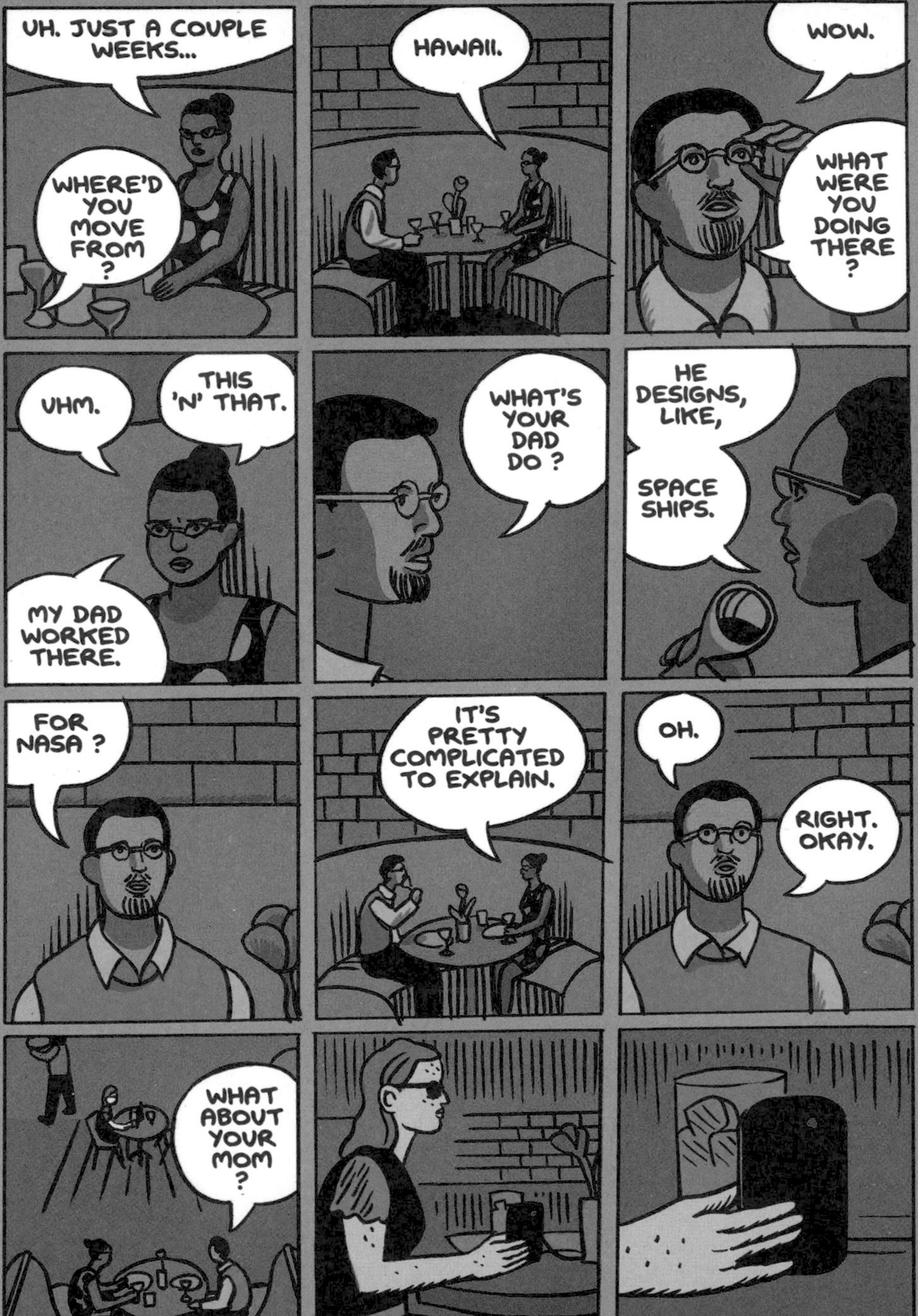
UH. JUST A COUPLE WEEKS...
WHERE'D YOU MOVE FROM ?
HAWAII.
WOW.
WHAT WERE YOU DOING THERE ?
UHM.
THIS 'N' THAT.
MY DAD WORKED THERE.
WHAT'S YOUR DAD DO ?
HE DESIGNS, LIKE,
SPACE SHIPS.
FOR NASA ?
IT'S PRETTY COMPLICATED TO EXPLAIN.
OH.
RIGHT. OKAY.
WHAT ABOUT YOUR MOM ?

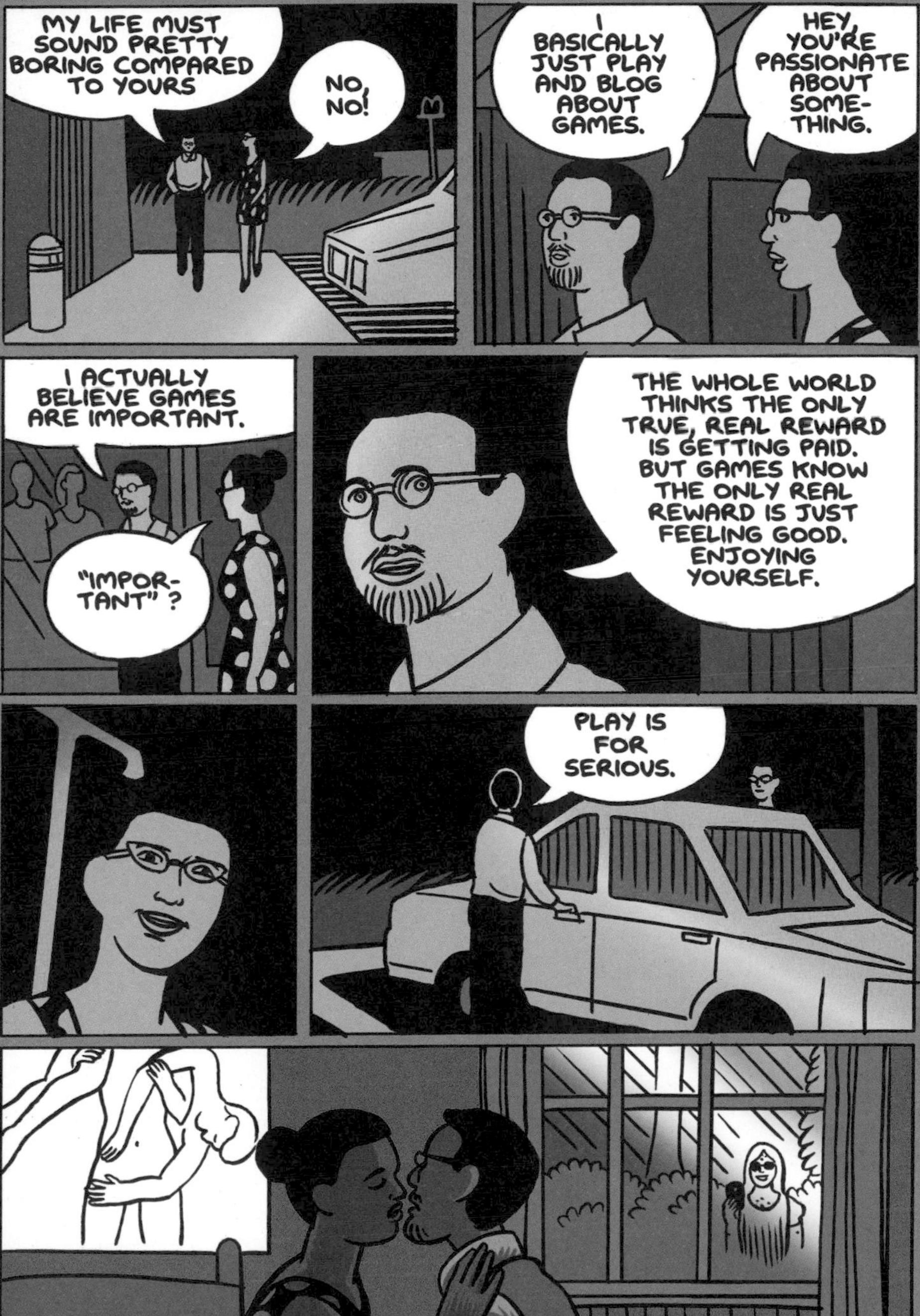
MY LIFE MUST SOUND PRETTY BORING COMPARED TO YOURS
NO, NO!
I BASICALLY JUST PLAY AND BLOG ABOUT GAMES.
HEY, YOU'RE PASSIONATE ABOUT SOME-THING.
I ACTUALLY BELIEVE GAMES ARE IMPORTANT.
"IMPOR-TANT" ?
THE WHOLE WORLD THINKS THE ONLY TRUE, REAL REWARD IS GETTING PAID. BUT GAMES KNOW THE ONLY REAL REWARD IS JUST FEELING GOOD. ENJOYING YOURSELF.
PLAY IS FOR SERIOUS.

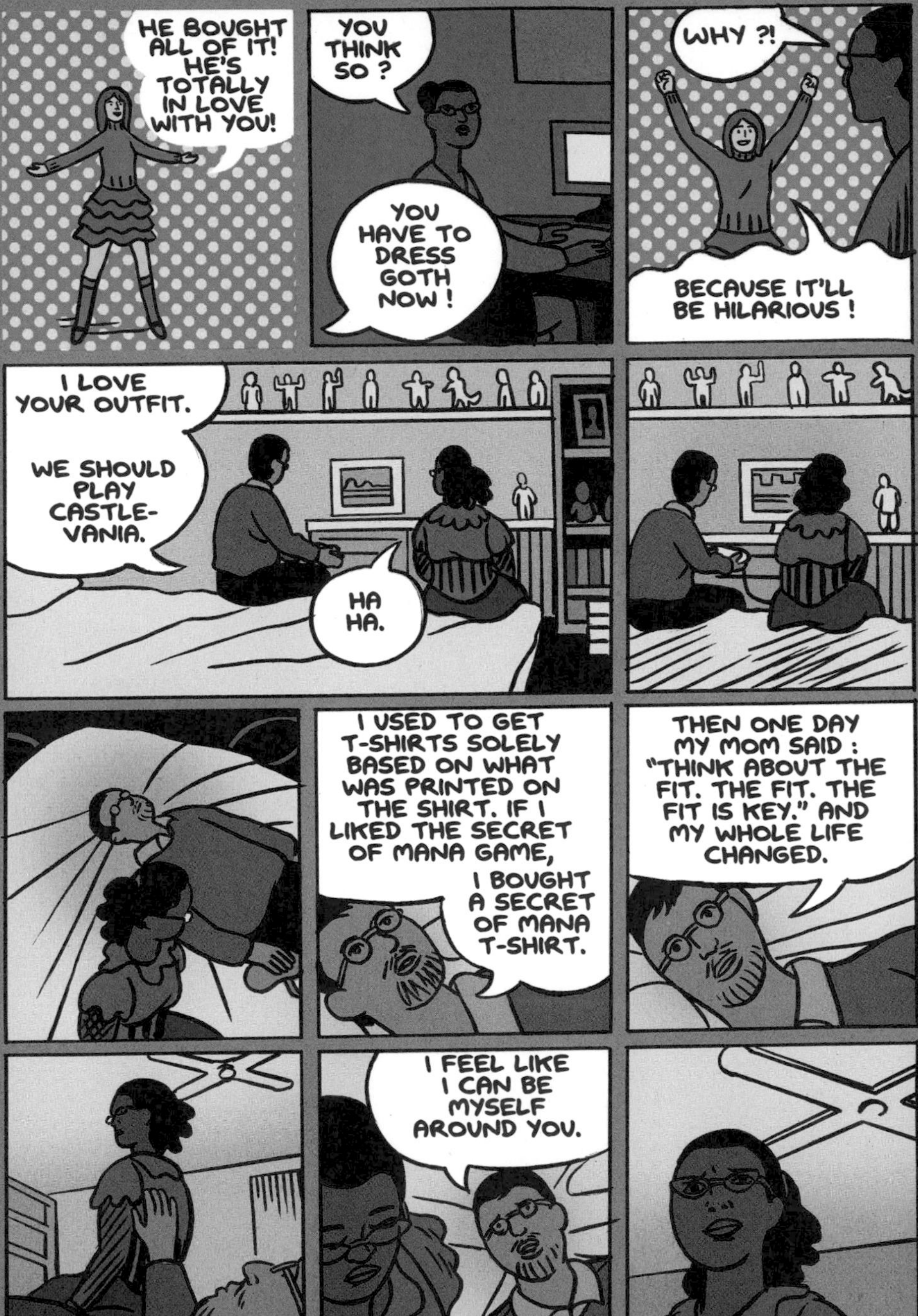
HE BOUGHT ALL OF IT! HE'S TOTALLY IN LOVE WITH YOU!
YOU THINK SO ?
YOU HAVE TO DRESS GOTH NOW !
WHY ?!
BECAUSE IT'LL BE HILARIOUS !
I LOVE YOUR OUTFIT.
WE SHOULD PLAY CASTLE-VANIA.
HA HA.
I USED TO GET T-SHIRTS SOLELY BASED ON WHAT WAS PRINTED ON THE SHIRT. IF I LIKED THE SECRET OF MANA GAME,
I BOUGHT A SECRET OF MANA T-SHIRT.
THEN ONE DAY MY MOM SAID : "THINK ABOUT THE FIT. THE FIT. THE FIT IS KEY." AND MY WHOLE LIFE CHANGED.
I FEEL LIKE I CAN BE MYSELF AROUND YOU.

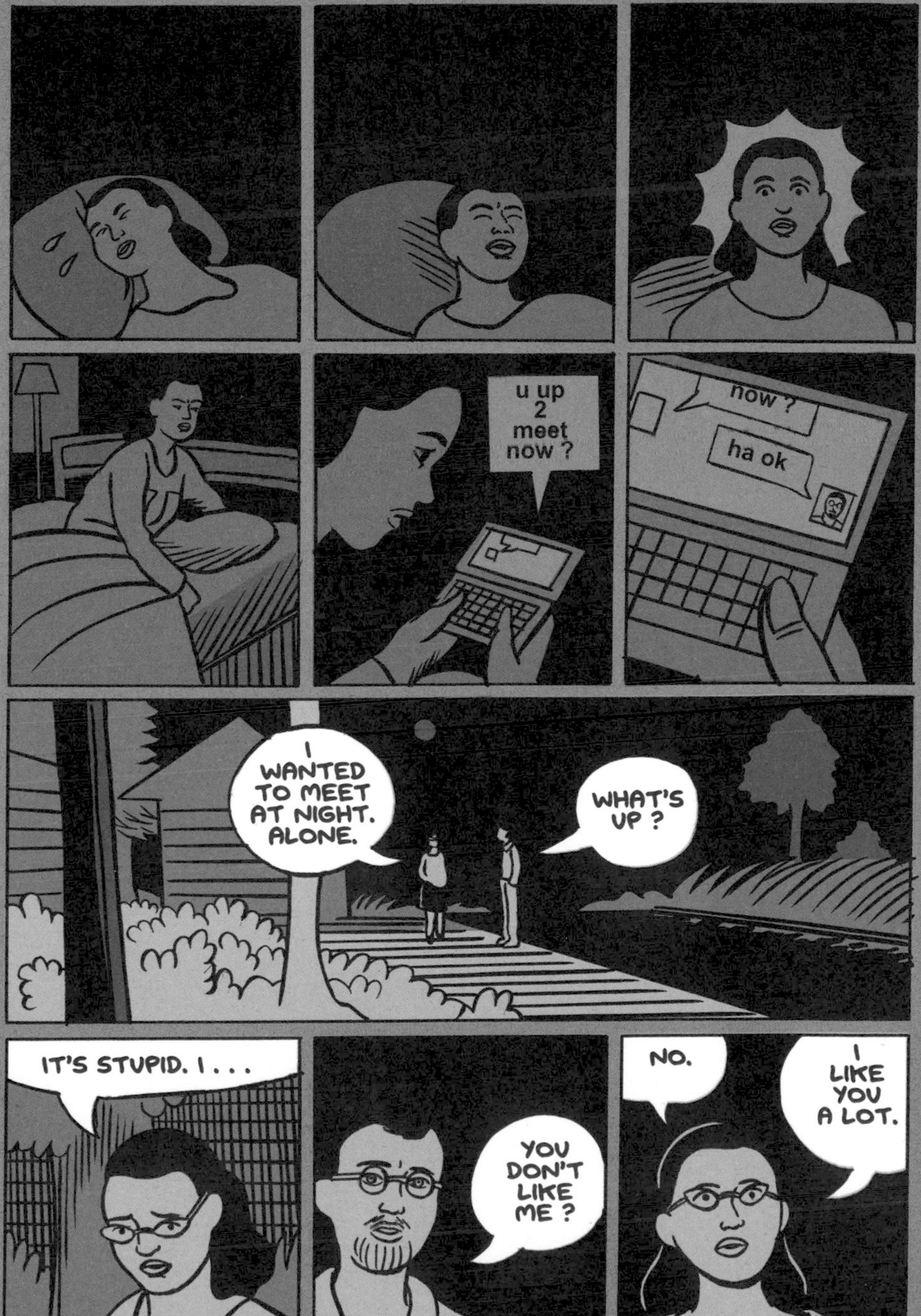
u up 2 meet now ?
now ?
ha ok
I WANTED TO MEET AT NIGHT. ALONE.
WHAT'S UP ?
IT'S STUPID. I . . .
YOU DON'T LIKE ME ?
NO.
I LIKE YOU A LOT.

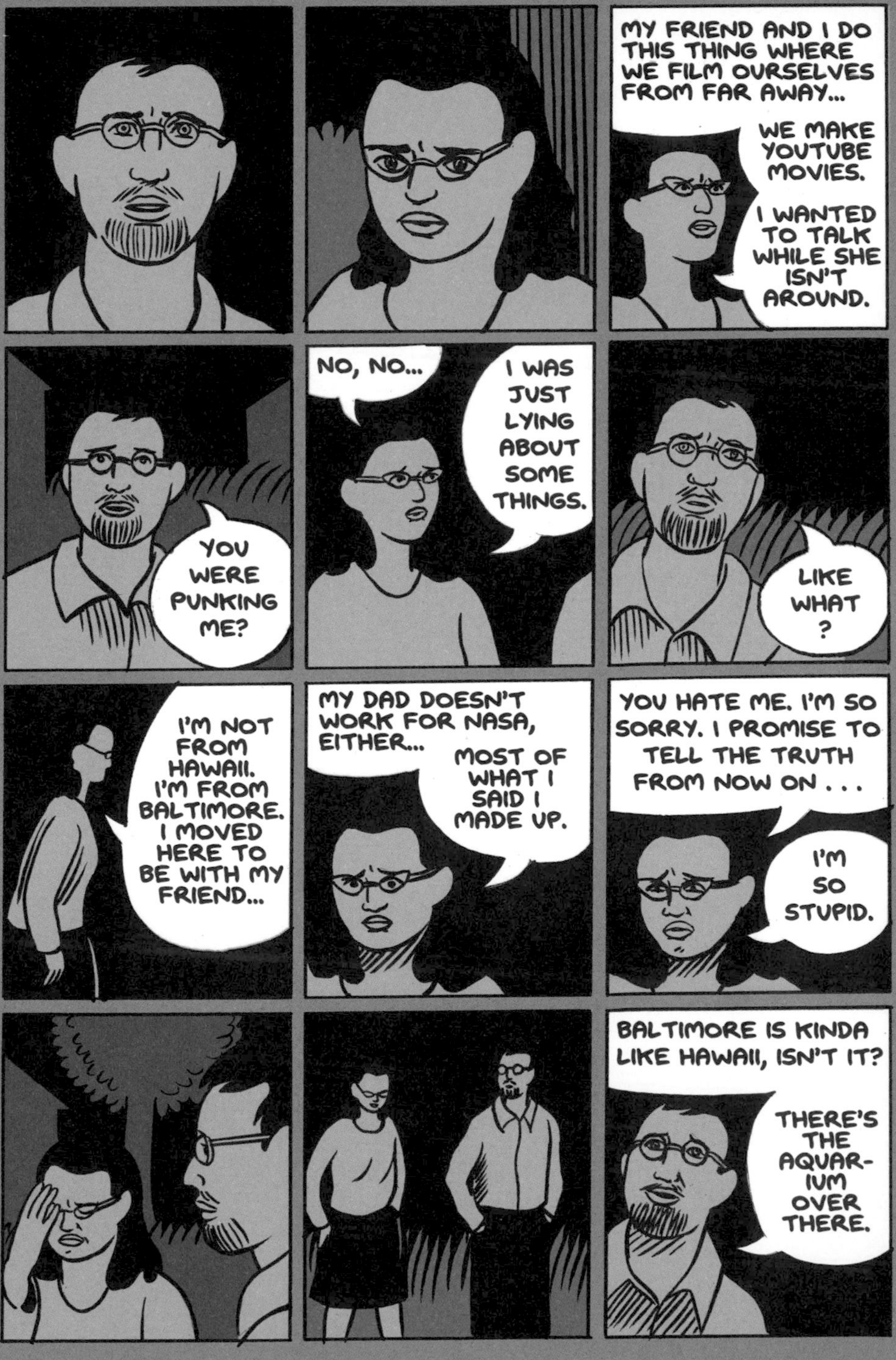
MY FRIEND AND I DO THIS THING WHERE WE FILM OURSELVES FROM FAR AWAY...
WE MAKE YOUTUBE MOVIES.
I WANTED TO TALK WHILE SHE ISN'T AROUND.
YOU WERE PUNKING ME?
NO, NO...
I WAS JUST LYING ABOUT SOME THINGS.
LIKE WHAT ?
I'M NOT FROM HAWAII. I'M FROM BALTIMORE. I MOVED HERE TO BE WITH MY FRIEND...
MY DAD DOESN'T WORK FOR NASA, EITHER...
MOST OF WHAT I SAID I MADE UP.
YOU HATE ME. I'M SO SORRY. I PROMISE TO TELL THE TRUTH FROM NOW ON . . .
I'M SO STUPID.
BALTIMORE IS KINDA LIKE HAWAII, ISN'T IT?
THERE'S THE AQUAR-IUM OVER THERE.

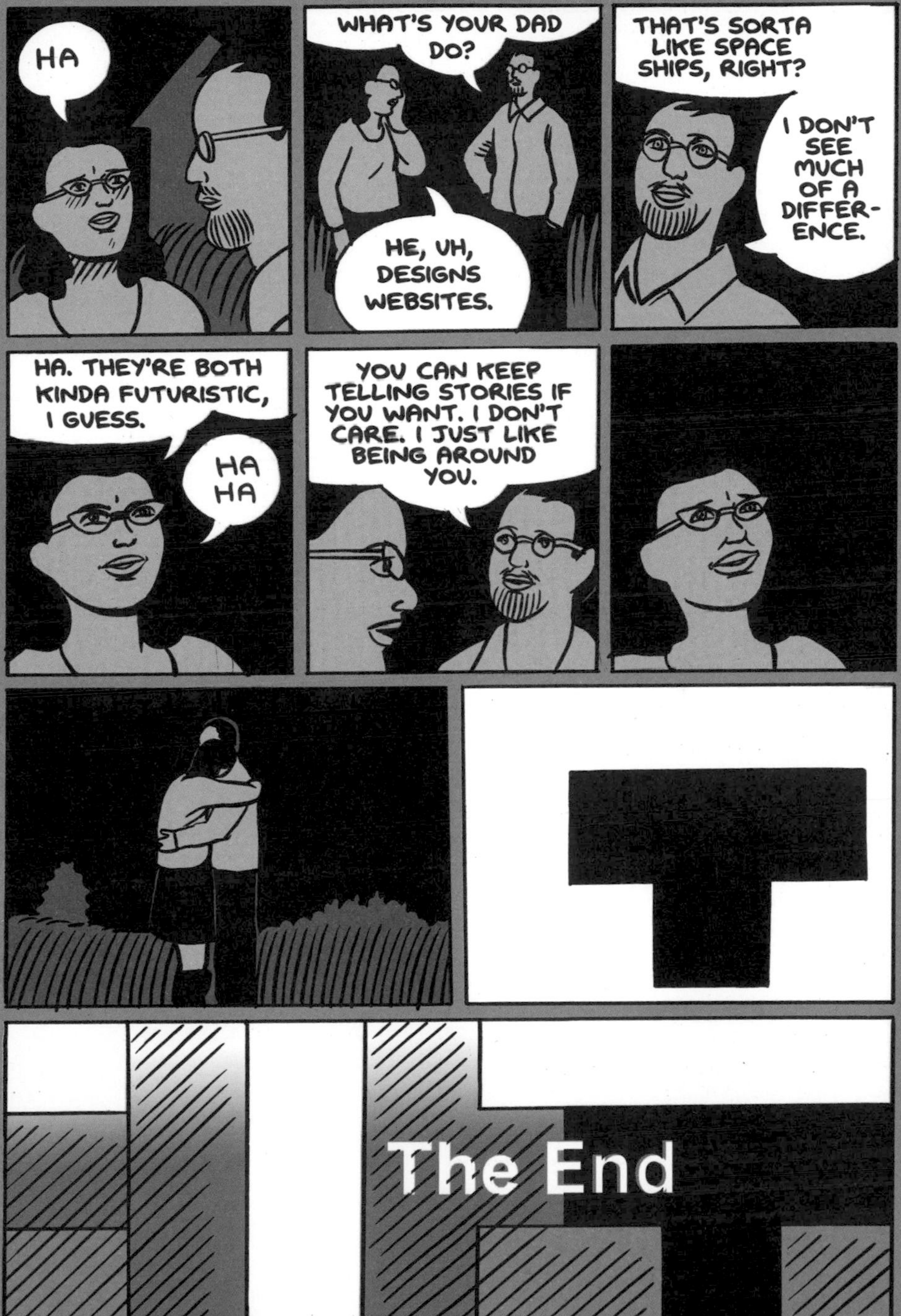
HA
WHAT'S YOUR DAD DO?
HE, UH, DESIGNS WEBSITES.
THAT'S SORTA LIKE SPACE SHIPS, RIGHT?
I DON'T SEE MUCH OF A DIFFERENCE.
HA. THEY'RE BOTH KINDA FUTURISTIC, I GUESS.
HA HA
YOU CAN KEEP TELLING STORIES IF YOU WANT. I DON'T CARE. I JUST LIKE BEING AROUND YOU.
The End

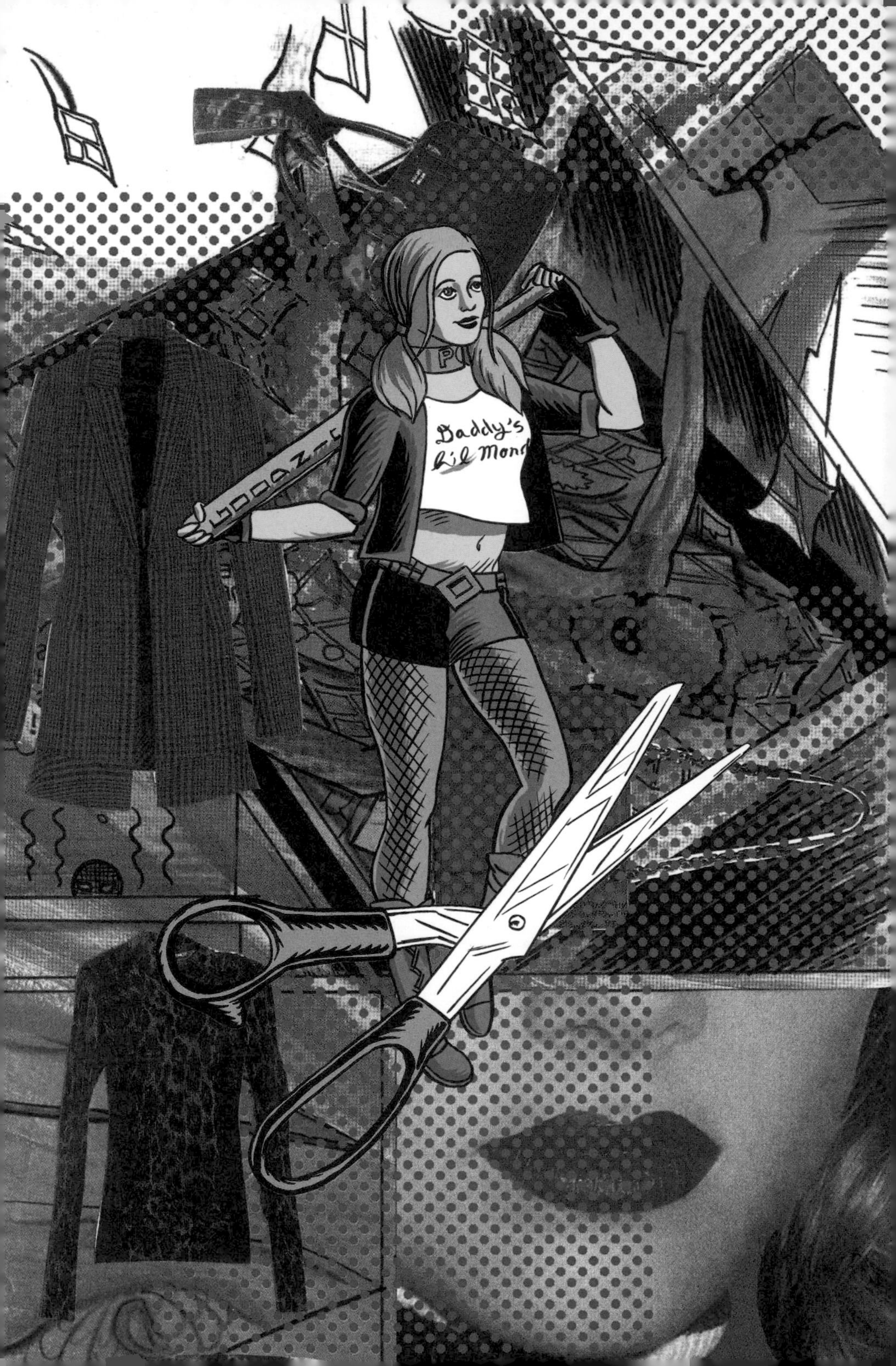
Daddy's Lil Monst

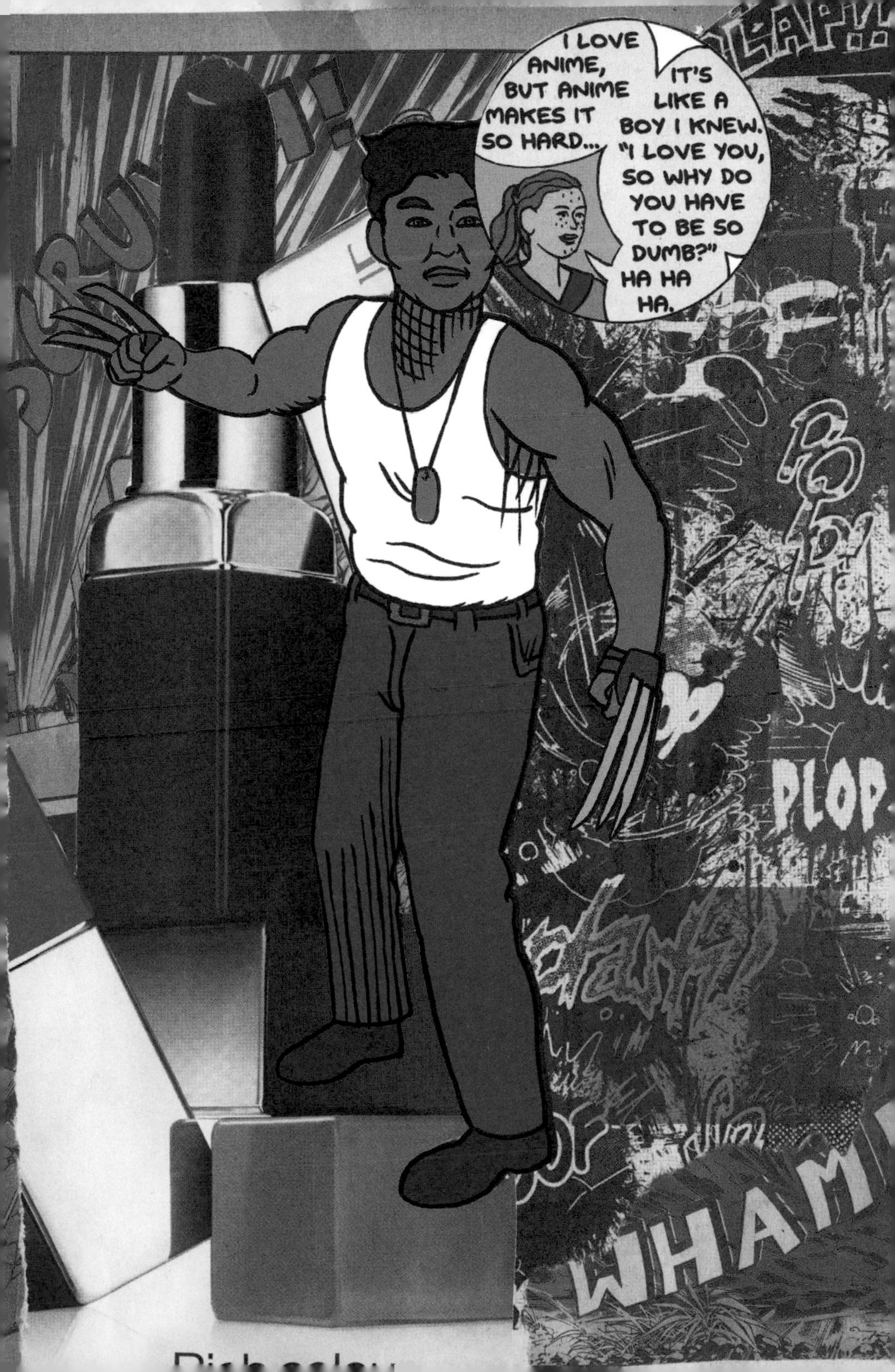
I LOVE ANIME, BUT ANIME MAKES IT SO HARD...
IT'S LIKE A BOY I KNEW. "I LOVE YOU, SO WHY DO YOU HAVE TO BE SO DUMB?" HA HA HA.
PLOP
WHAM

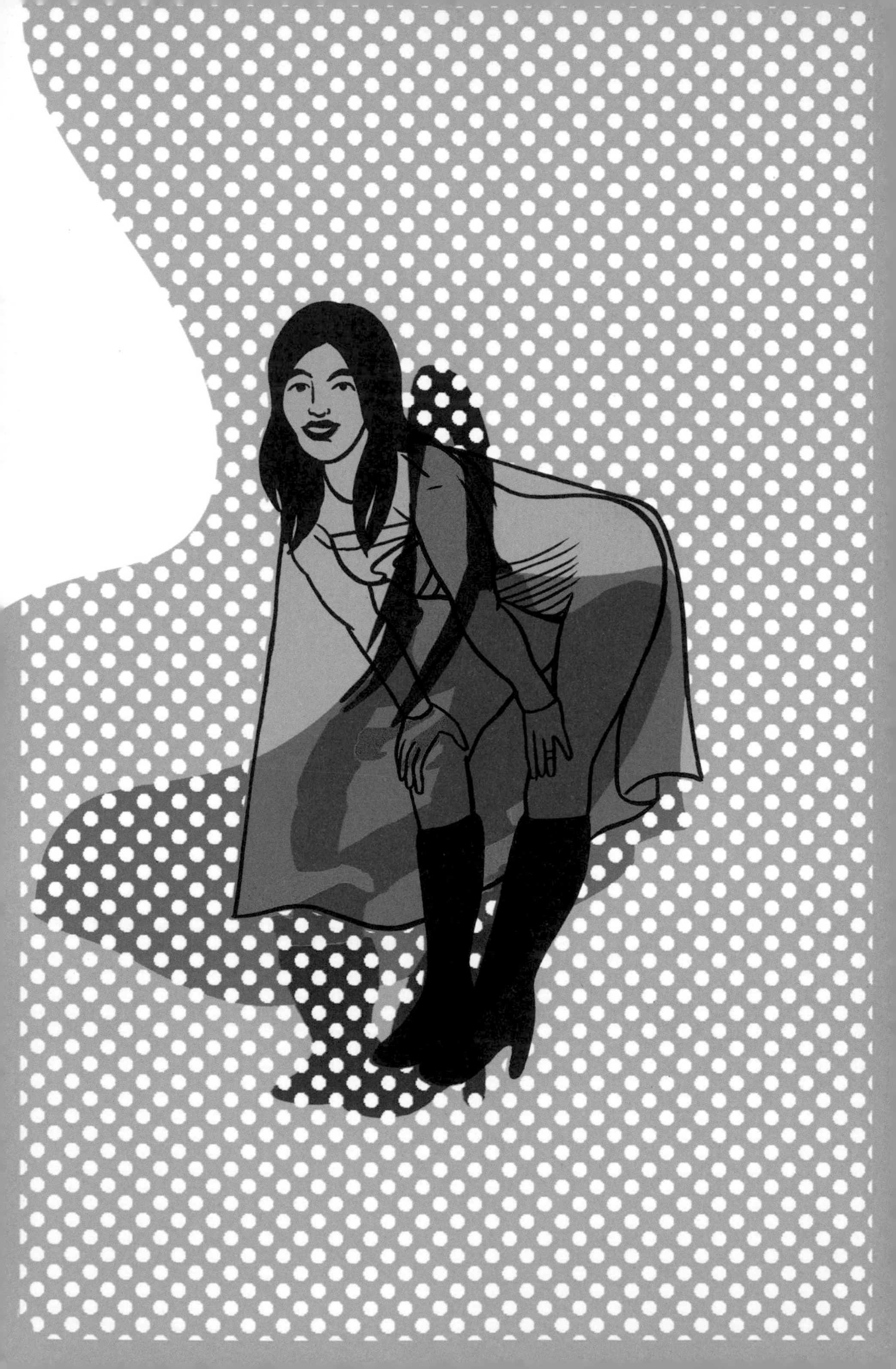

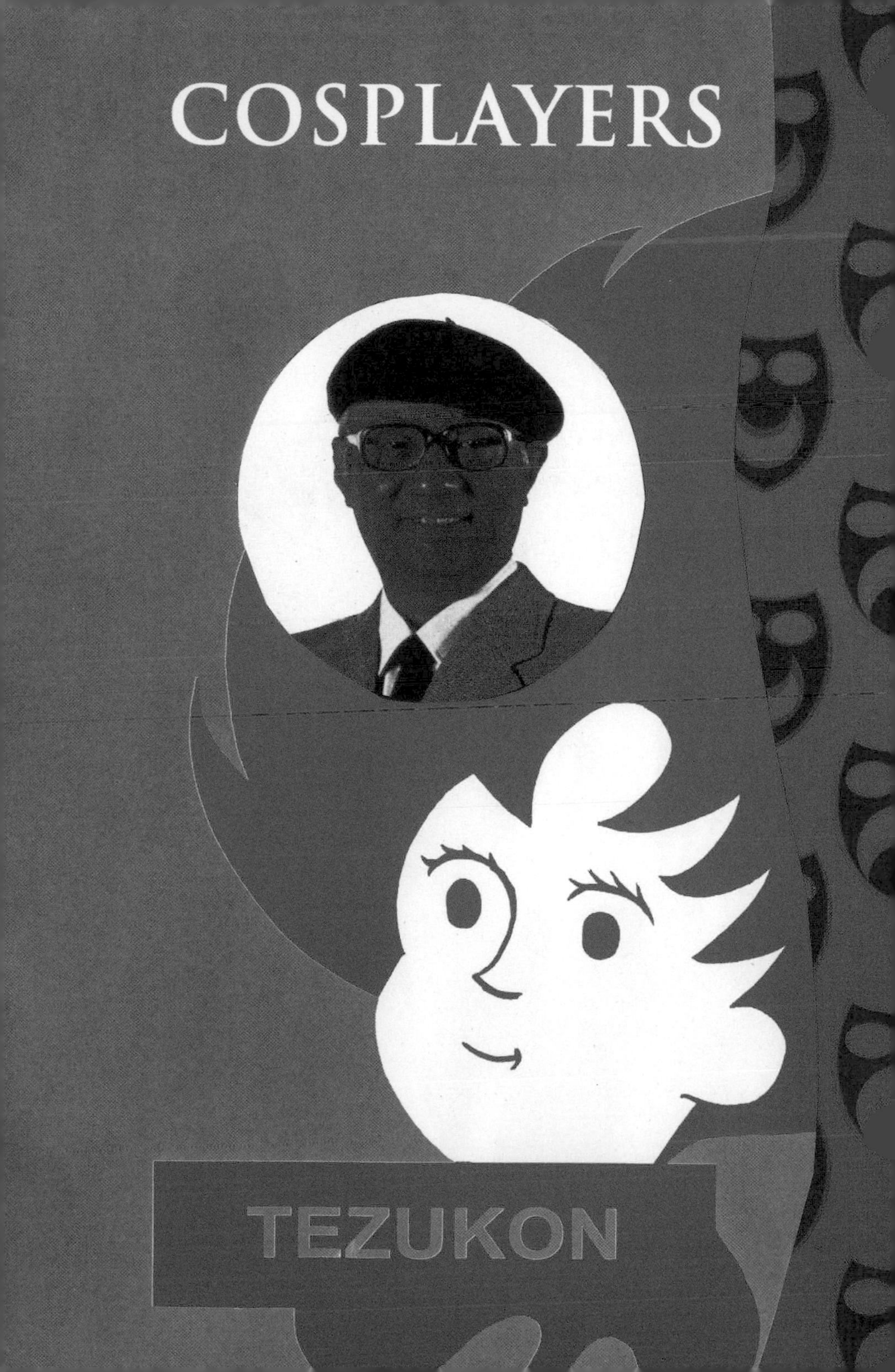
COSPLAYERS
TEZUKON

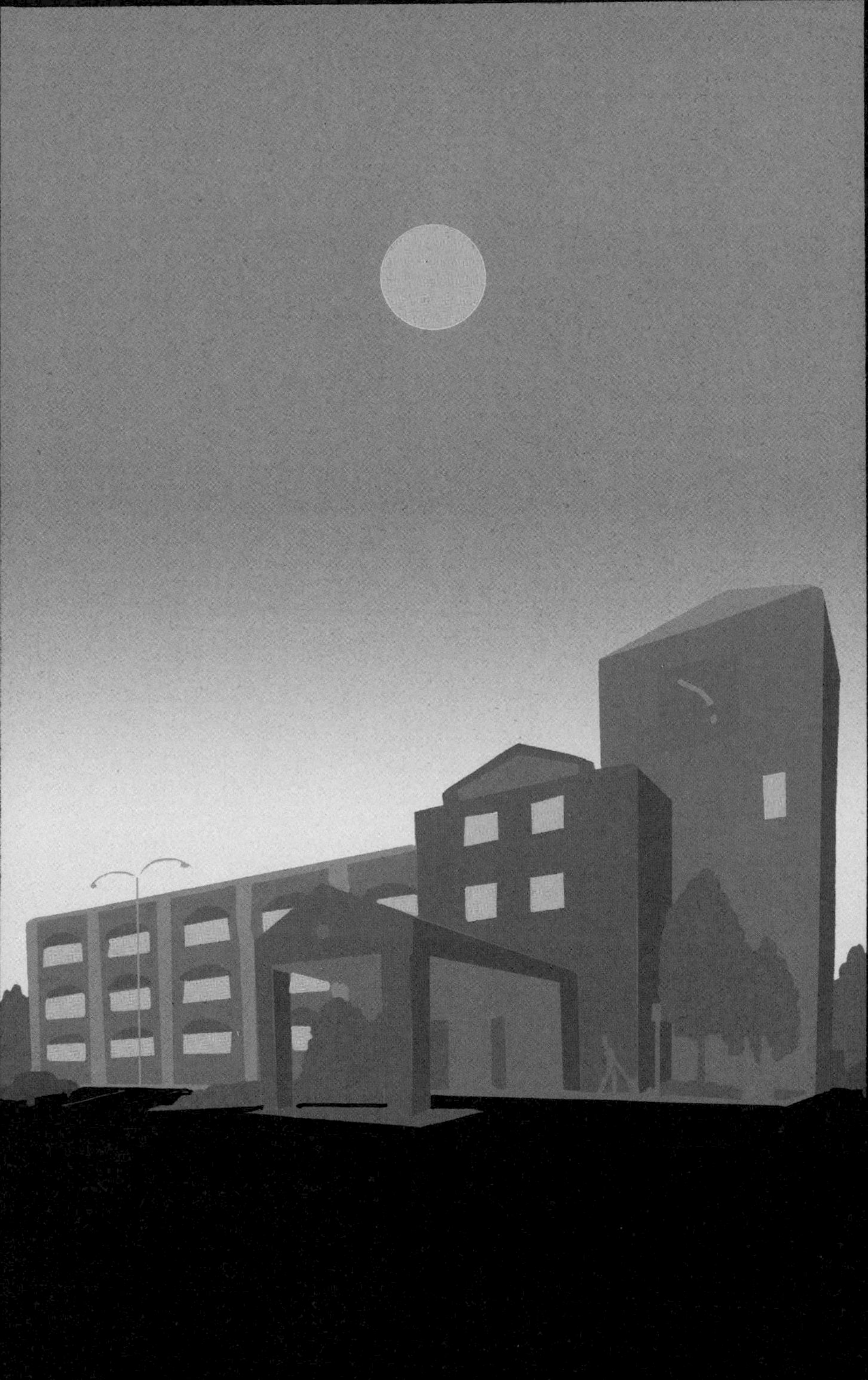

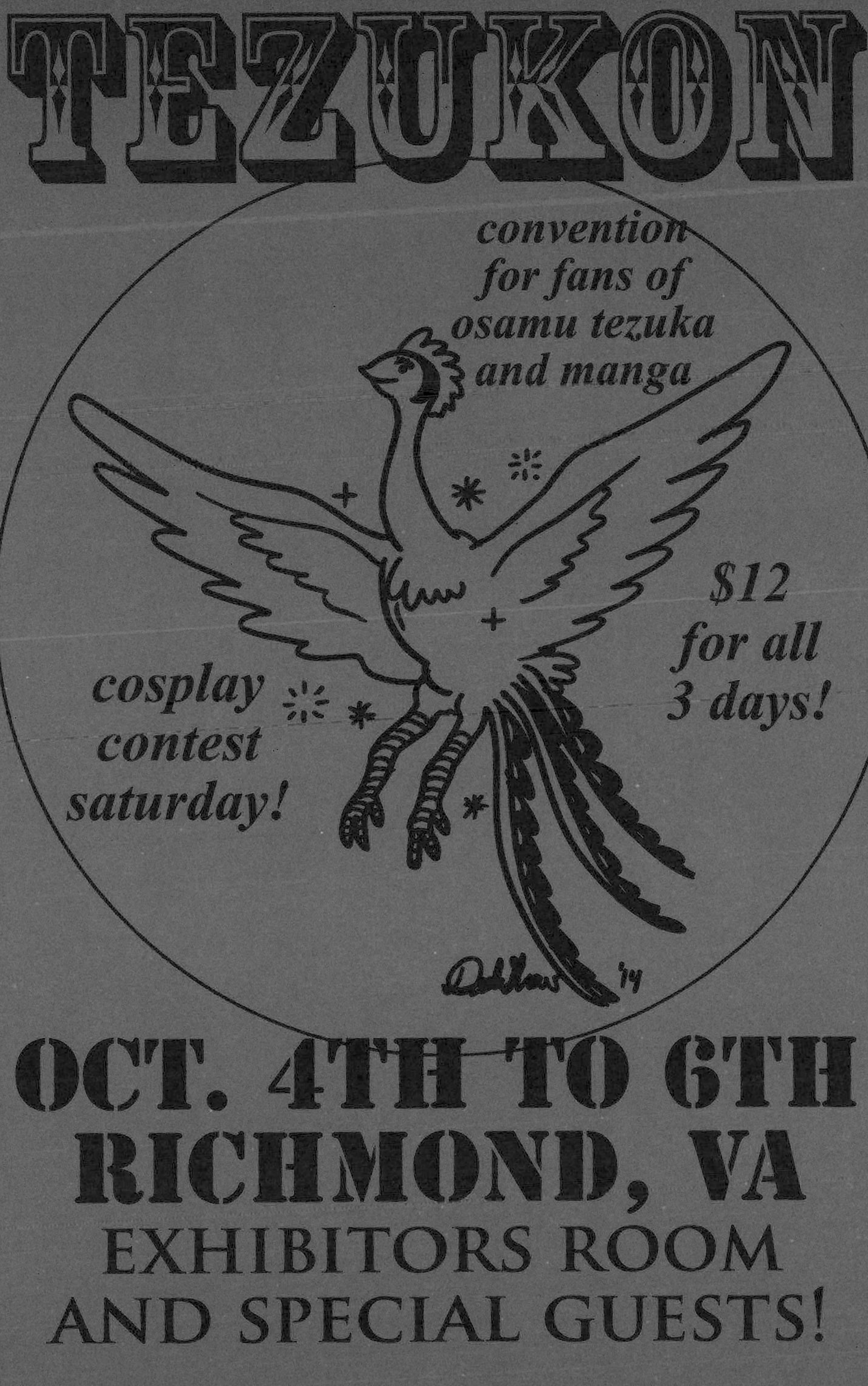
TEZUKON
convention for fans of osamu tezuka and manga
$12 for all 3 days!
cosplay contest saturday!
OCT. 4TH TO 6TH
RICHMOND, VA
EXHIBITORS ROOM
AND SPECIAL GUESTS!

Exhibitors Floor open Friday 5-7pm, Saturday 9am-7pm, Sunday 10am-5pm

FRIDAY

Panels Room		Screenings Room	
Time	Event	Time	Film
5pm	West to East: Anime Adaptations.	5pm	Kemonozune
6pm	Becky Cloonan Q&A	7pm	To-Y
7pm	8 bit and 16 bit DJ Night	8pm	Odin: Photon Sailor Starlight

SATURDAY

Panels Room		Screenings Room	
9am	Anime/Manga Scholar Ben Baxter on Tezuka's Legacy	10am	Bobby's Girl
10am	Cosplay Competition	11am	Midori
12pm	Anime Fandom: Then & Now	12pm	Robot Carnival
1pm	Robotech Tribute Panel	2pm	Night on the Galactic Railroad
3pm	Hope Larson Q&A	4pm	Neo-Tokyo
4pm	Draw Your Own Manga Workshop	6pm	Lupin III : Legend of the Gold of Babylon
5pm	Cosplay Winners Announced	8pm	The Sensualist
6pm	Into to J-Pop	10pm	Belladonna of the Sadness
7pm	Karaoke Night	12am	Angel's Egg

SUNDAY

Panels Room		Screenings Room	
11am	Anime News Network Discussion Panel	11am	Cat Soup
12pm	Katie Skelly Q&A	12pm	Giant Robo (1992)
1pm	Manga Scholar Ryan Holmberg on Garo	1pm	A Thousand & One Nights (Animerama)
2pm	Toonami: A Look Back	3pm	Tezuka's Experimental Shorts
3pm	Gundam Plastic Model Kits Demonstration	4pm	Astro Boy (Original Series)
4pm	Roundtable on Manga's Enduring Influence	5pm	Royal Space Force: The Wings of Honneamise
		7pm	The End of Evangelion

BE SAFE !

Friday

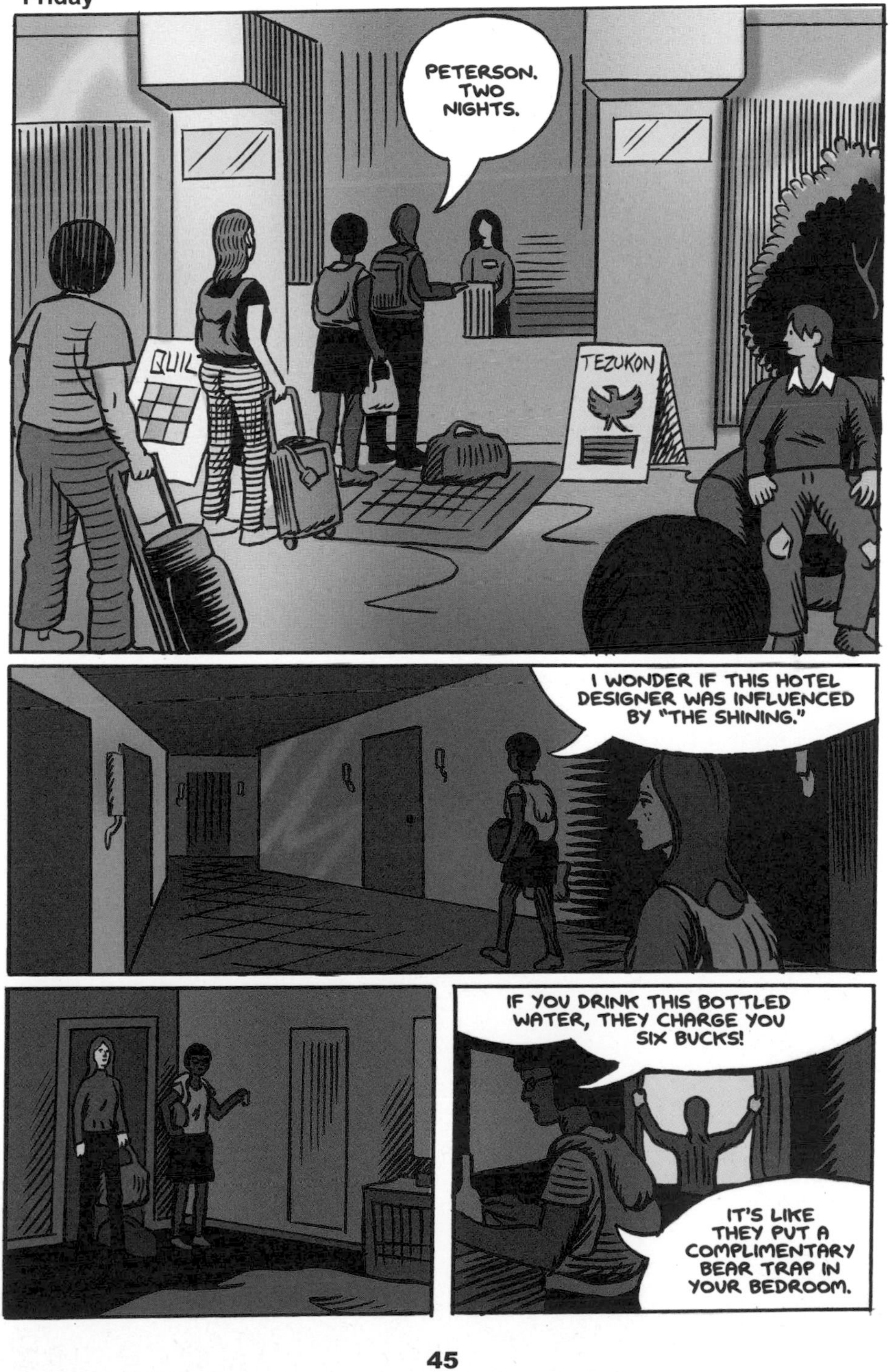

PETERSON. TWO NIGHTS.
QUIL
TEZUKON
I WONDER IF THIS HOTEL DESIGNER WAS INFLUENCED BY "THE SHINING."
IF YOU DRINK THIS BOTTLED WATER, THEY CHARGE YOU SIX BUCKS!
IT'S LIKE THEY PUT A COMPLIMENTARY BEAR TRAP IN YOUR BEDROOM.

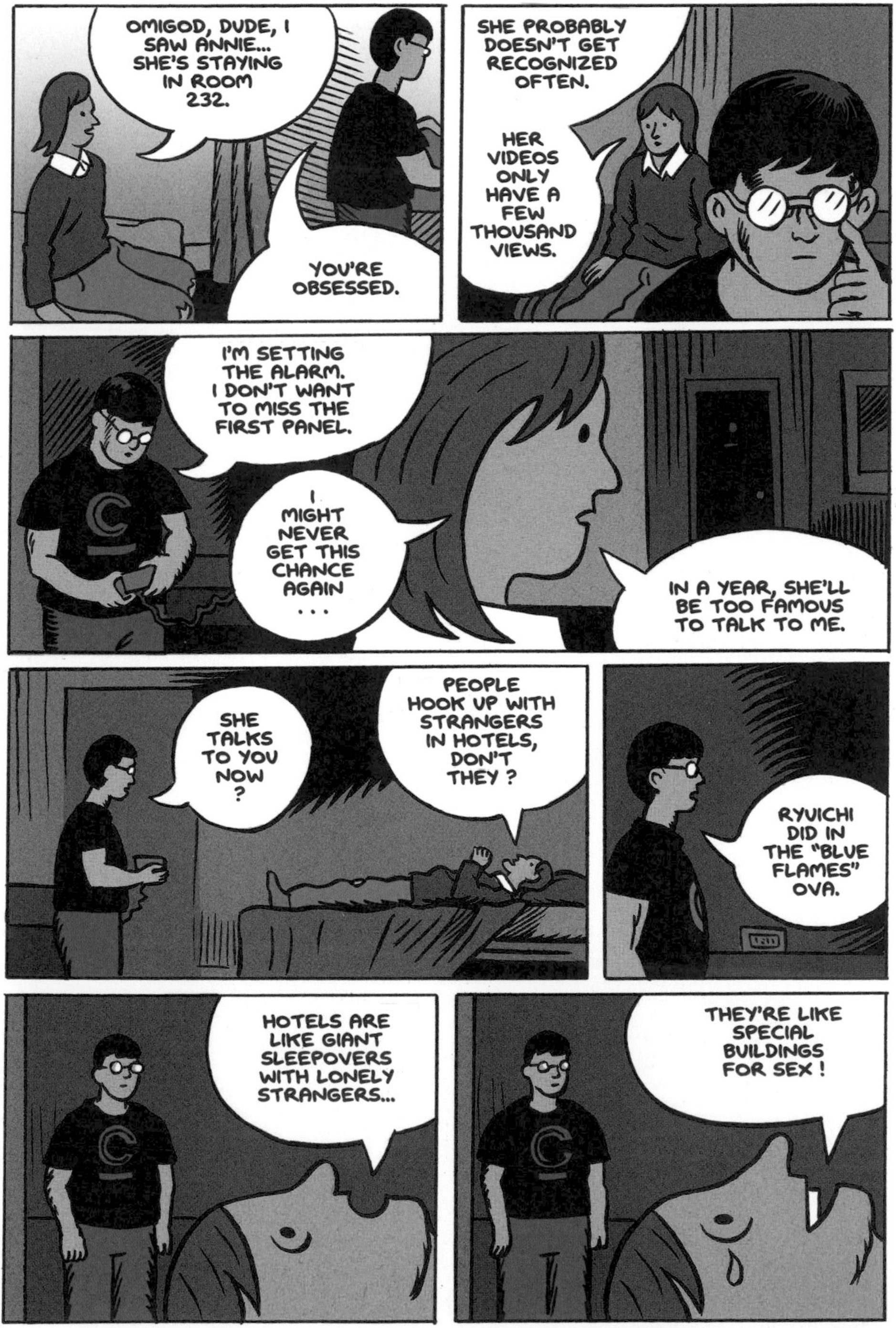
OMIGOD, DUDE, I SAW ANNIE... SHE'S STAYING IN ROOM 232.
YOU'RE OBSESSED.
SHE PROBABLY DOESN'T GET RECOGNIZED OFTEN.
HER VIDEOS ONLY HAVE A FEW THOUSAND VIEWS.
I'M SETTING THE ALARM. I DON'T WANT TO MISS THE FIRST PANEL.
I MIGHT NEVER GET THIS CHANCE AGAIN . . .
IN A YEAR, SHE'LL BE TOO FAMOUS TO TALK TO ME.
SHE TALKS TO YOU NOW ?
PEOPLE HOOK UP WITH STRANGERS IN HOTELS, DON'T THEY ?
RYUICHI DID IN THE "BLUE FLAMES" OVA.
HOTELS ARE LIKE GIANT SLEEPOVERS WITH LONELY STRANGERS...
THEY'RE LIKE SPECIAL BUILDINGS FOR SEX !

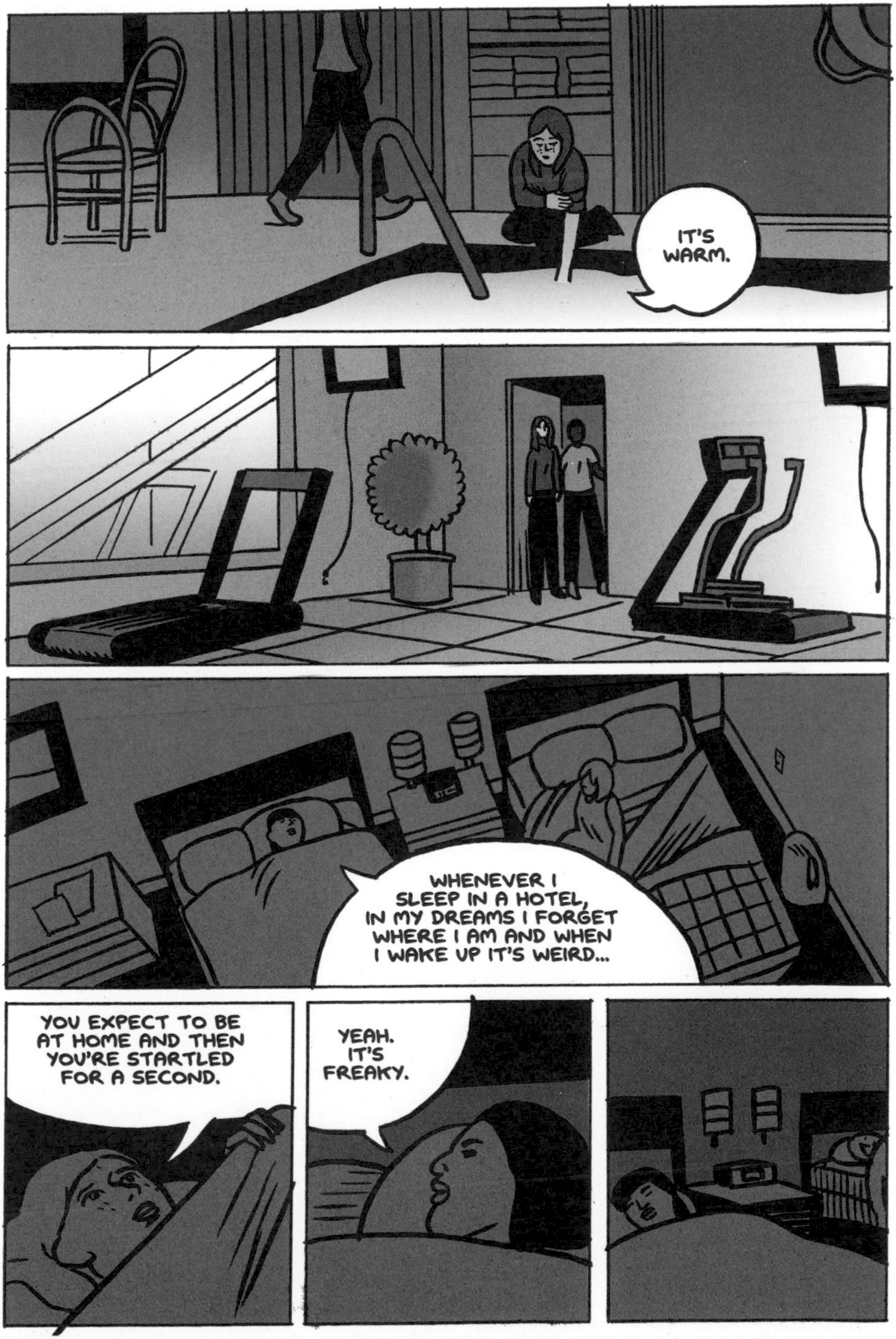
IT'S WARM.
WHENEVER I SLEEP IN A HOTEL, IN MY DREAMS I FORGET WHERE I AM AND WHEN I WAKE UP IT'S WEIRD...
YOU EXPECT TO BE AT HOME AND THEN YOU'RE STARTLED FOR A SECOND.
YEAH. IT'S FREAKY.

Saturday

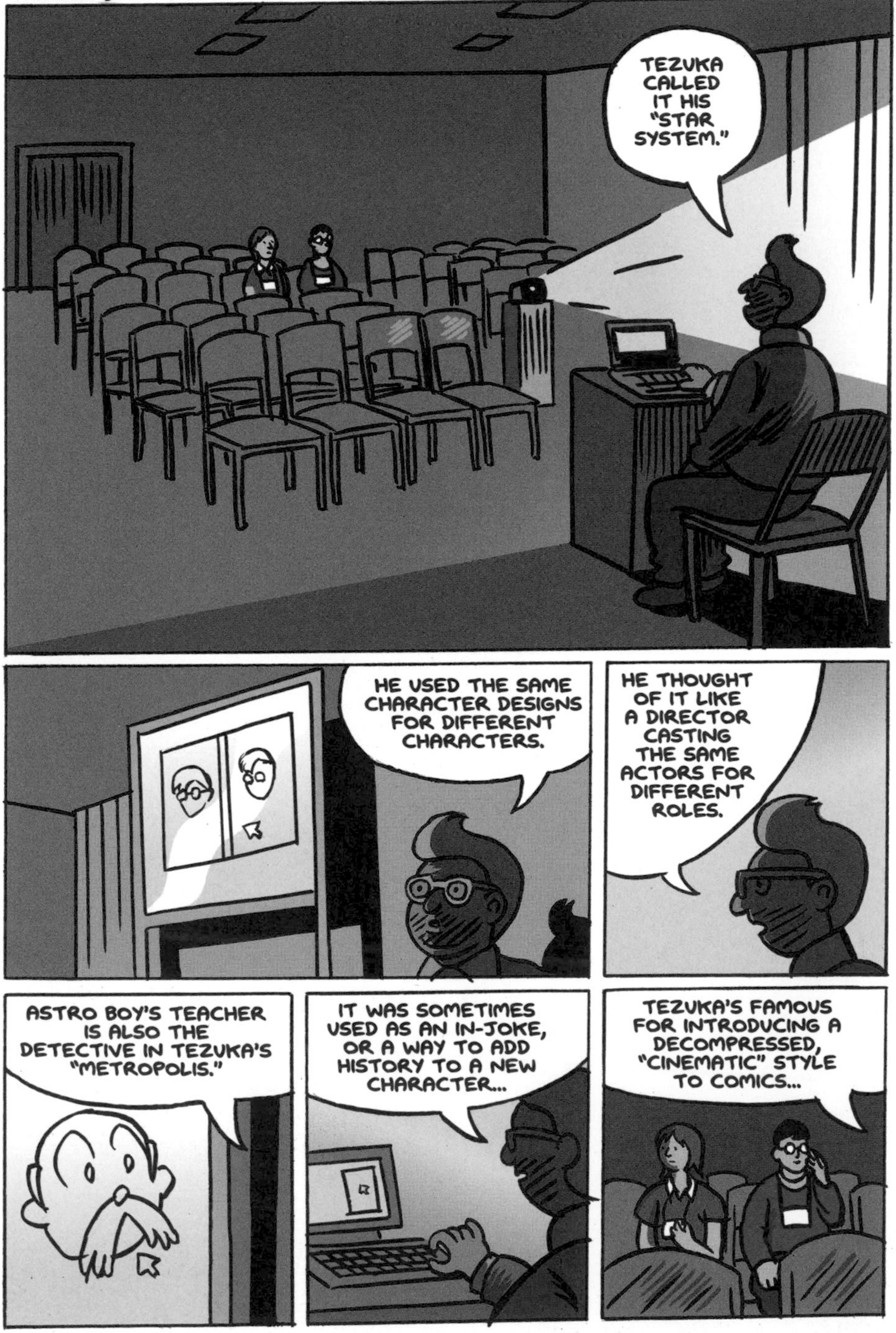
TEZUKA CALLED IT HIS "STAR SYSTEM."
HE USED THE SAME CHARACTER DESIGNS FOR DIFFERENT CHARACTERS.
HE THOUGHT OF IT LIKE A DIRECTOR CASTING THE SAME ACTORS FOR DIFFERENT ROLES.
ASTRO BOY'S TEACHER IS ALSO THE DETECTIVE IN TEZUKA'S "METROPOLIS."
IT WAS SOMETIMES USED AS AN IN-JOKE, OR A WAY TO ADD HISTORY TO A NEW CHARACTER...
TEZUKA'S FAMOUS FOR INTRODUCING A DECOMPRESSED, "CINEMATIC" STYLE TO COMICS...

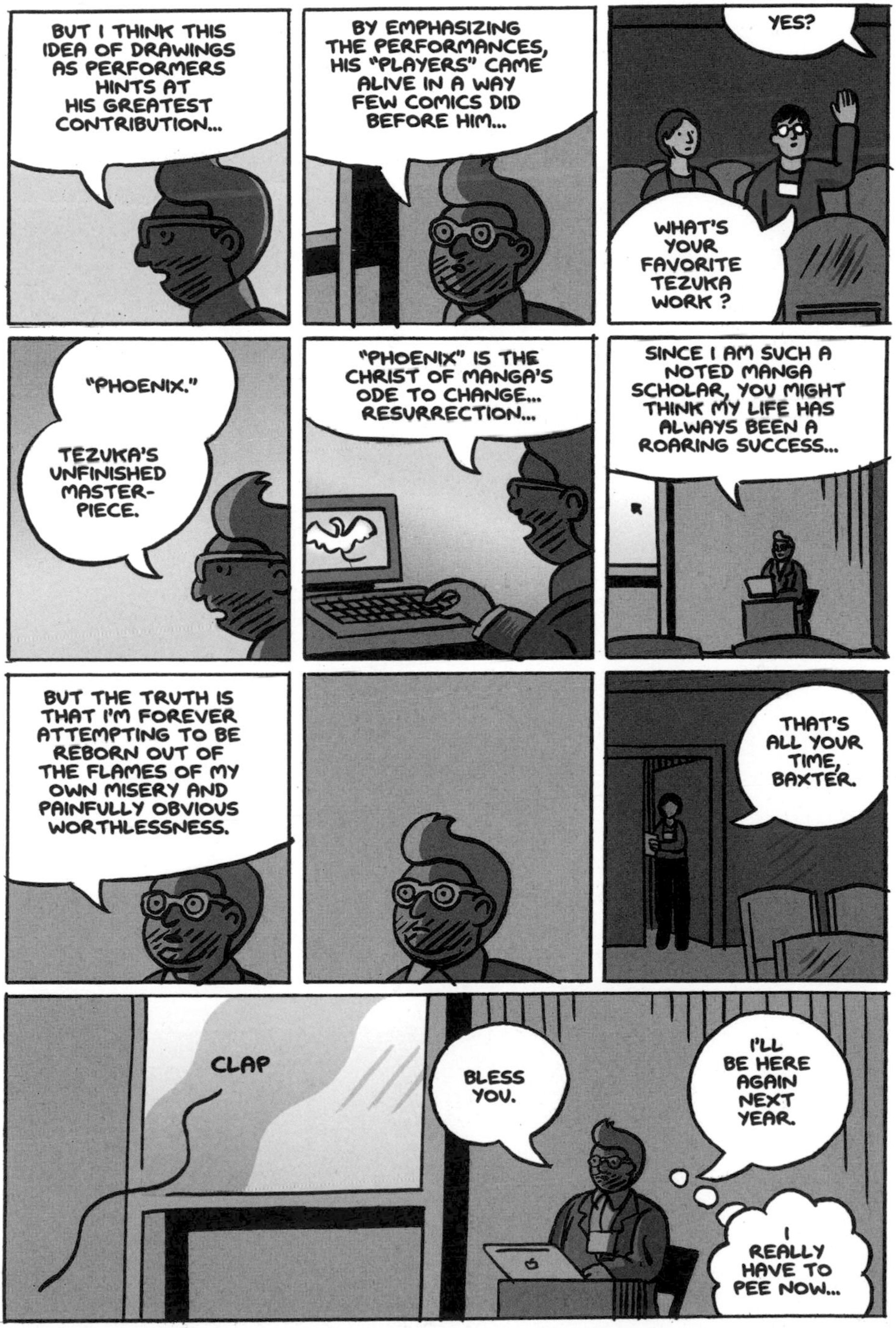
BUT I THINK THIS IDEA OF DRAWINGS AS PERFORMERS HINTS AT HIS GREATEST CONTRIBUTION...
BY EMPHASIZING THE PERFORMANCES, HIS "PLAYERS" CAME ALIVE IN A WAY FEW COMICS DID BEFORE HIM...
YES?
WHAT'S YOUR FAVORITE TEZUKA WORK ?
"PHOENIX."
TEZUKA'S UNFINISHED MASTER-PIECE.
"PHOENIX" IS THE CHRIST OF MANGA'S ODE TO CHANGE... RESURRECTION...
SINCE I AM SUCH A NOTED MANGA SCHOLAR, YOU MIGHT THINK MY LIFE HAS ALWAYS BEEN A ROARING SUCCESS...
BUT THE TRUTH IS THAT I'M FOREVER ATTEMPTING TO BE REBORN OUT OF THE FLAMES OF MY OWN MISERY AND PAINFULLY OBVIOUS WORTHLESSNESS.
THAT'S ALL YOUR TIME, BAXTER.
CLAP
BLESS YOU.
I'LL BE HERE AGAIN NEXT YEAR.
I REALLY HAVE TO PEE NOW...

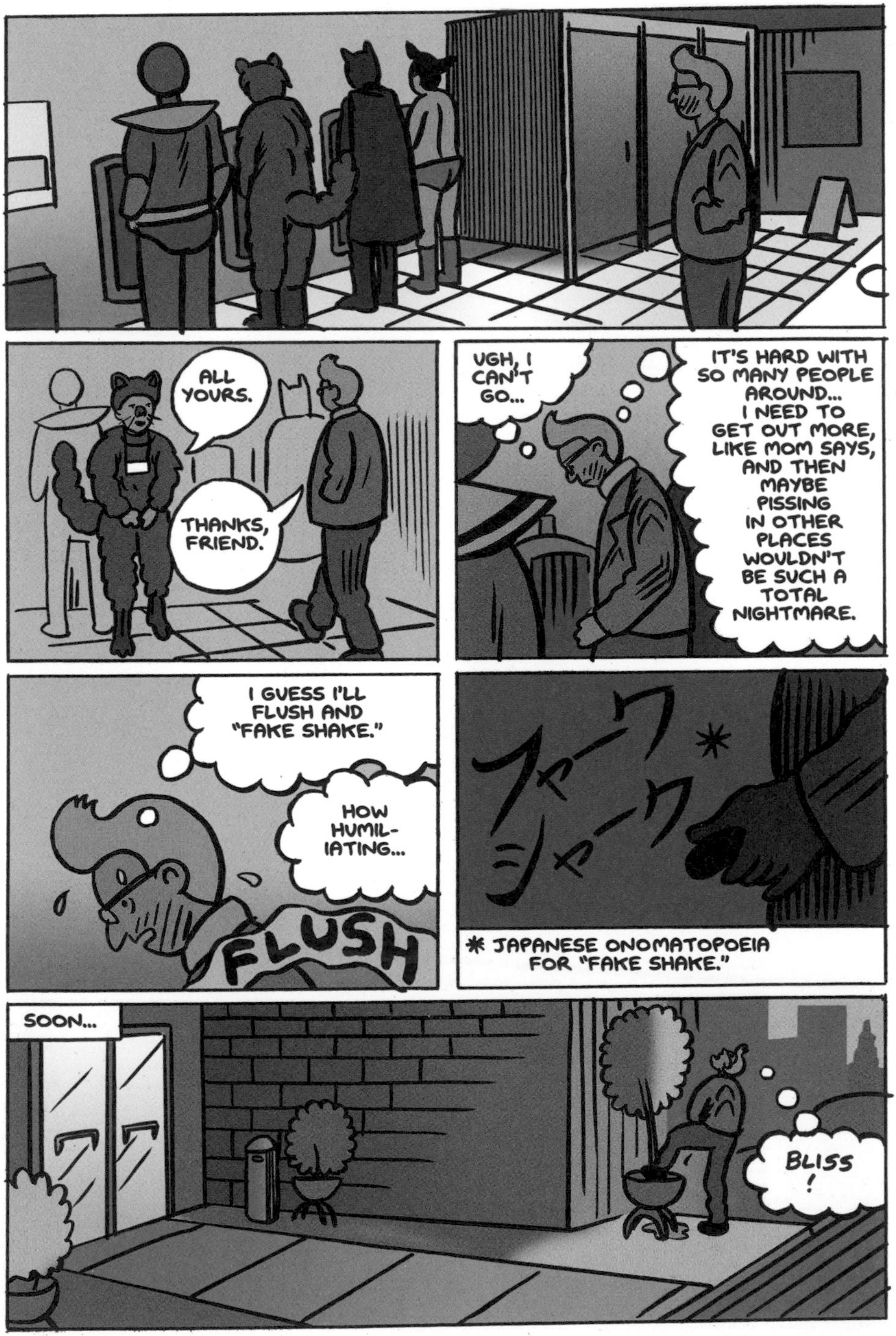
ALL YOURS.
THANKS, FRIEND.
UGH, I CAN'T GO...
IT'S HARD WITH SO MANY PEOPLE AROUND... I NEED TO GET OUT MORE, LIKE MOM SAYS, AND THEN MAYBE PISSING IN OTHER PLACES WOULDN'T BE SUCH A TOTAL NIGHTMARE.
I GUESS I'LL FLUSH AND "FAKE SHAKE."
HOW HUMIL-IATING...
FLUSH
* JAPANESE ONOMATOPOEIA FOR "FAKE SHAKE."
SOON...
BLISS!

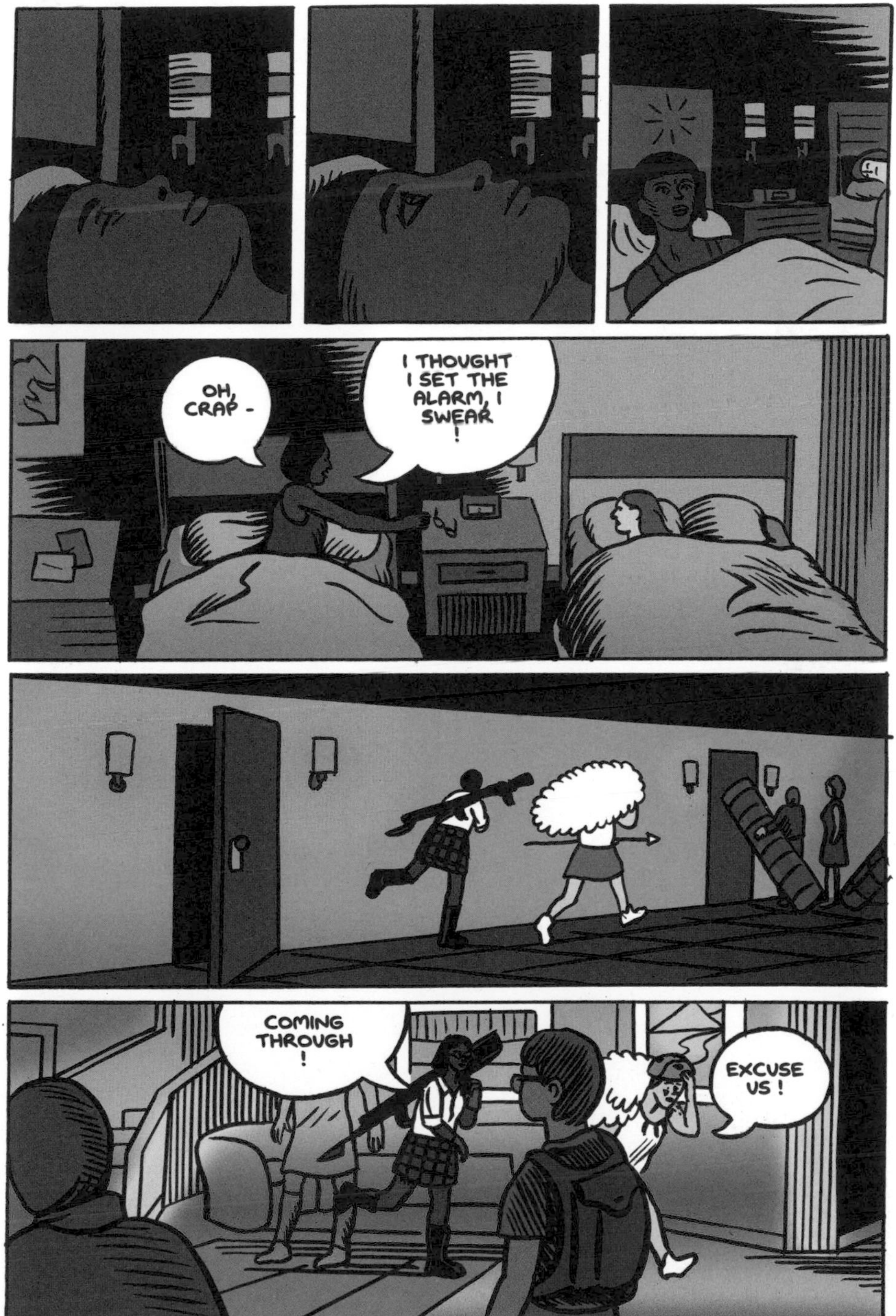
OH, CRAP -
I THOUGHT I SET THE ALARM, I SWEAR !
COMING THROUGH !
EXCUSE US !

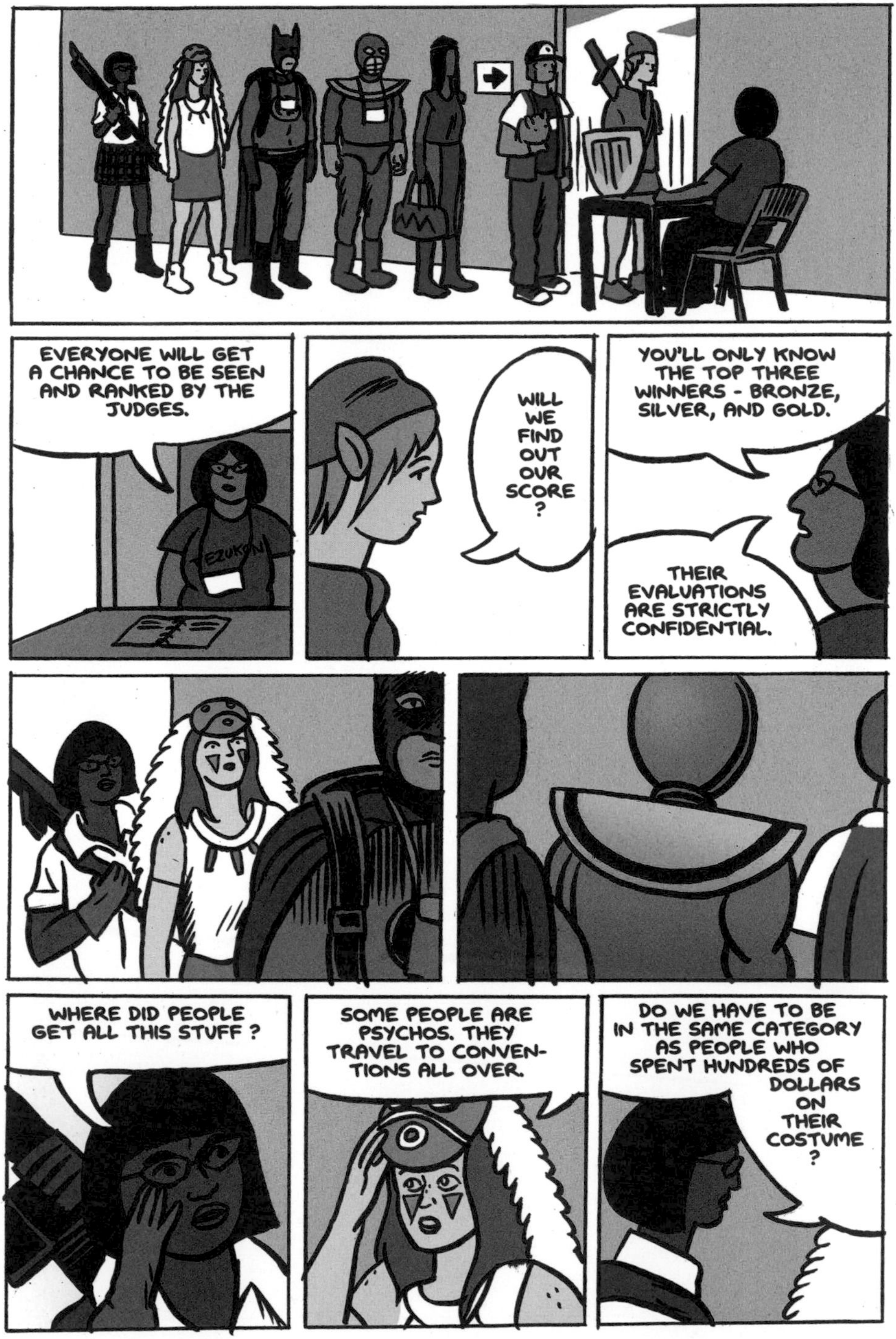
EVERYONE WILL GET A CHANCE TO BE SEEN AND RANKED BY THE JUDGES.
TEZUKON
WILL WE FIND OUT OUR SCORE ?
YOU'LL ONLY KNOW THE TOP THREE WINNERS - BRONZE, SILVER, AND GOLD.
THEIR EVALUATIONS ARE STRICTLY CONFIDENTIAL.
WHERE DID PEOPLE GET ALL THIS STUFF ?
SOME PEOPLE ARE PSYCHOS. THEY TRAVEL TO CONVEN-TIONS ALL OVER.
DO WE HAVE TO BE IN THE SAME CATEGORY AS PEOPLE WHO SPENT HUNDREDS OF DOLLARS ON THEIR COSTUME ?

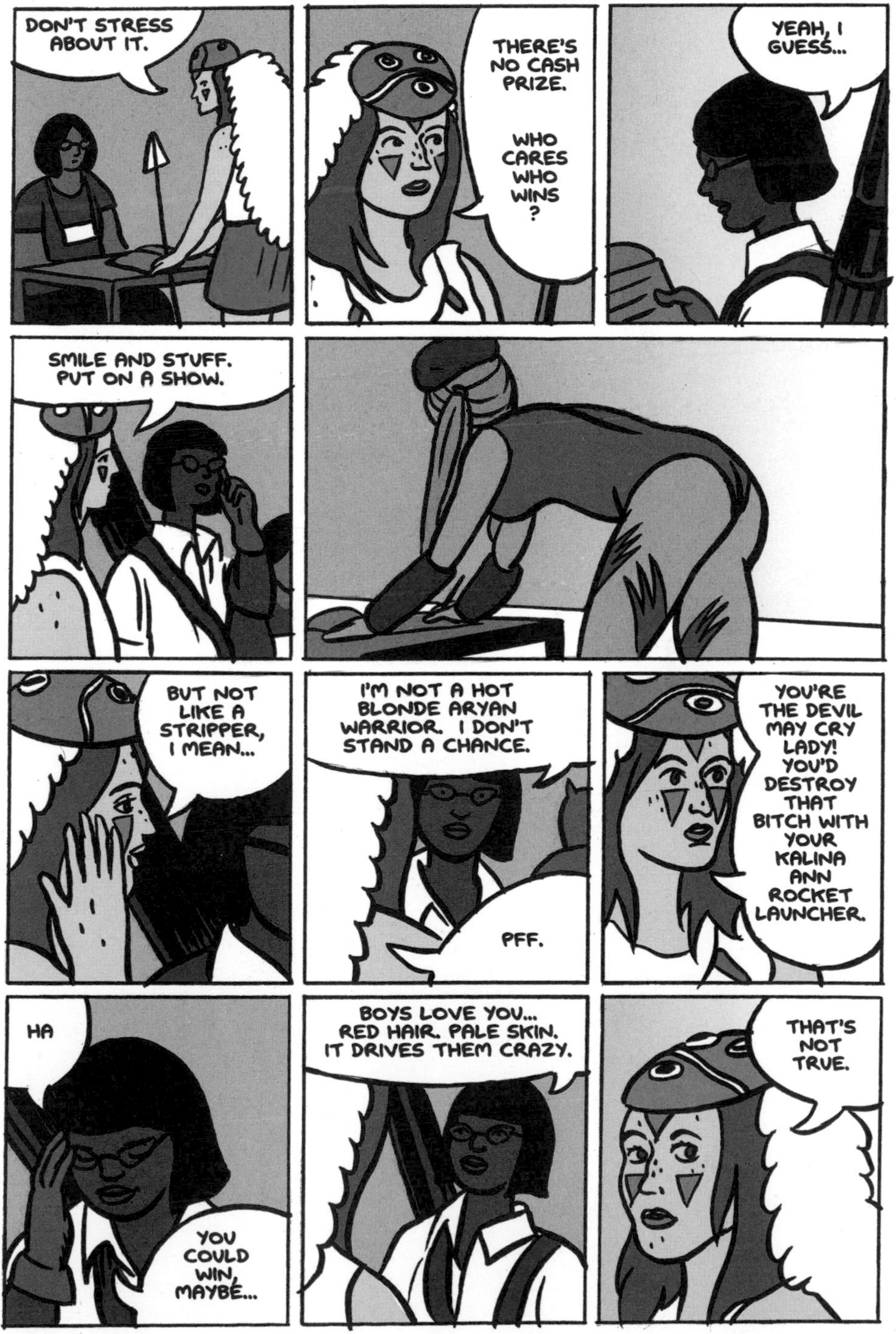
DON'T STRESS ABOUT IT.
THERE'S NO CASH PRIZE.
WHO CARES WHO WINS?
YEAH, I GUESS...
SMILE AND STUFF. PUT ON A SHOW.
BUT NOT LIKE A STRIPPER, I MEAN...
I'M NOT A HOT BLONDE ARYAN WARRIOR. I DON'T STAND A CHANCE.
PFF.
YOU'RE THE DEVIL MAY CRY LADY! YOU'D DESTROY THAT BITCH WITH YOUR KALINA ANN ROCKET LAUNCHER.
HA
YOU COULD WIN, MAYBE...
BOYS LOVE YOU... RED HAIR. PALE SKIN. IT DRIVES THEM CRAZY.
THAT'S NOT TRUE.

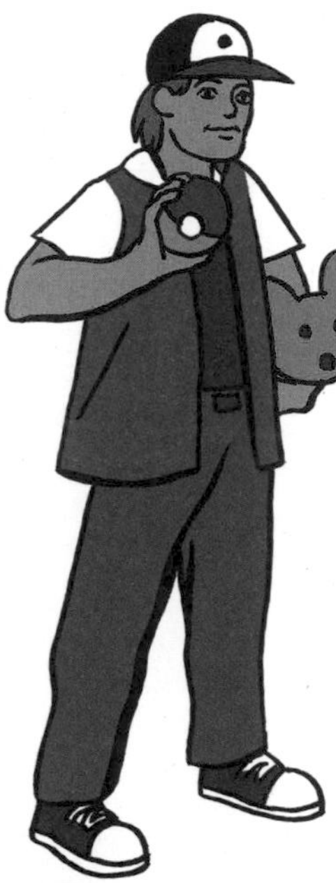
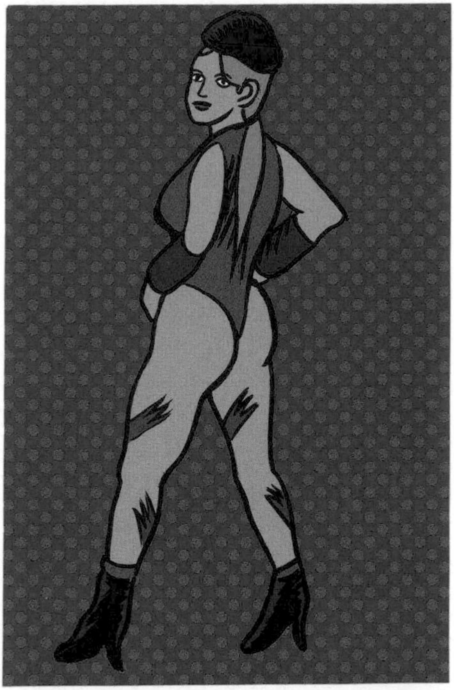
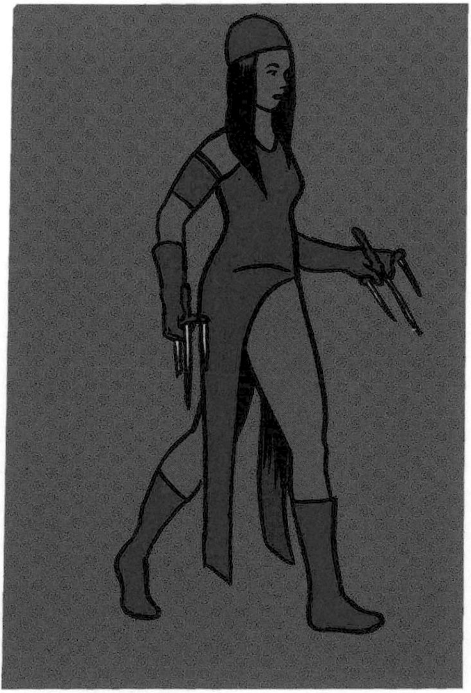
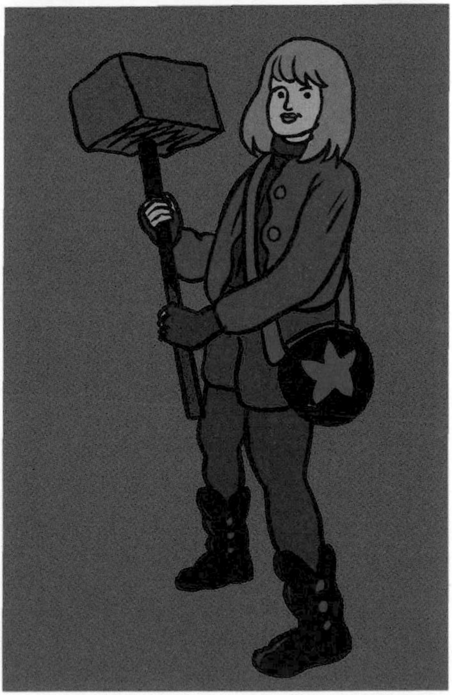

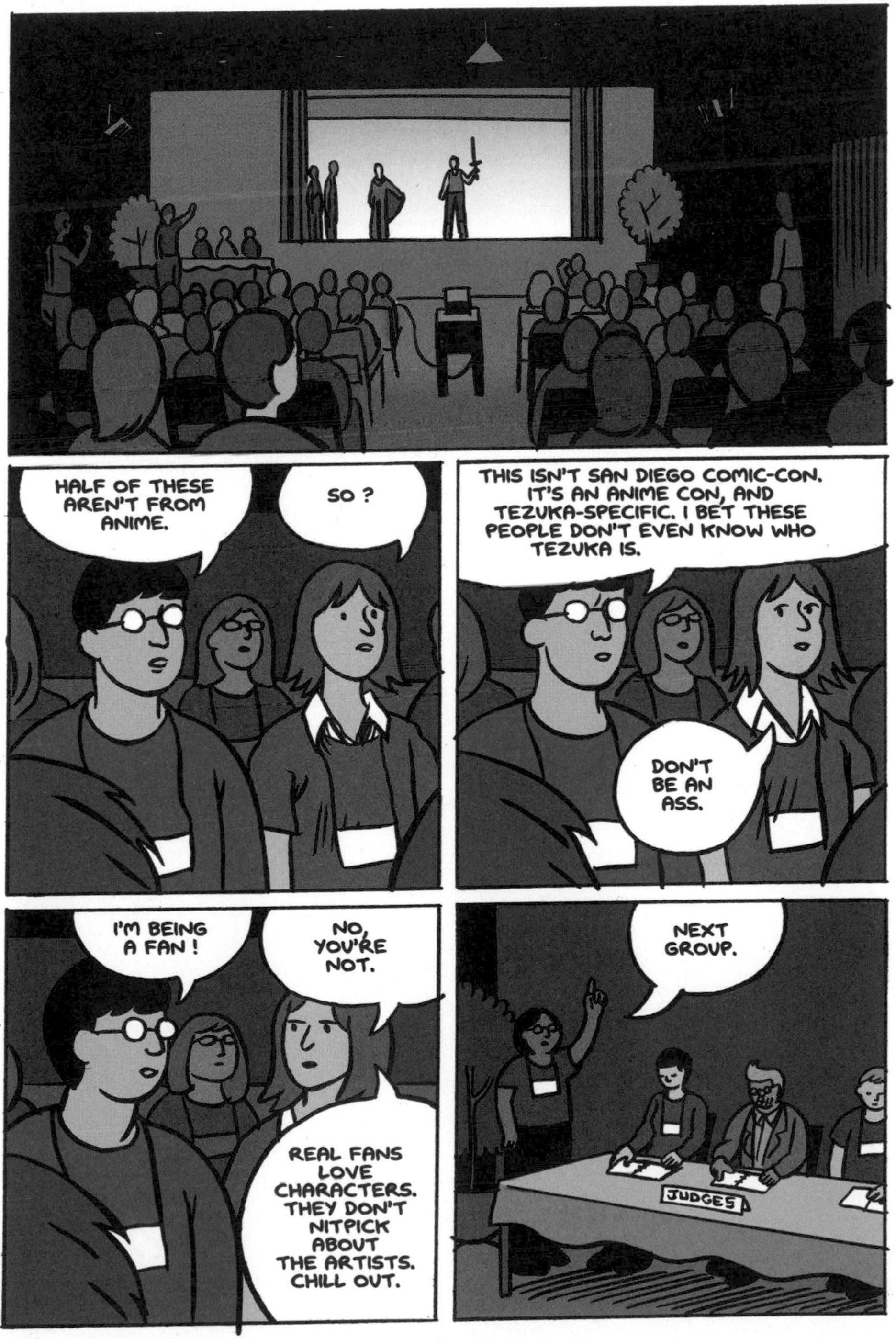
HALF OF THESE AREN'T FROM ANIME.
SO ?
THIS ISN'T SAN DIEGO COMIC-CON. IT'S AN ANIME CON, AND TEZUKA-SPECIFIC. I BET THESE PEOPLE DON'T EVEN KNOW WHO TEZUKA IS.
DON'T BE AN ASS.
I'M BEING A FAN !
NO, YOU'RE NOT.
REAL FANS LOVE CHARACTERS. THEY DON'T NITPICK ABOUT THE ARTISTS. CHILL OUT.
NEXT GROUP.
JUDGES

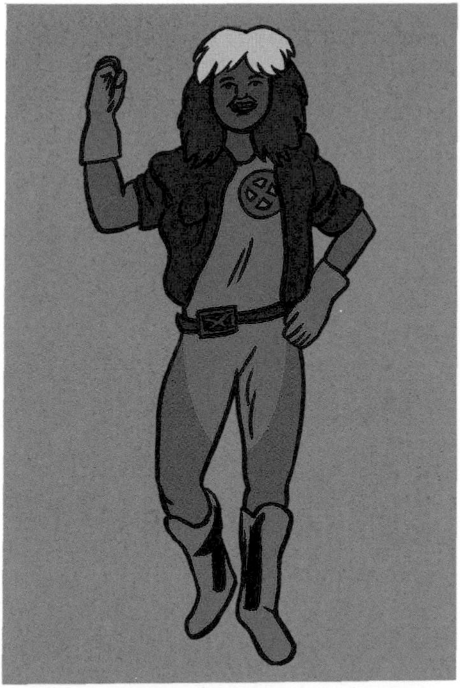

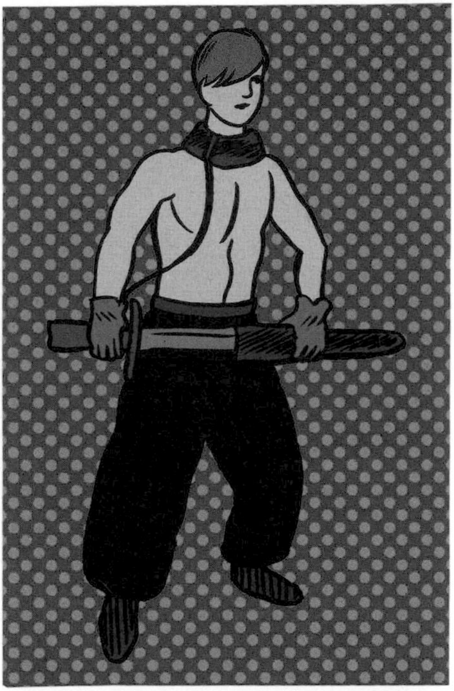

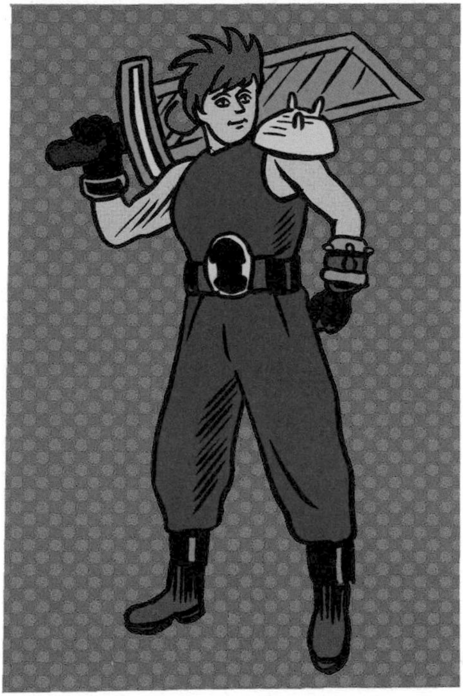

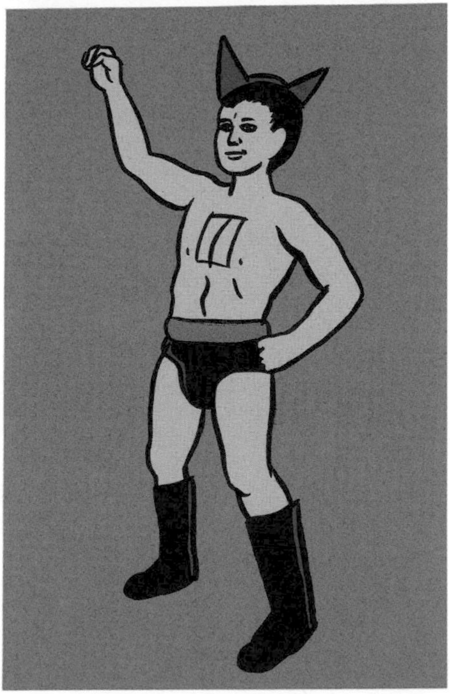

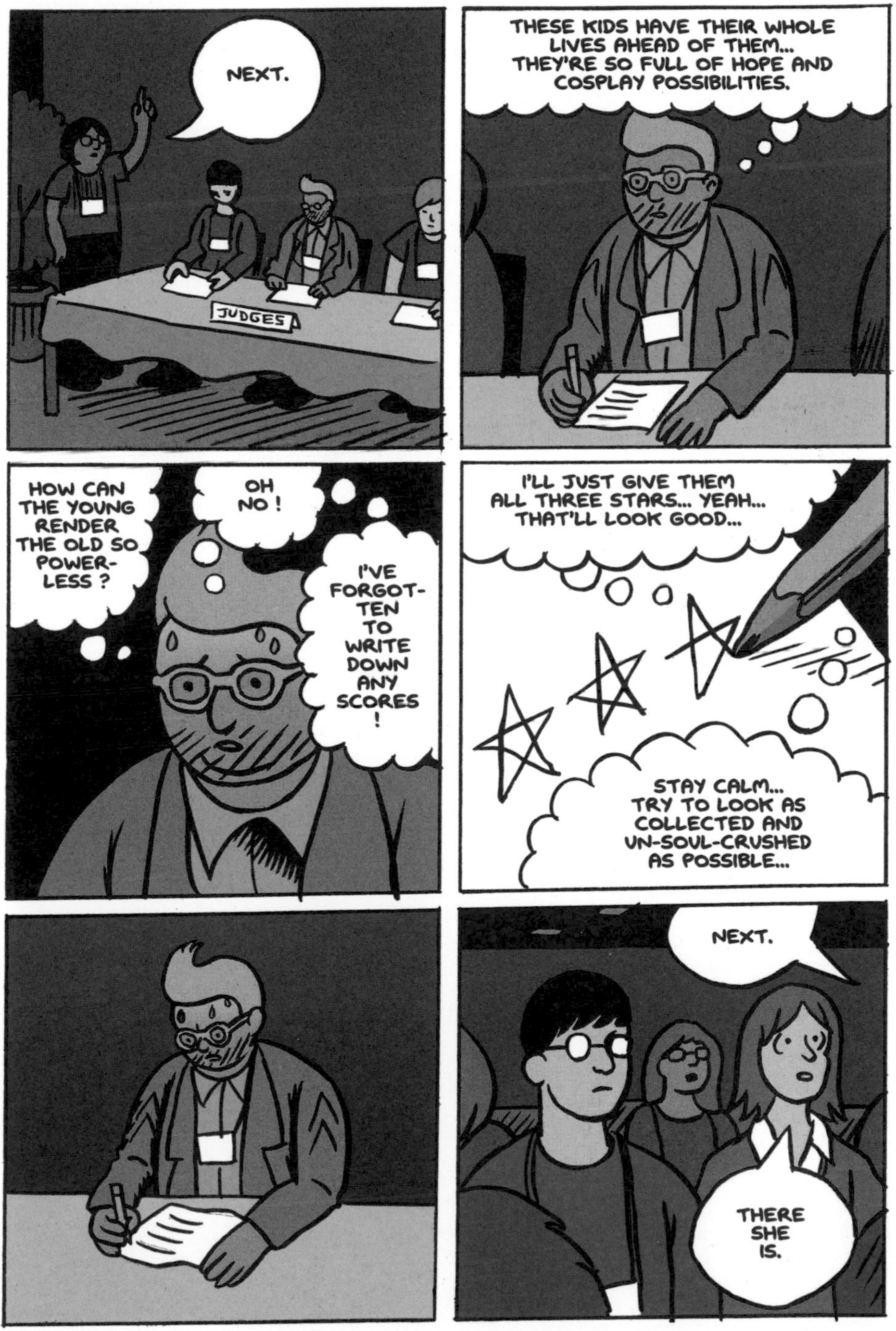
NEXT.
JUDGES
THESE KIDS HAVE THEIR WHOLE LIVES AHEAD OF THEM... THEY'RE SO FULL OF HOPE AND COSPLAY POSSIBILITIES.
HOW CAN THE YOUNG RENDER THE OLD SO POWER-LESS ?
OH NO !
I'VE FORGOT-TEN TO WRITE DOWN ANY SCORES !
I'LL JUST GIVE THEM ALL THREE STARS... YEAH... THAT'LL LOOK GOOD...
STAY CALM... TRY TO LOOK AS COLLECTED AND UN-SOUL-CRUSHED AS POSSIBLE...
NEXT.
THERE SHE IS.

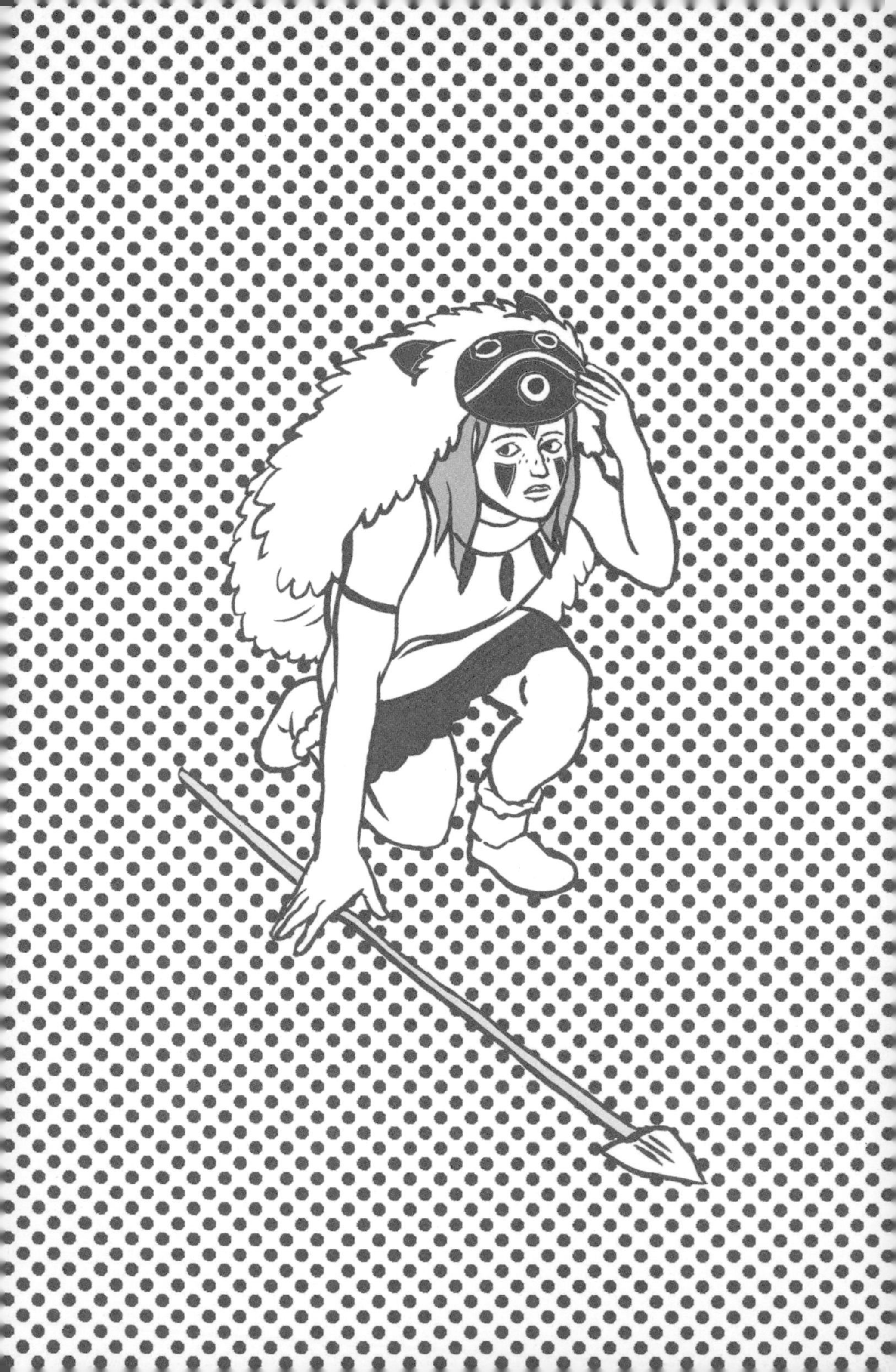

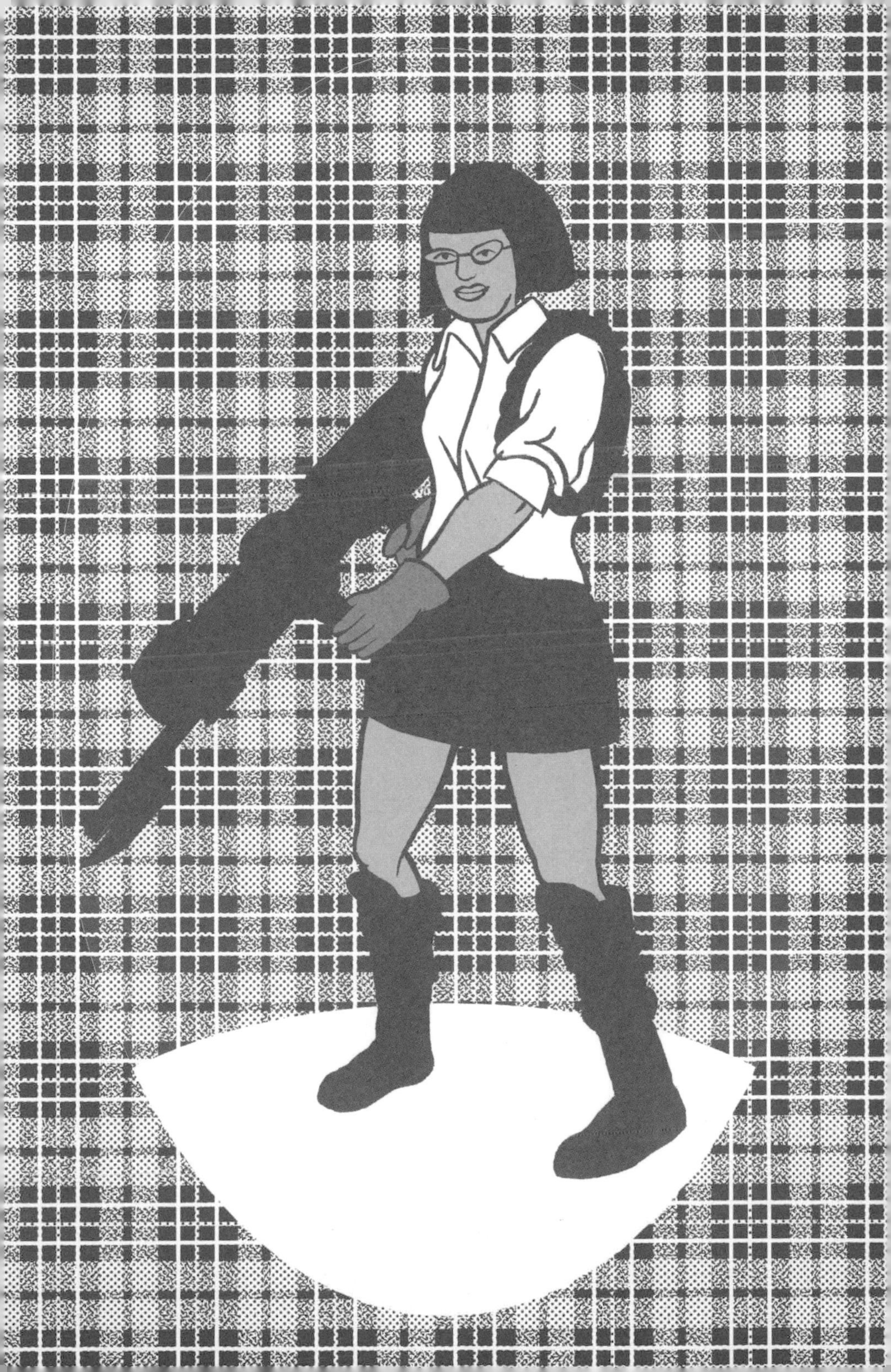

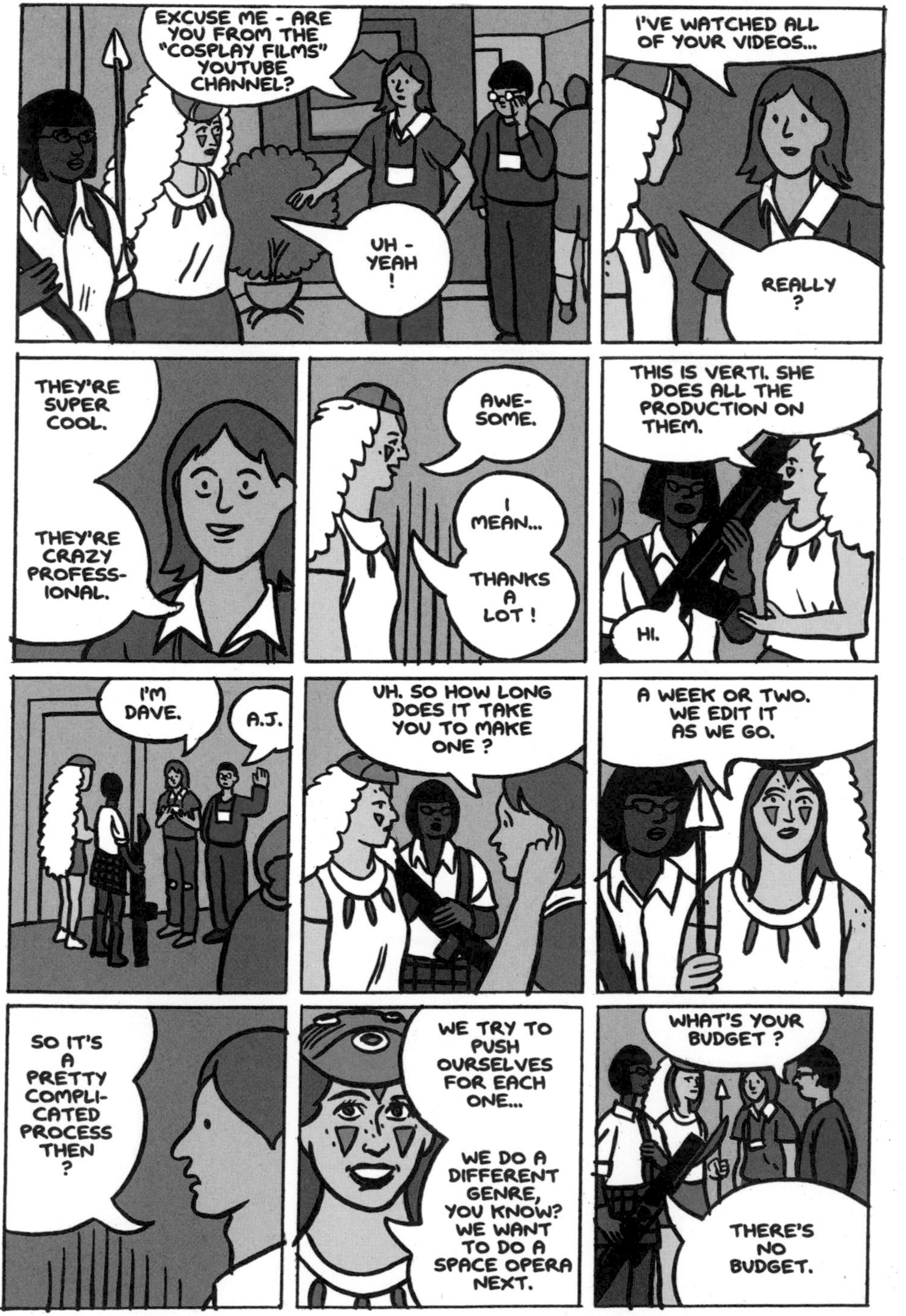
EXCUSE ME - ARE YOU FROM THE "COSPLAY FILMS" YOUTUBE CHANNEL?
UH - YEAH !
I'VE WATCHED ALL OF YOUR VIDEOS...
REALLY ?
THEY'RE SUPER COOL.
THEY'RE CRAZY PROFESS- IONAL.
AWE- SOME.
I MEAN...
THANKS A LOT !
THIS IS VERTI. SHE DOES ALL THE PRODUCTION ON THEM.
HI.
I'M DAVE.
A.J.
UH. SO HOW LONG DOES IT TAKE YOU TO MAKE ONE ?
A WEEK OR TWO. WE EDIT IT AS WE GO.
SO IT'S A PRETTY COMPLI- CATED PROCESS THEN ?
WE TRY TO PUSH OURSELVES FOR EACH ONE...
WE DO A DIFFERENT GENRE, YOU KNOW? WE WANT TO DO A SPACE OPERA NEXT.
WHAT'S YOUR BUDGET ?
THERE'S NO BUDGET.

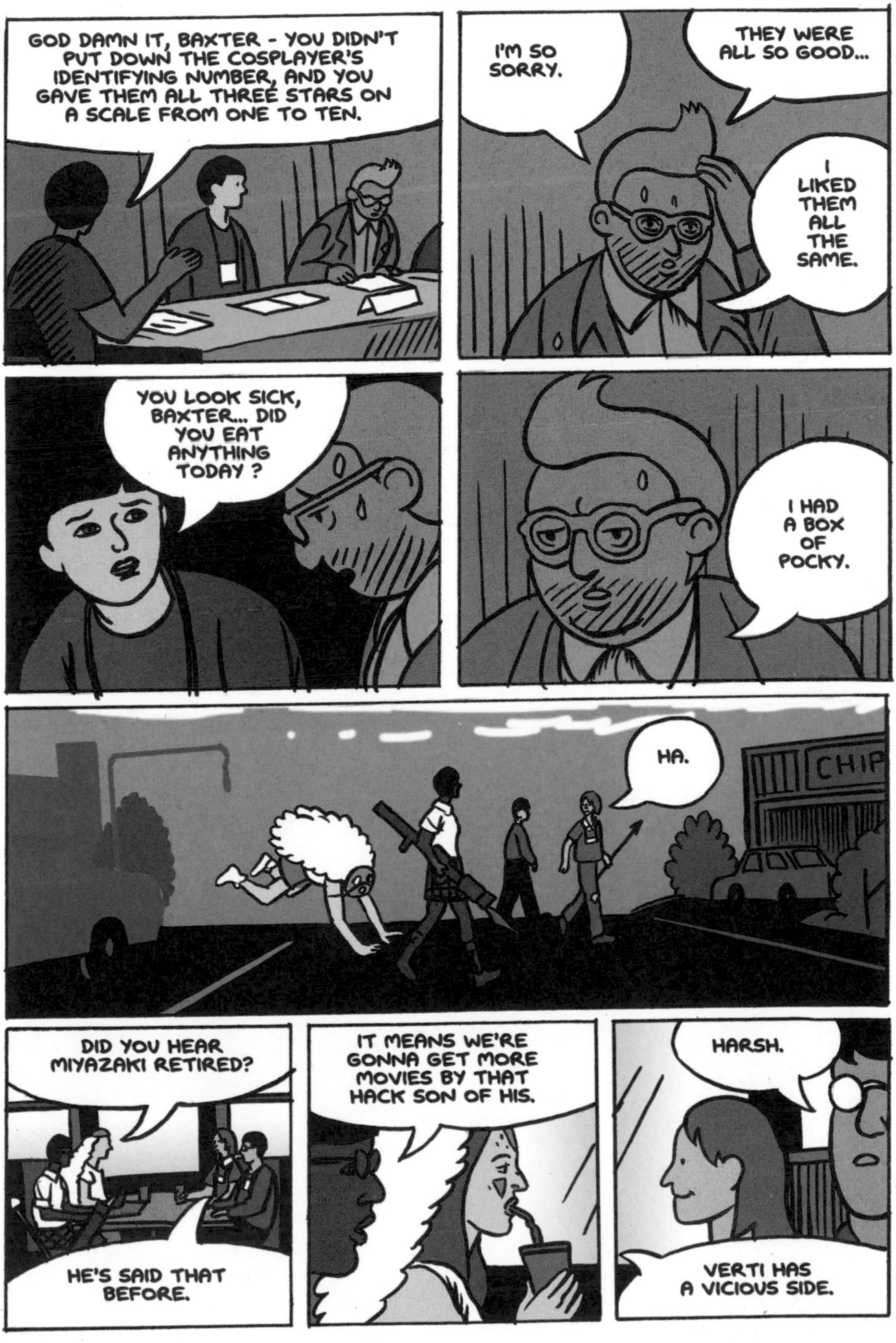
GOD DAMN IT, BAXTER - YOU DIDN'T PUT DOWN THE COSPLAYER'S IDENTIFYING NUMBER, AND YOU GAVE THEM ALL THREE STARS ON A SCALE FROM ONE TO TEN.
I'M SO SORRY.
THEY WERE ALL SO GOOD...
I LIKED THEM ALL THE SAME.
YOU LOOK SICK, BAXTER... DID YOU EAT ANYTHING TODAY ?
I HAD A BOX OF POCKY.
HA.
CHIP
DID YOU HEAR MIYAZAKI RETIRED?
HE'S SAID THAT BEFORE.
IT MEANS WE'RE GONNA GET MORE MOVIES BY THAT HACK SON OF HIS.
HARSH.
VERTI HAS A VICIOUS SIDE.

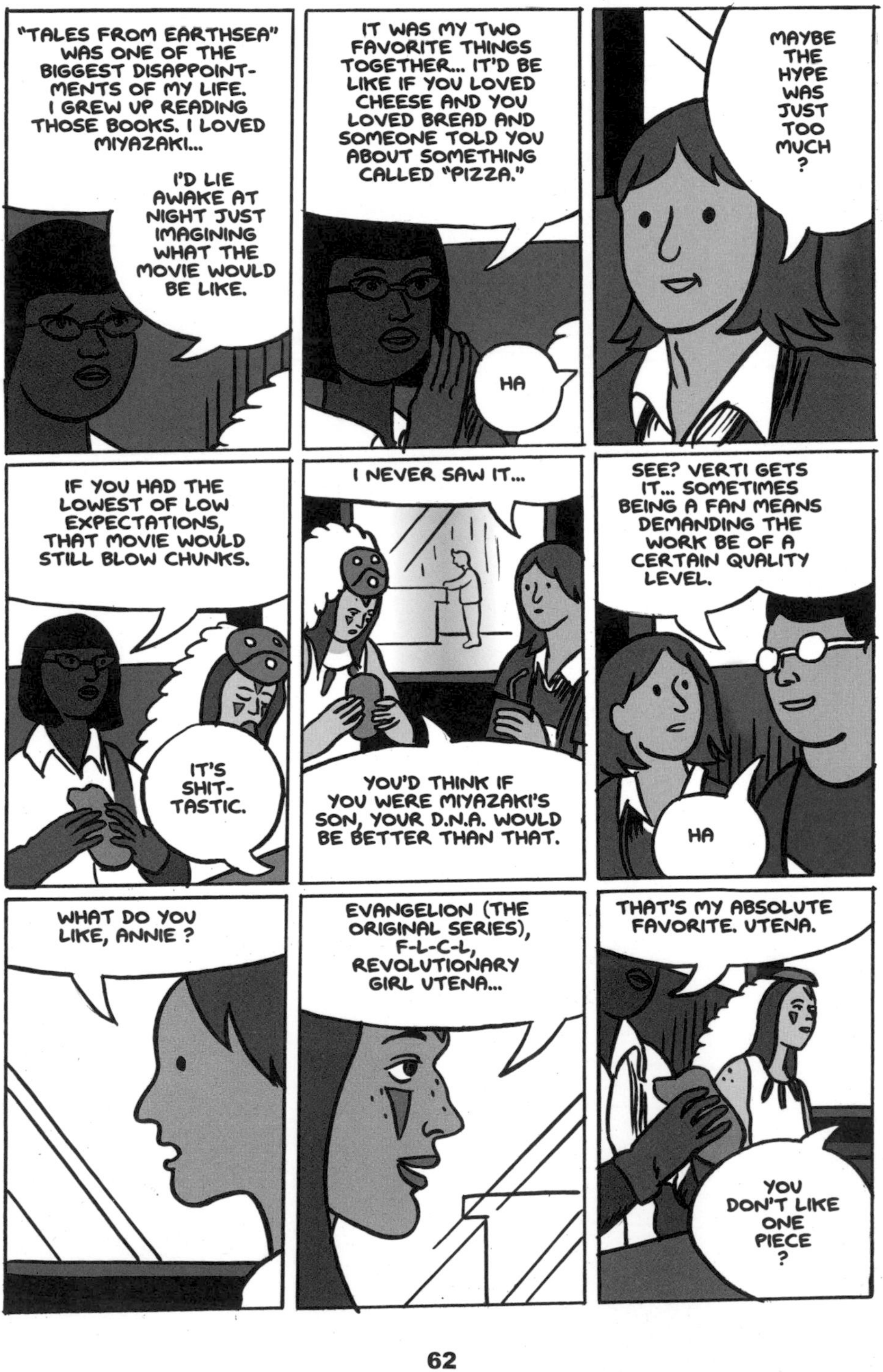
"TALES FROM EARTHSEA" WAS ONE OF THE BIGGEST DISAPPOINT-MENTS OF MY LIFE. I GREW UP READING THOSE BOOKS. I LOVED MIYAZAKI...
I'D LIE AWAKE AT NIGHT JUST IMAGINING WHAT THE MOVIE WOULD BE LIKE.
IT WAS MY TWO FAVORITE THINGS TOGETHER... IT'D BE LIKE IF YOU LOVED CHEESE AND YOU LOVED BREAD AND SOMEONE TOLD YOU ABOUT SOMETHING CALLED "PIZZA."
HA
MAYBE THE HYPE WAS JUST TOO MUCH ?
IF YOU HAD THE LOWEST OF LOW EXPECTATIONS, THAT MOVIE WOULD STILL BLOW CHUNKS.
IT'S SHIT-TASTIC.
I NEVER SAW IT...
YOU'D THINK IF YOU WERE MIYAZAKI'S SON, YOUR D.N.A. WOULD BE BETTER THAN THAT.
SEE? VERTI GETS IT... SOMETIMES BEING A FAN MEANS DEMANDING THE WORK BE OF A CERTAIN QUALITY LEVEL.
HA
WHAT DO YOU LIKE, ANNIE ?
EVANGELION (THE ORIGINAL SERIES), F-L-C-L, REVOLUTIONARY GIRL UTENA...
THAT'S MY ABSOLUTE FAVORITE. UTENA.
YOU DON'T LIKE ONE PIECE ?

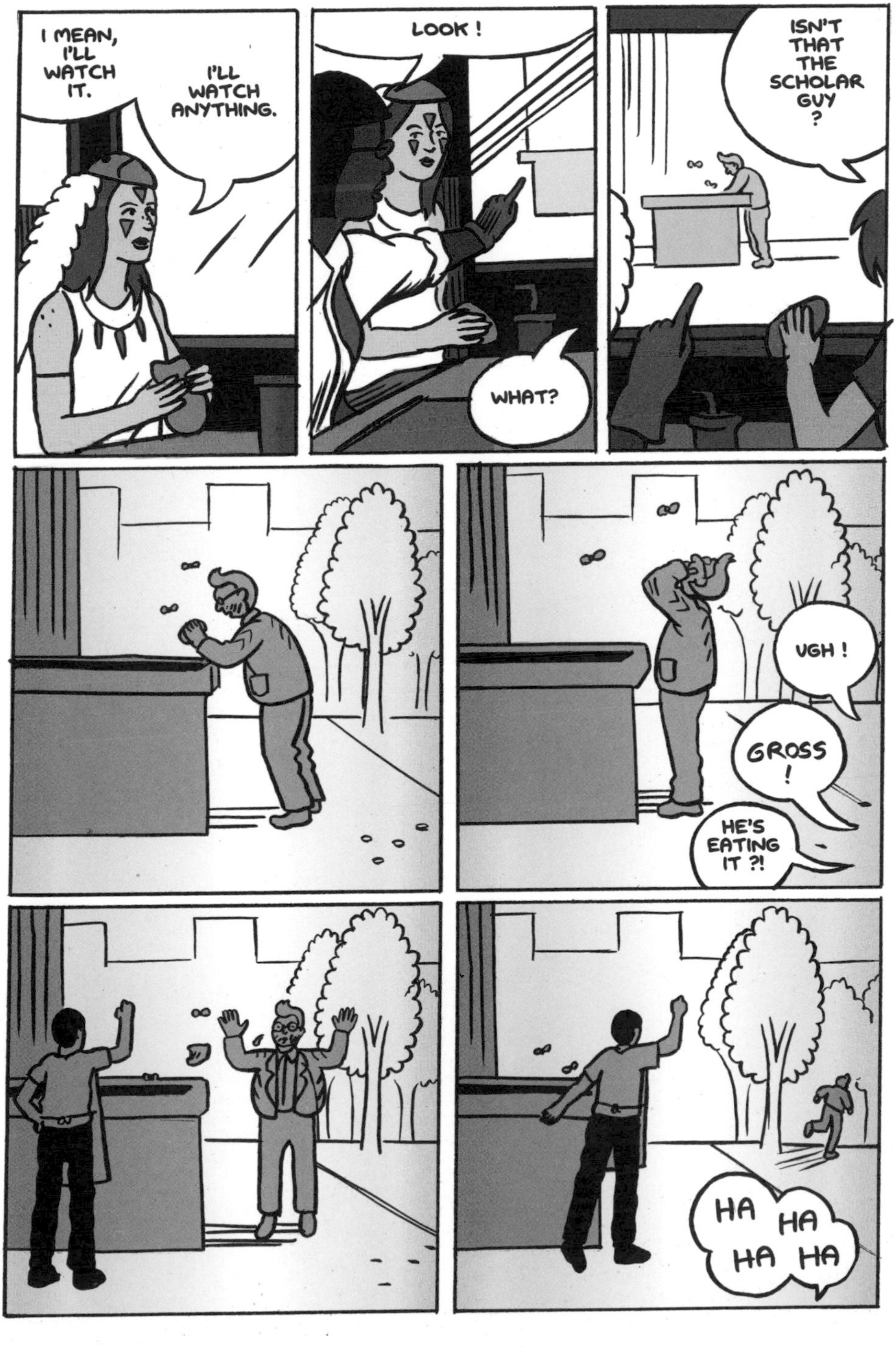
I MEAN, I'LL WATCH IT.
I'LL WATCH ANYTHING.
LOOK !
WHAT?
ISN'T THAT THE SCHOLAR GUY ?
UGH !
GROSS !
HE'S EATING IT ?!
HA HA HA HA

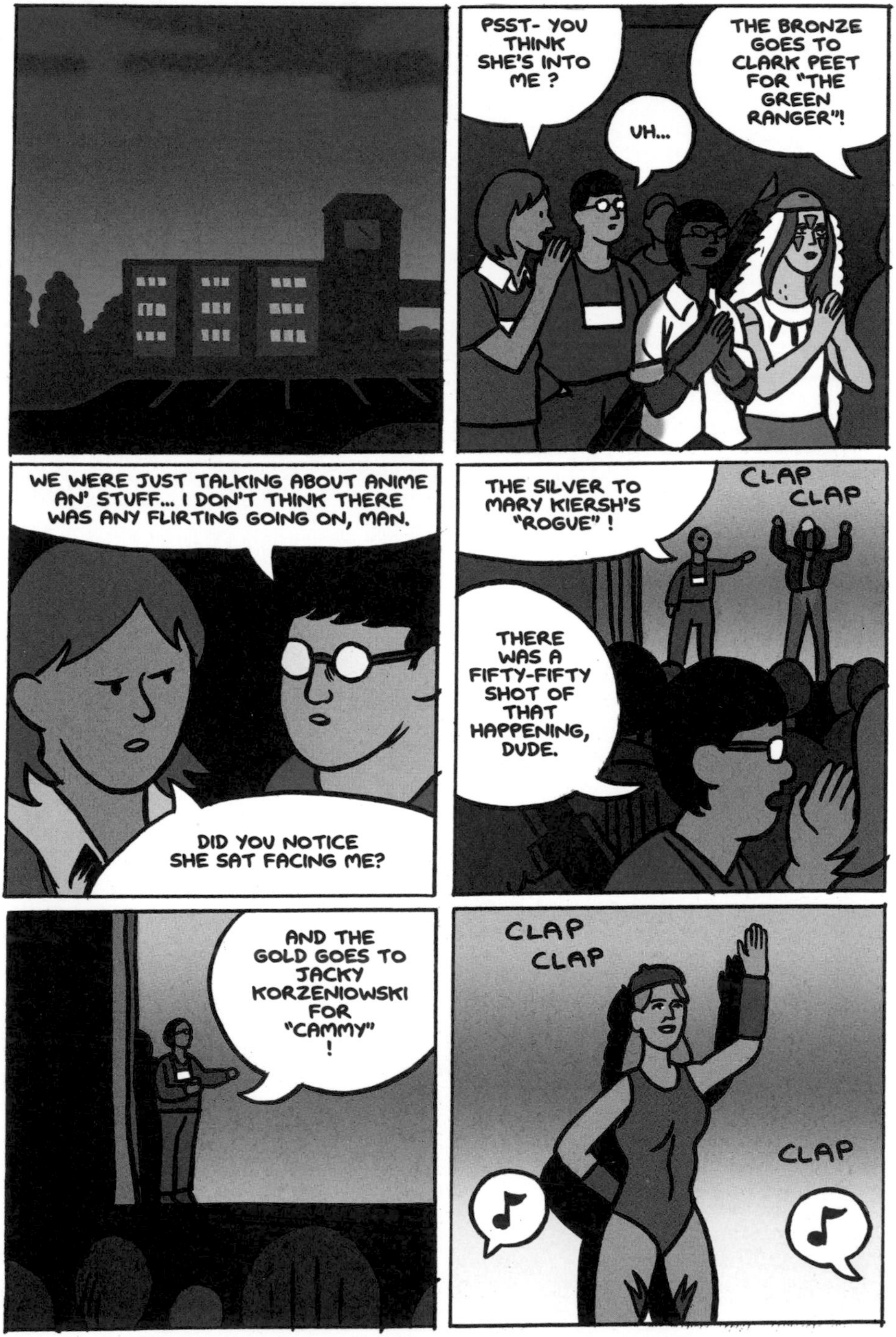
PSST- YOU THINK SHE'S INTO ME ?
UH...
THE BRONZE GOES TO CLARK PEET FOR "THE GREEN RANGER"!
WE WERE JUST TALKING ABOUT ANIME AN' STUFF... I DON'T THINK THERE WAS ANY FLIRTING GOING ON, MAN.
DID YOU NOTICE SHE SAT FACING ME?
THE SILVER TO MARY KIERSH'S "ROGUE" !
CLAP CLAP
THERE WAS A FIFTY-FIFTY SHOT OF THAT HAPPENING, DUDE.
AND THE GOLD GOES TO JACKY KORZENIOWSKI FOR "CAMMY" !
CLAP CLAP
CLAP

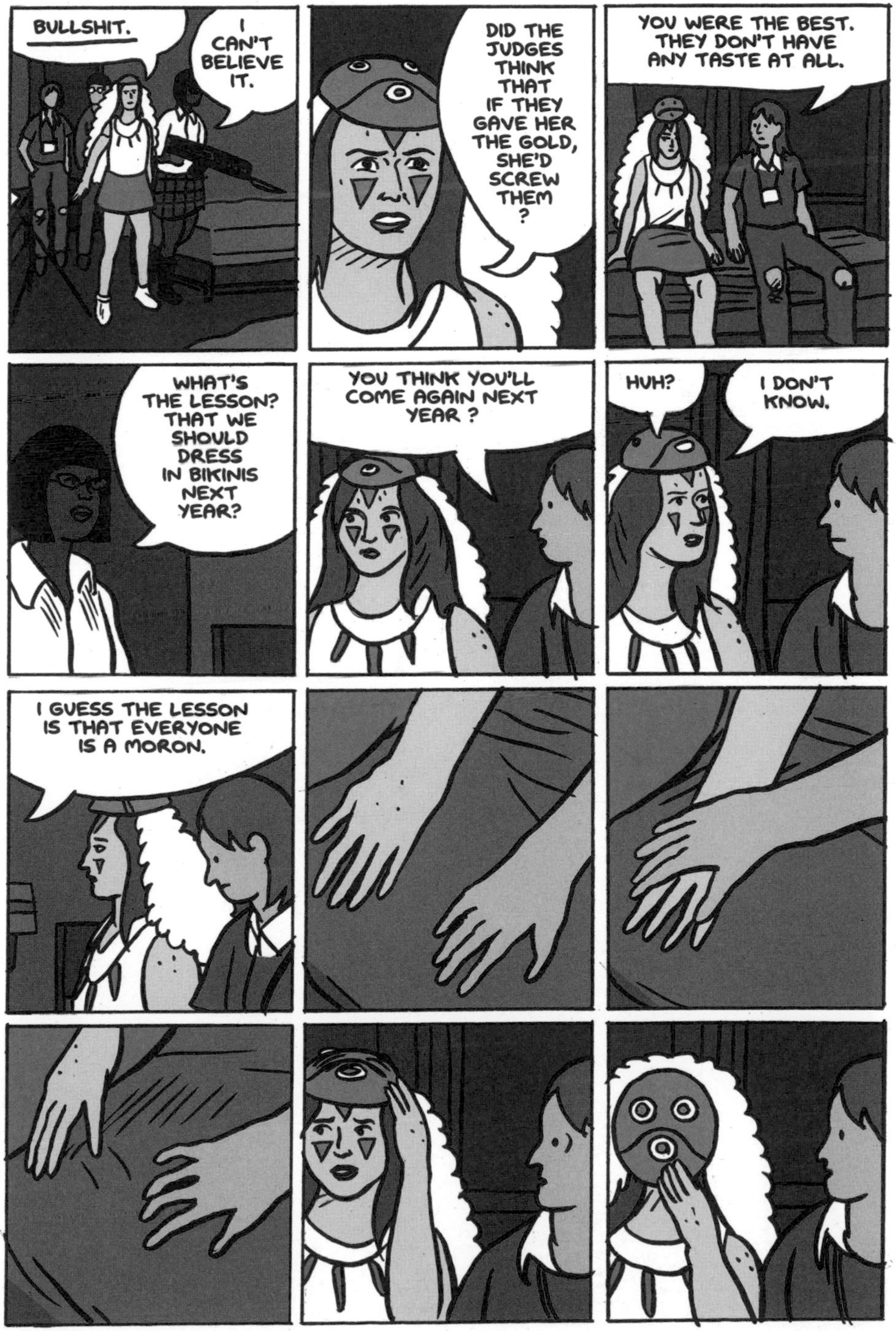
BULLSHIT.
I CAN'T BELIEVE IT.
DID THE JUDGES THINK THAT IF THEY GAVE HER THE GOLD, SHE'D SCREW THEM ?
YOU WERE THE BEST. THEY DON'T HAVE ANY TASTE AT ALL.
WHAT'S THE LESSON? THAT WE SHOULD DRESS IN BIKINIS NEXT YEAR?
YOU THINK YOU'LL COME AGAIN NEXT YEAR ?
HUH?
I DON'T KNOW.
I GUESS THE LESSON IS THAT EVERYONE IS A MORON.

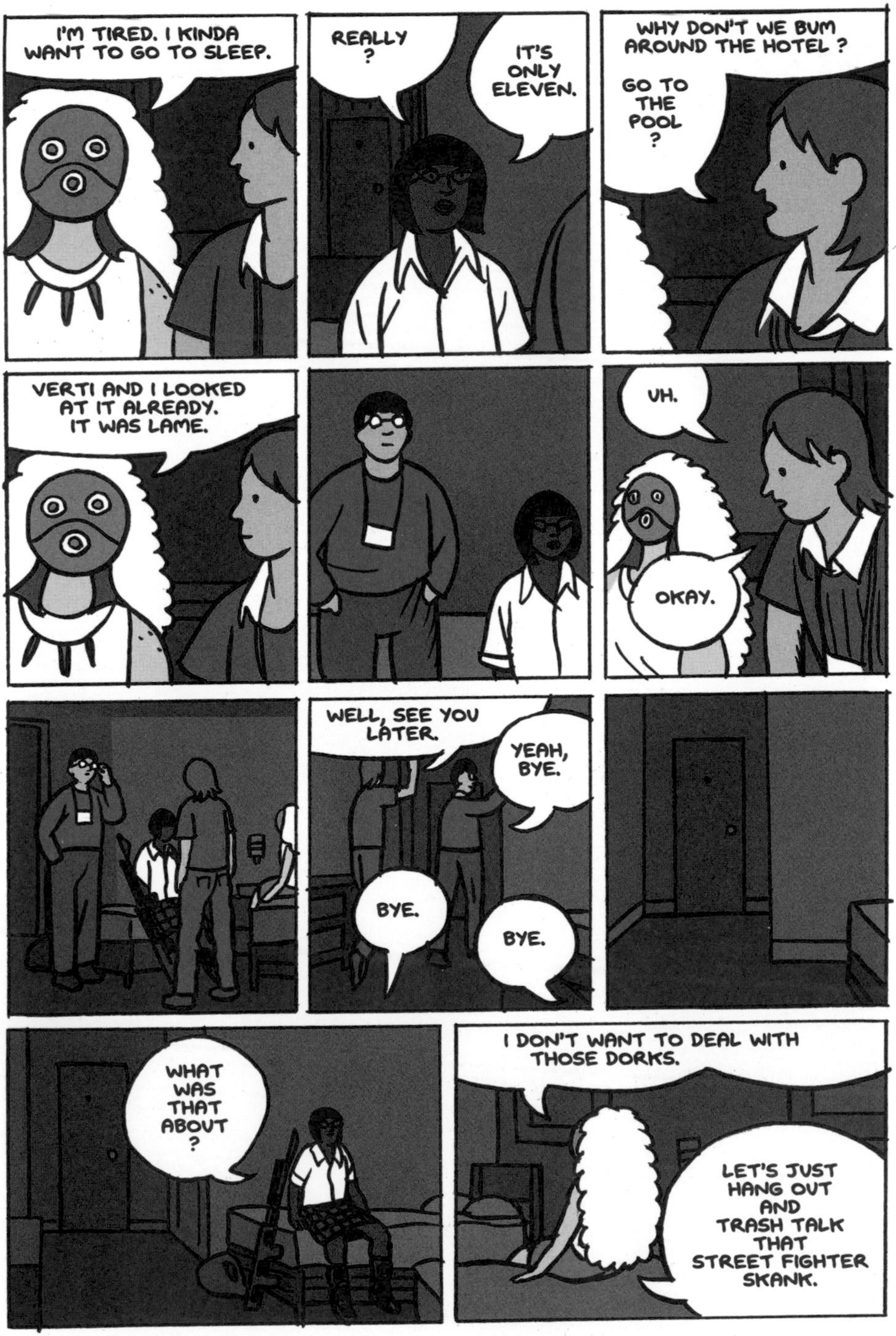
I'M TIRED. I KINDA WANT TO GO TO SLEEP.
REALLY ?
IT'S ONLY ELEVEN.
WHY DON'T WE BUM AROUND THE HOTEL ?
GO TO THE POOL ?
VERTI AND I LOOKED AT IT ALREADY. IT WAS LAME.
UH.
OKAY.
WELL, SEE YOU LATER.
YEAH, BYE.
BYE.
BYE.
WHAT WAS THAT ABOUT ?
I DON'T WANT TO DEAL WITH THOSE DORKS.
LET'S JUST HANG OUT AND TRASH TALK THAT STREET FIGHTER SKANK.

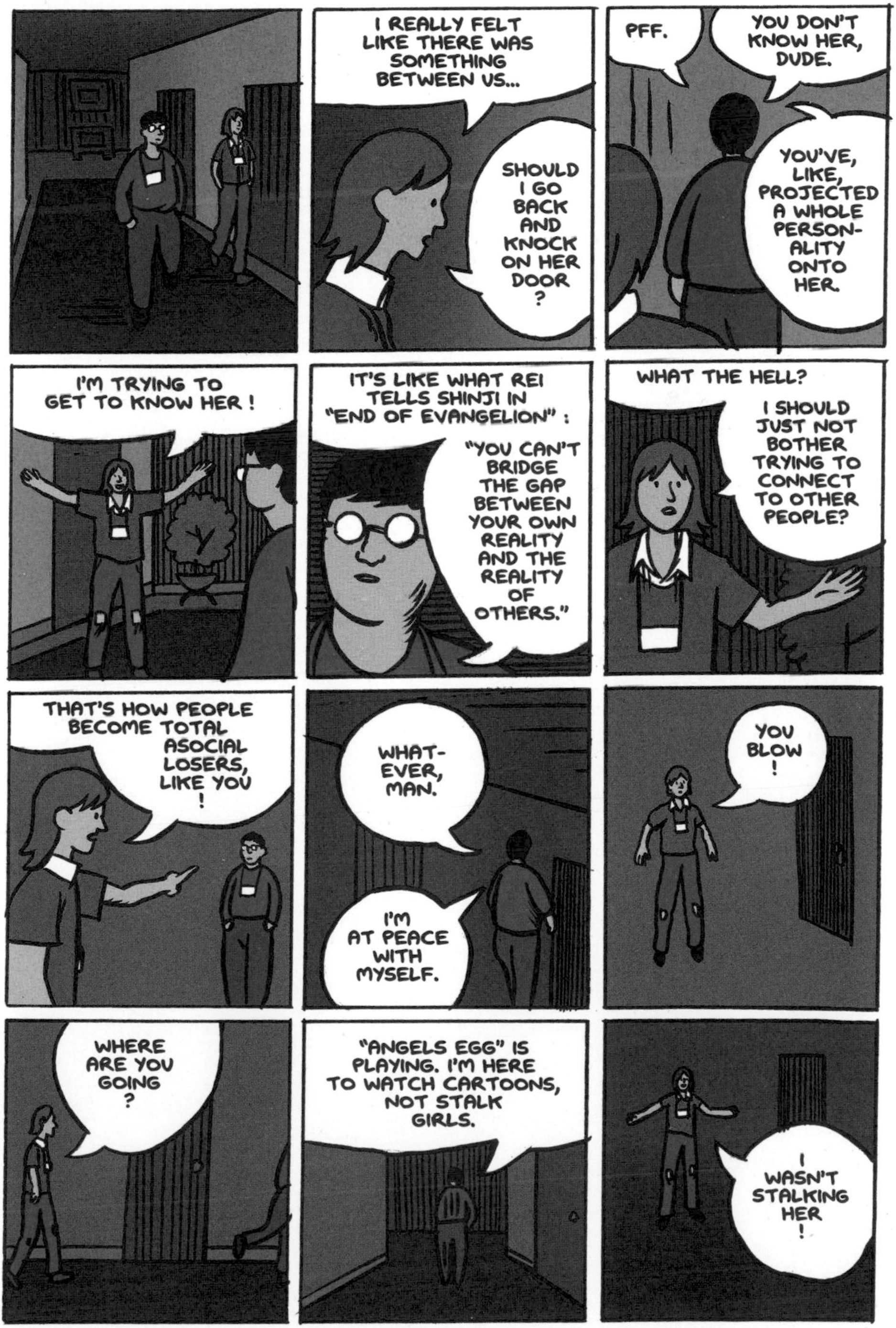
I REALLY FELT LIKE THERE WAS SOMETHING BETWEEN US...
SHOULD I GO BACK AND KNOCK ON HER DOOR ?
PFF.
YOU DON'T KNOW HER, DUDE.
YOU'VE, LIKE, PROJECTED A WHOLE PERSON-ALITY ONTO HER.
I'M TRYING TO GET TO KNOW HER !
IT'S LIKE WHAT REI TELLS SHINJI IN "END OF EVANGELION" :
"YOU CAN'T BRIDGE THE GAP BETWEEN YOUR OWN REALITY AND THE REALITY OF OTHERS."
WHAT THE HELL?
I SHOULD JUST NOT BOTHER TRYING TO CONNECT TO OTHER PEOPLE?
THAT'S HOW PEOPLE BECOME TOTAL ASOCIAL LOSERS, LIKE YOU !
WHAT-EVER, MAN.
I'M AT PEACE WITH MYSELF.
YOU BLOW !
WHERE ARE YOU GOING ?
"ANGELS EGG" IS PLAYING. I'M HERE TO WATCH CARTOONS, NOT STALK GIRLS.
I WASN'T STALKING HER !

Technically Sunday (Since it's past midnight)

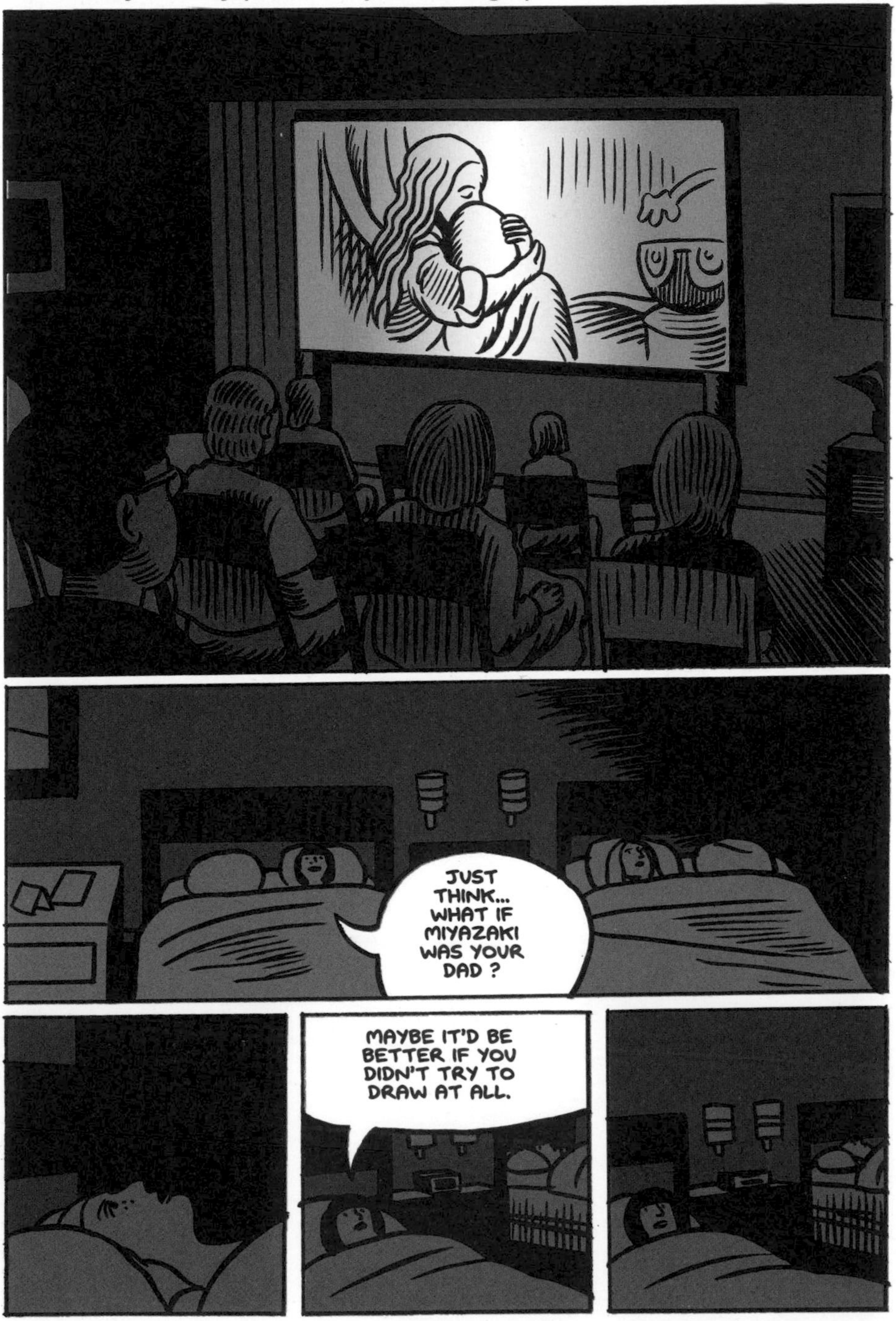

JUST THINK... WHAT IF MIYAZAKI WAS YOUR DAD ?
MAYBE IT'D BE BETTER IF YOU DIDN'T TRY TO DRAW AT ALL.

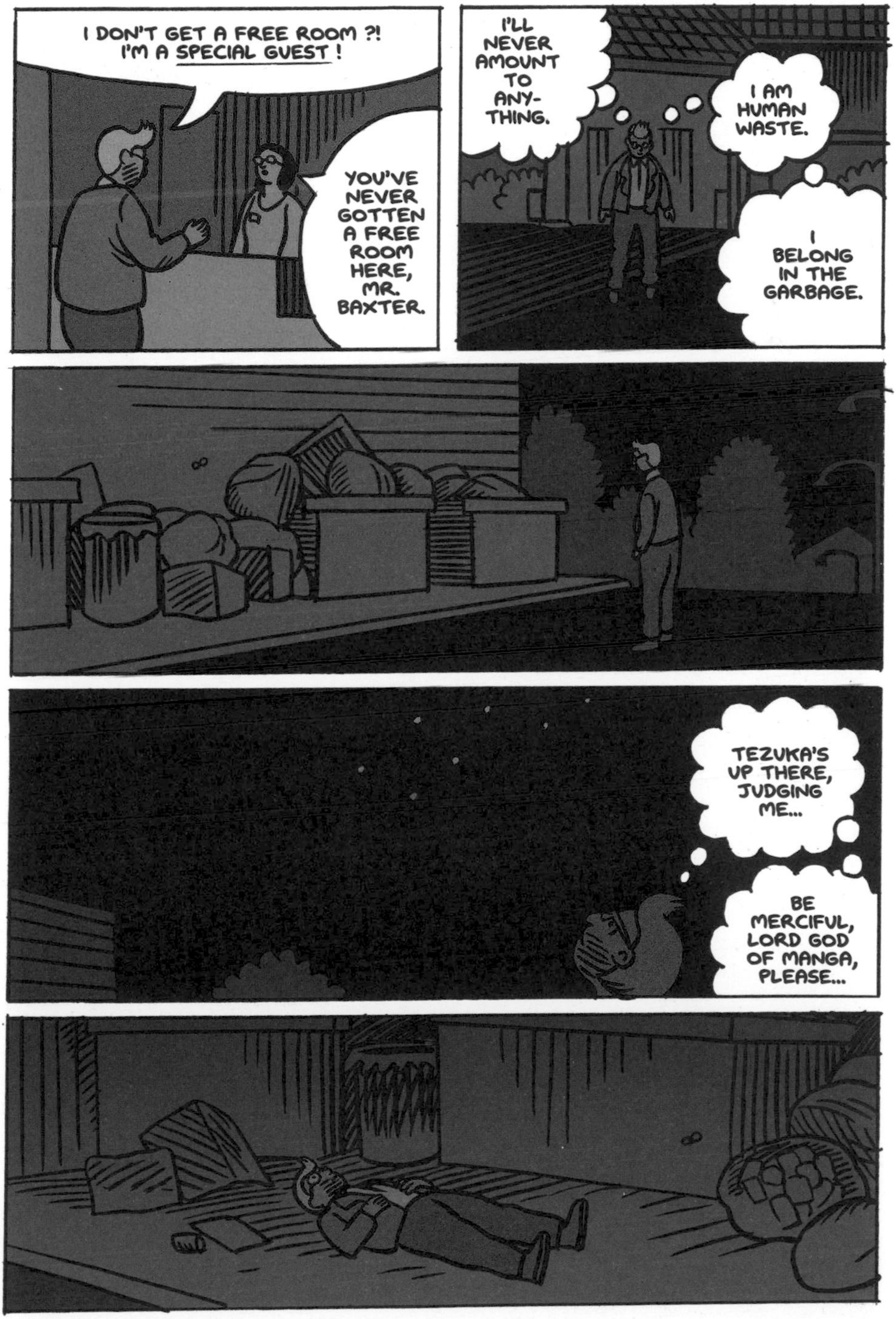
I DON'T GET A FREE ROOM ?! I'M A SPECIAL GUEST !
YOU'VE NEVER GOTTEN A FREE ROOM HERE, MR. BAXTER.
I'LL NEVER AMOUNT TO ANY-THING.
I AM HUMAN WASTE.
I BELONG IN THE GARBAGE.
TEZUKA'S UP THERE, JUDGING ME...
BE MERCIFUL, LORD GOD OF MANGA, PLEASE...

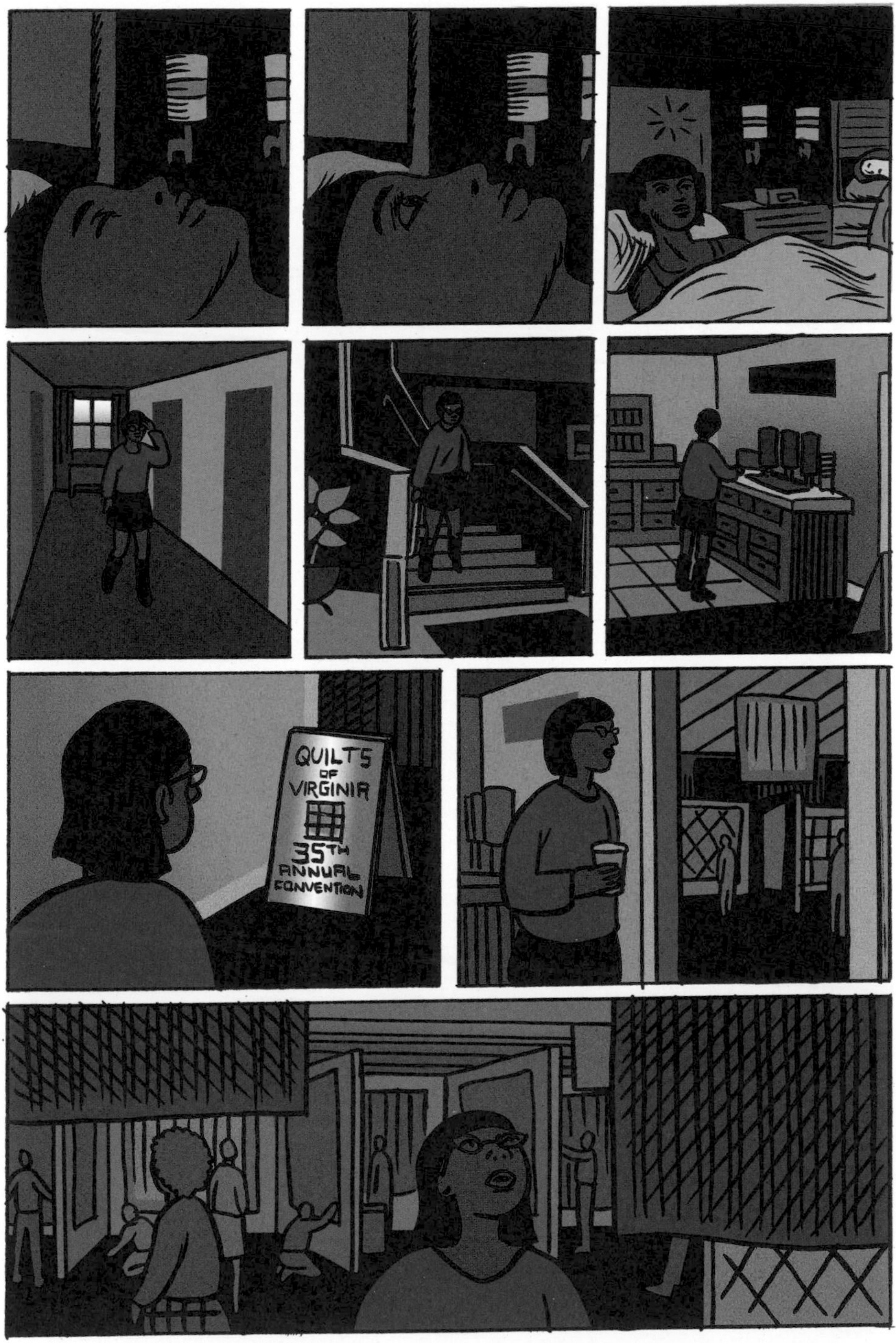
QUILTS OF VIRGINIA
35TH ANNUAL CONVENTION

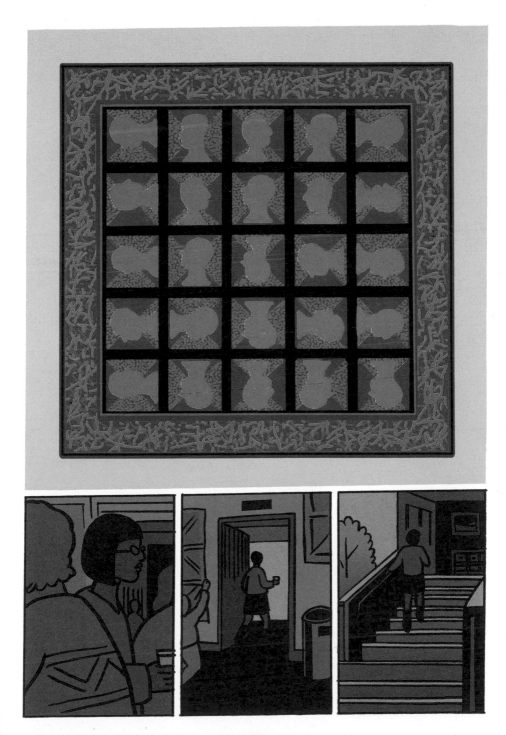

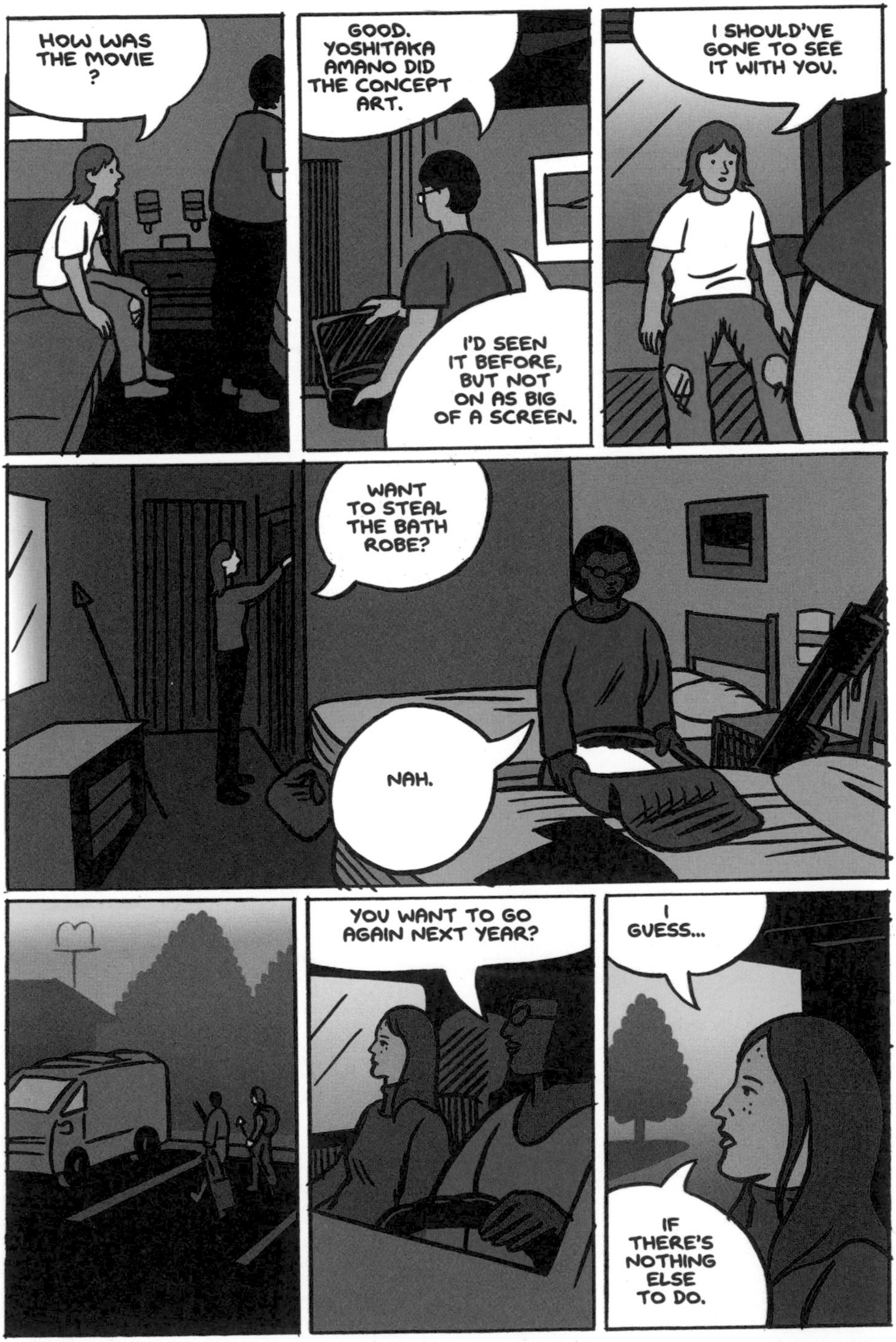
HOW WAS THE MOVIE ?
GOOD. YOSHITAKA AMANO DID THE CONCEPT ART.
I'D SEEN IT BEFORE, BUT NOT ON AS BIG OF A SCREEN.
I SHOULD'VE GONE TO SEE IT WITH YOU.
WANT TO STEAL THE BATH ROBE?
NAH.
YOU WANT TO GO AGAIN NEXT YEAR?
I GUESS...
IF THERE'S NOTHING ELSE TO DO.

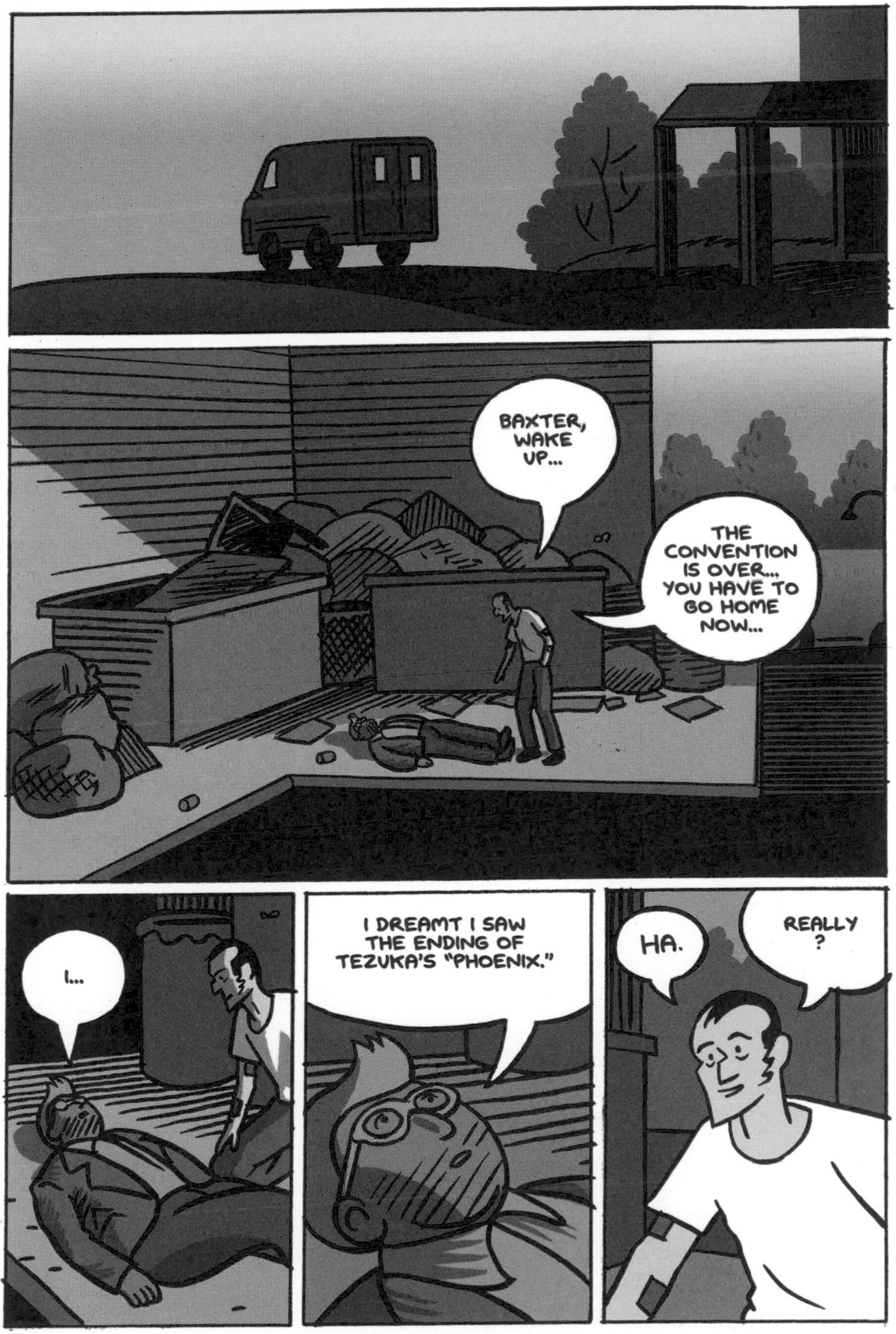
BAXTER, WAKE UP...
THE CONVENTION IS OVER... YOU HAVE TO GO HOME NOW...
I...
I DREAMT I SAW THE ENDING OF TEZUKA'S "PHOENIX."
HA.
REALLY ?

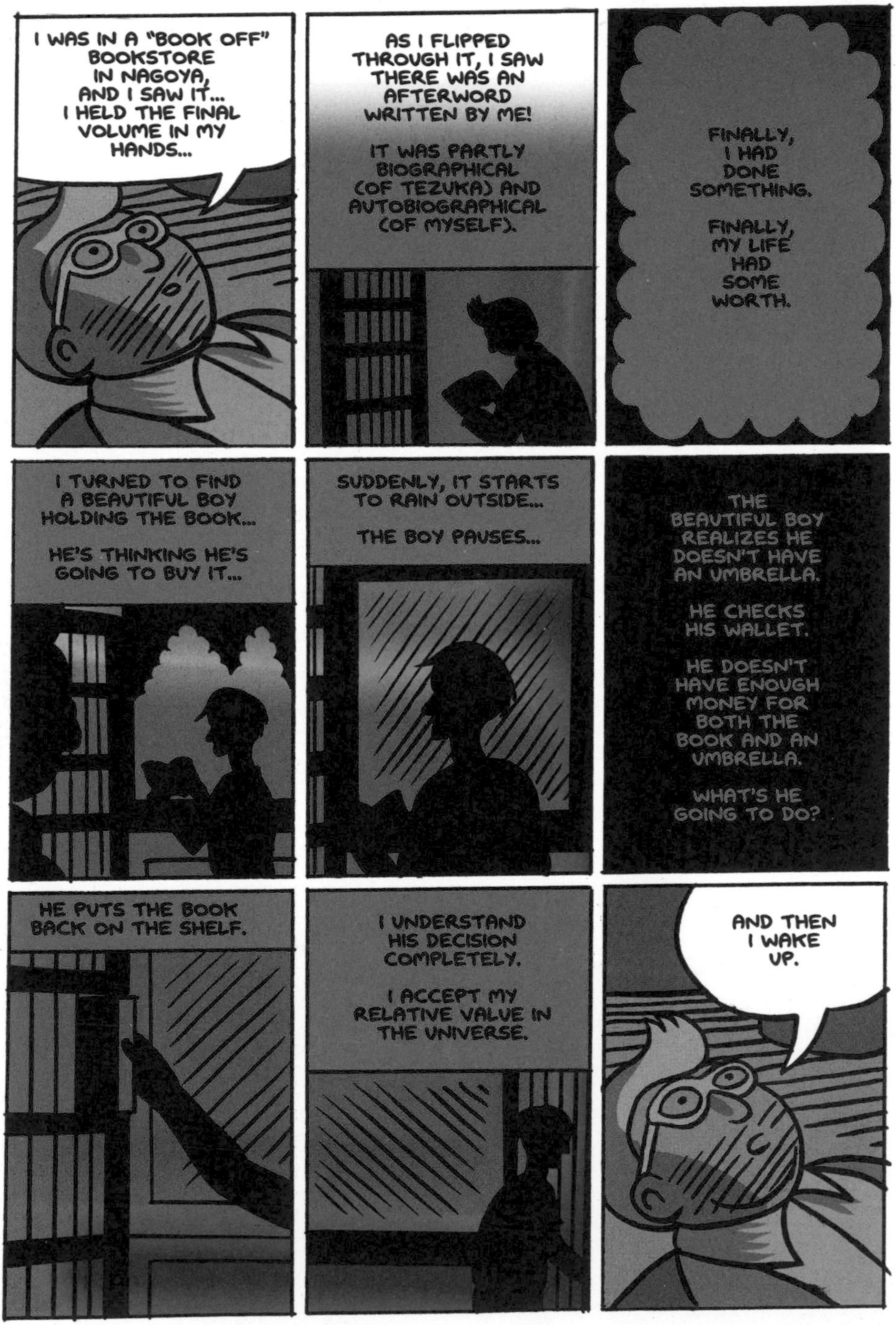
I WAS IN A "BOOK OFF" BOOKSTORE IN NAGOYA, AND I SAW IT... I HELD THE FINAL VOLUME IN MY HANDS...
AS I FLIPPED THROUGH IT, I SAW THERE WAS AN AFTERWORD WRITTEN BY ME!
IT WAS PARTLY BIOGRAPHICAL (OF TEZUKA) AND AUTOBIOGRAPHICAL (OF MYSELF).
FINALLY, I HAD DONE SOMETHING.
FINALLY, MY LIFE HAD SOME WORTH.
I TURNED TO FIND A BEAUTIFUL BOY HOLDING THE BOOK...
HE'S THINKING HE'S GOING TO BUY IT...
SUDDENLY, IT STARTS TO RAIN OUTSIDE...
THE BOY PAUSES...
THE BEAUTIFUL BOY REALIZES HE DOESN'T HAVE AN UMBRELLA.
HE CHECKS HIS WALLET.
HE DOESN'T HAVE ENOUGH MONEY FOR BOTH THE BOOK AND AN UMBRELLA.
WHAT'S HE GOING TO DO?
HE PUTS THE BOOK BACK ON THE SHELF.
I UNDERSTAND HIS DECISION COMPLETELY.
I ACCEPT MY RELATIVE VALUE IN THE UNIVERSE.
AND THEN I WAKE UP.

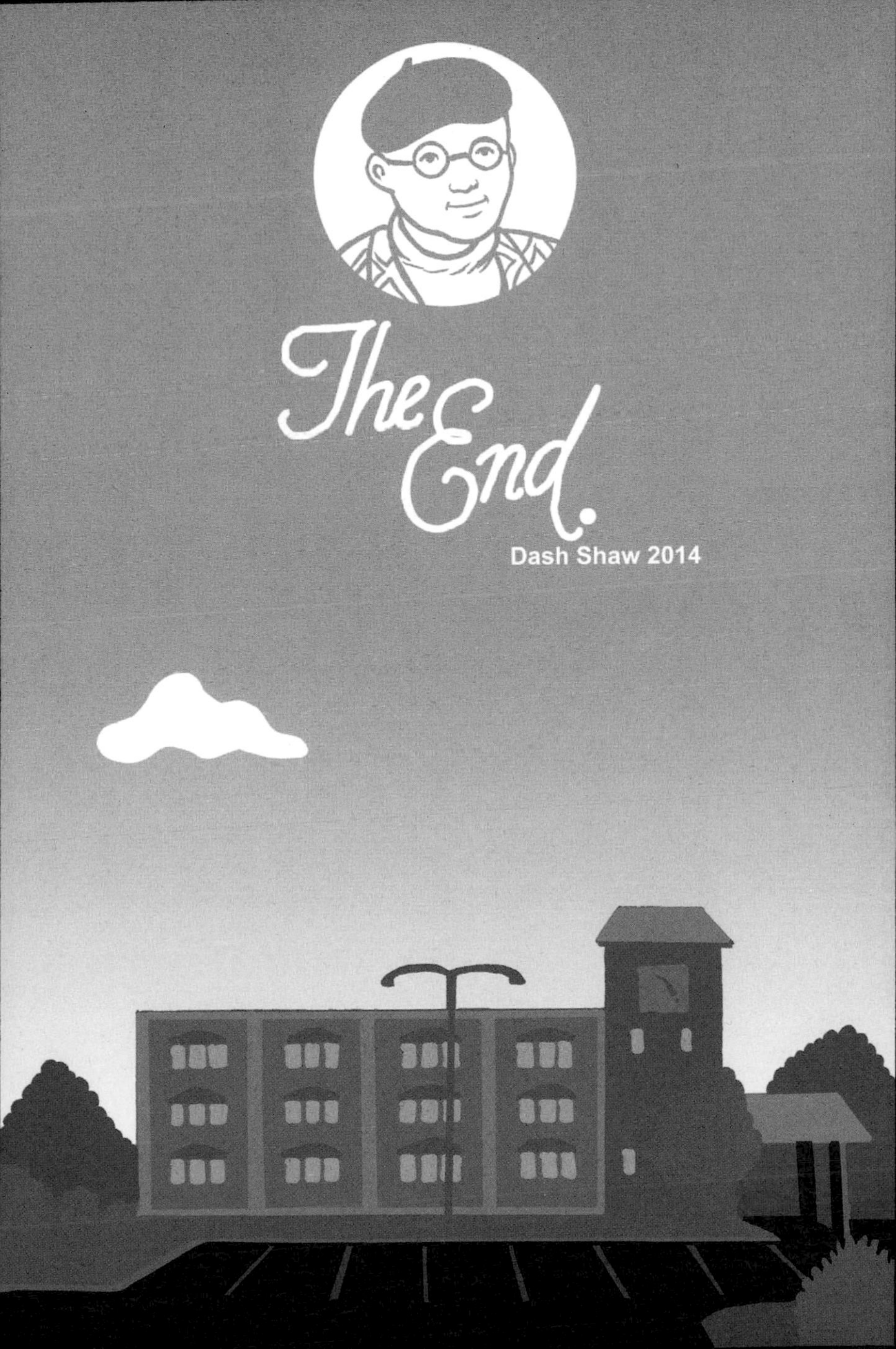
The End.
Dash Shaw 2014

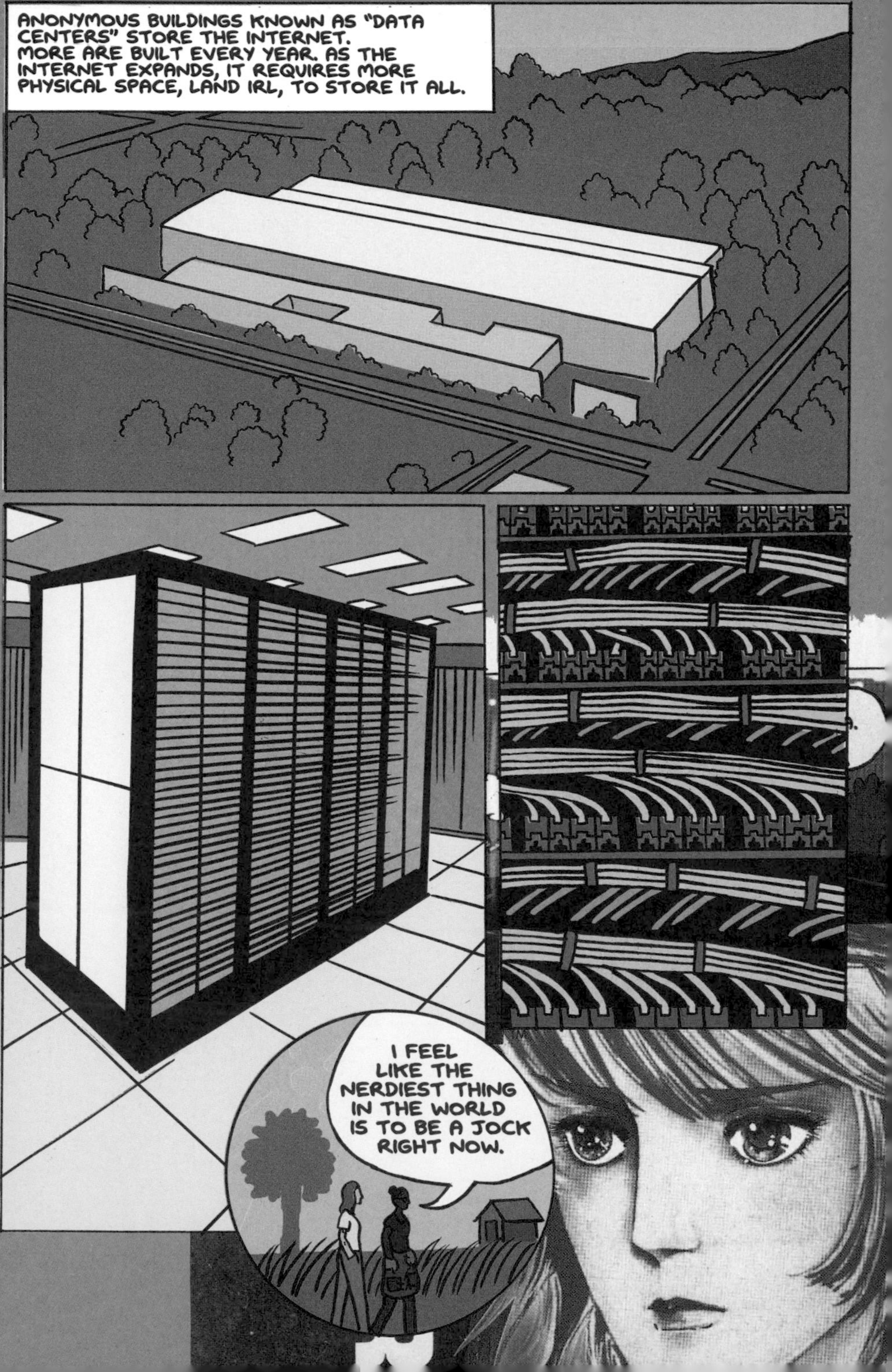
ANONYMOUS BUILDINGS KNOWN AS "DATA CENTERS" STORE THE INTERNET.
MORE ARE BUILT EVERY YEAR. AS THE INTERNET EXPANDS, IT REQUIRES MORE PHYSICAL SPACE, LAND IRL, TO STORE IT ALL.
I FEEL LIKE THE NERDIEST THING IN THE WORLD IS TO BE A JOCK RIGHT NOW.

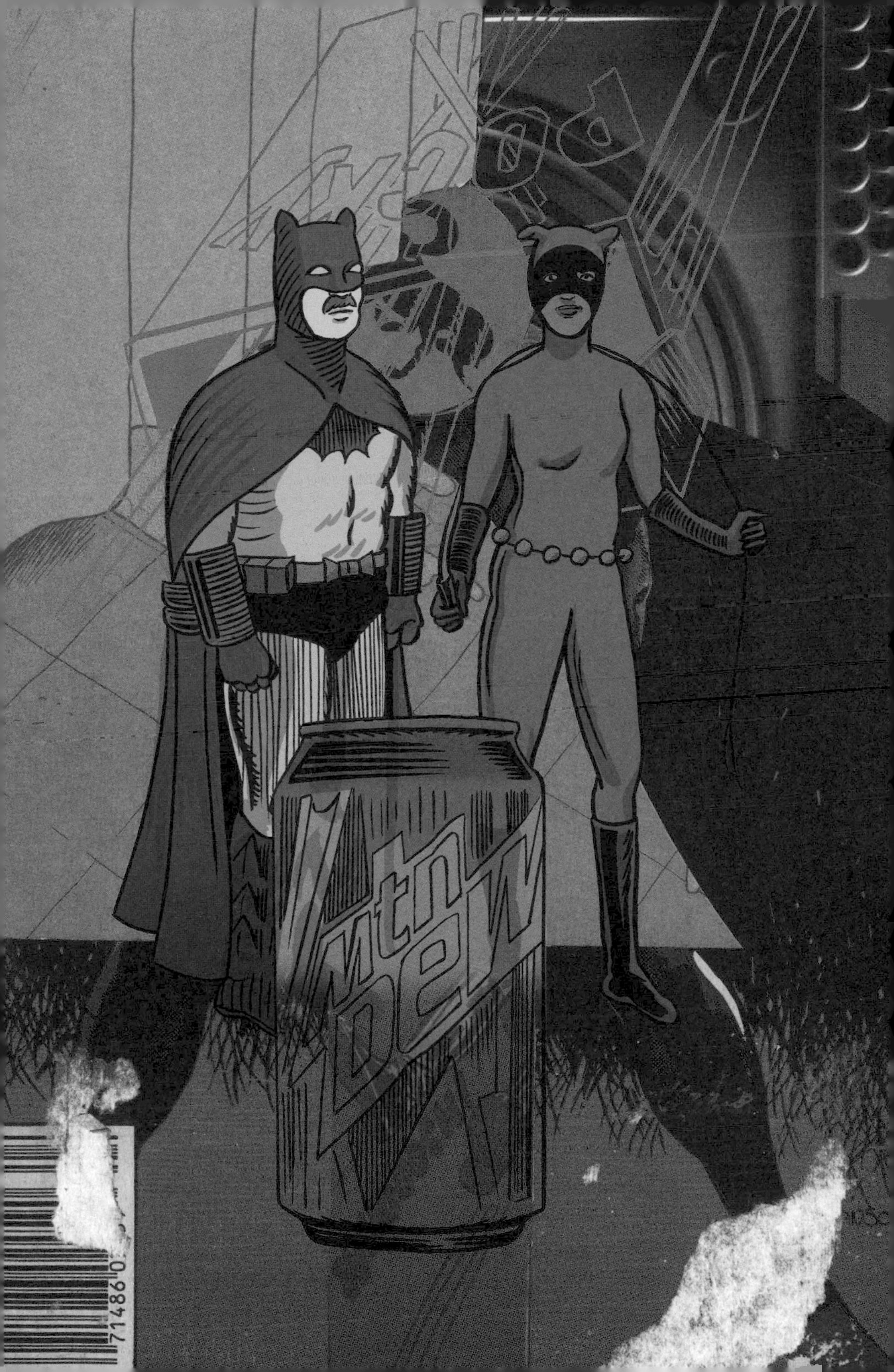
mtn dew

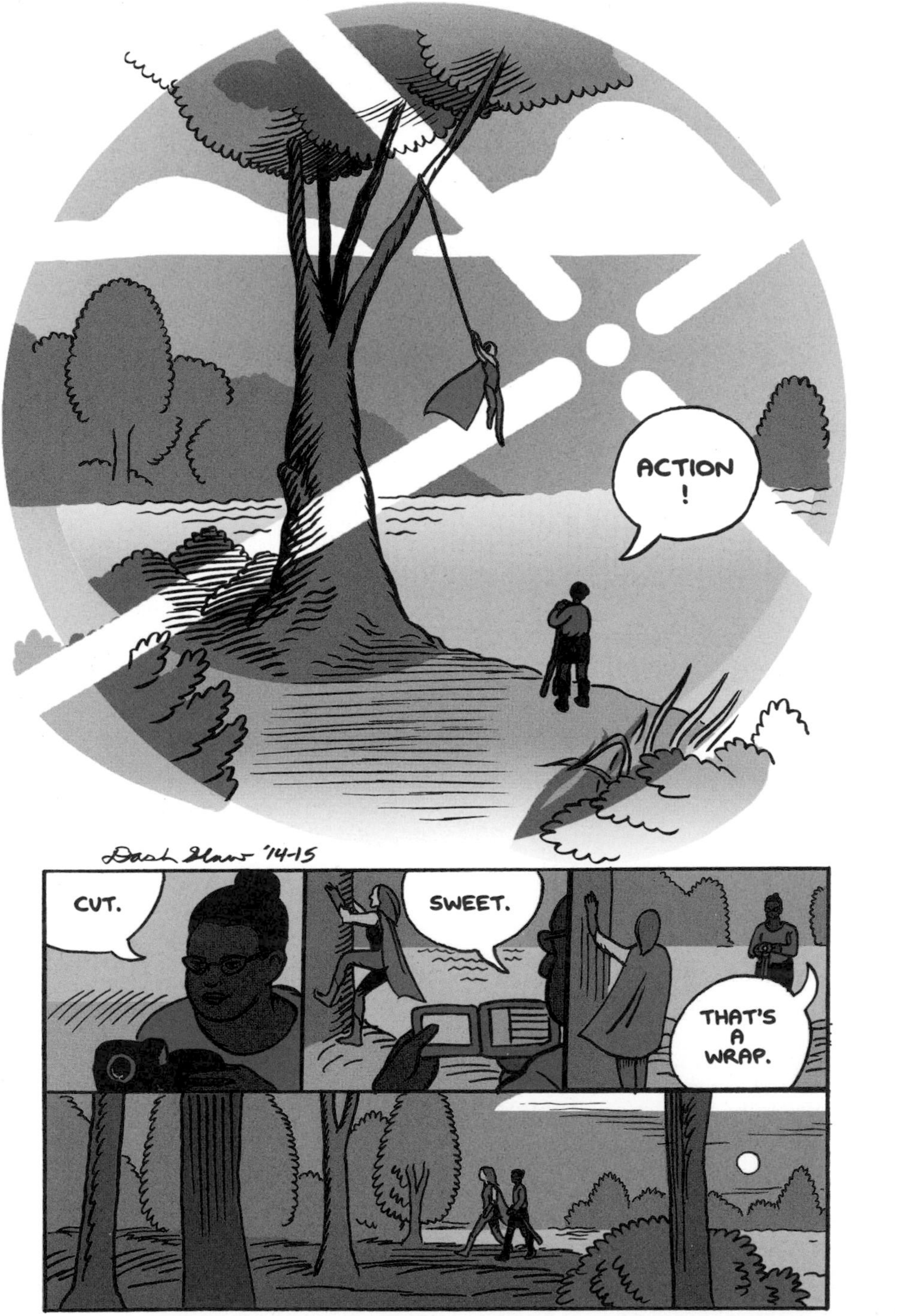
ACTION !
Dash Shaw '14-15
CUT.
SWEET.
THAT'S A WRAP.

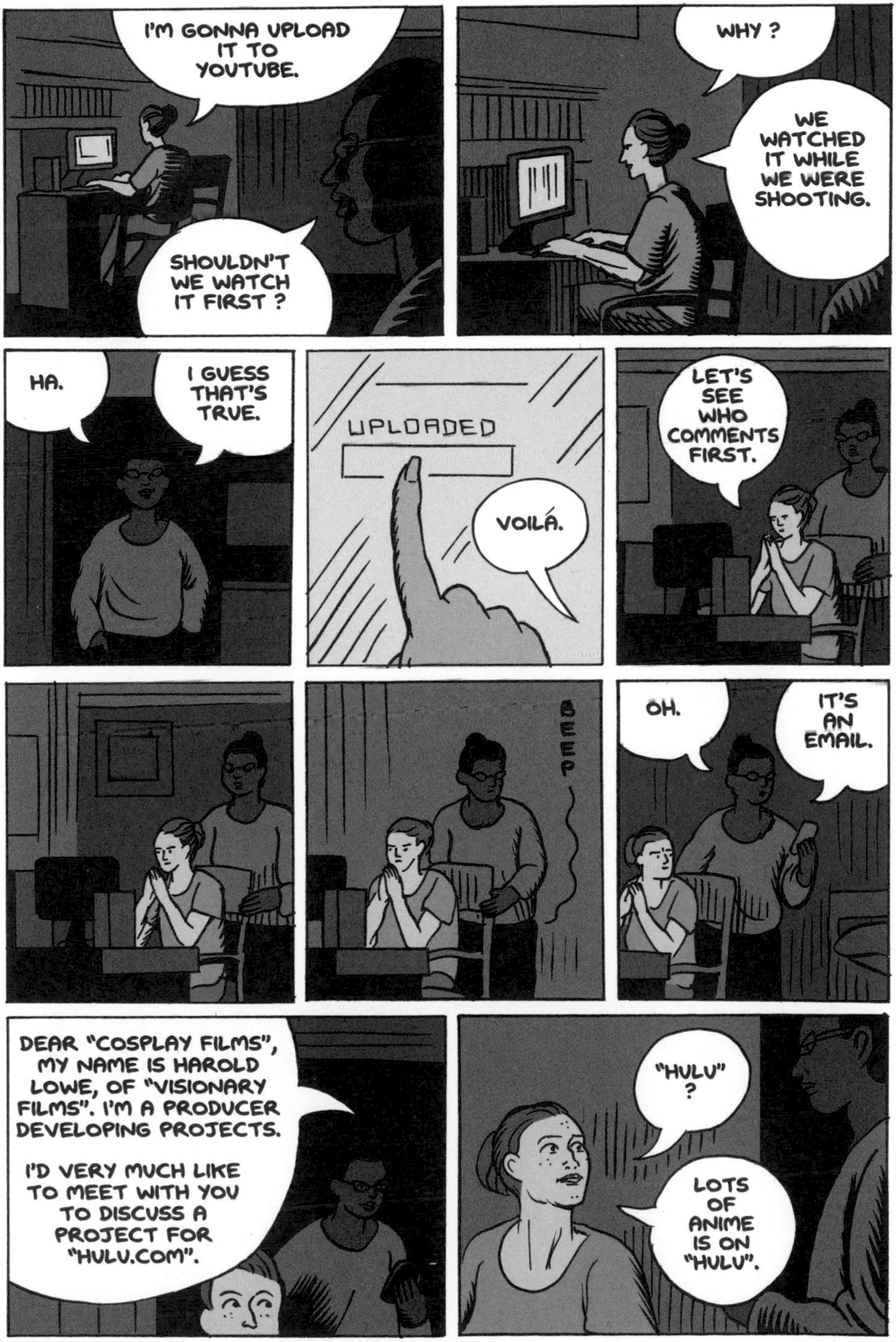
I'M GONNA UPLOAD IT TO YOUTUBE.
SHOULDN'T WE WATCH IT FIRST ?
WHY ?
WE WATCHED IT WHILE WE WERE SHOOTING.
HA.
I GUESS THAT'S TRUE.
UPLOADED
VOILÁ.
LET'S SEE WHO COMMENTS FIRST.
BEEP
OH.
IT'S AN EMAIL.
DEAR "COSPLAY FILMS", MY NAME IS HAROLD LOWE, OF "VISIONARY FILMS". I'M A PRODUCER DEVELOPING PROJECTS.
I'D VERY MUCH LIKE TO MEET WITH YOU TO DISCUSS A PROJECT FOR "HULU.COM".
"HULU" ?
LOTS OF ANIME IS ON "HULU".

AND SO...

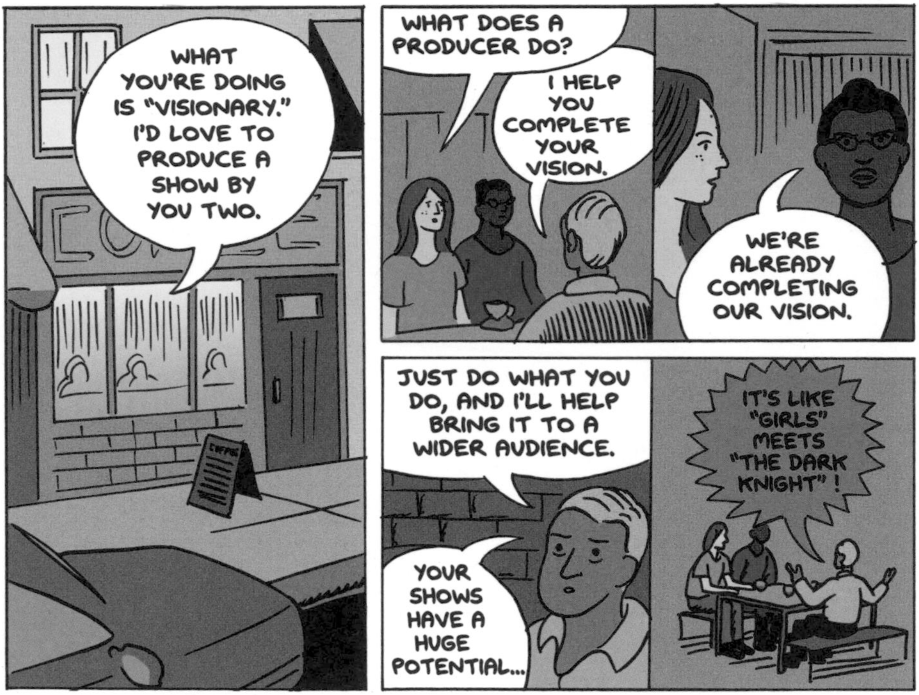
WHAT YOU'RE DOING IS "VISIONARY." I'D LOVE TO PRODUCE A SHOW BY YOU TWO.
WHAT DOES A PRODUCER DO?
I HELP YOU COMPLETE YOUR VISION.
WE'RE ALREADY COMPLETING OUR VISION.
JUST DO WHAT YOU DO, AND I'LL HELP BRING IT TO A WIDER AUDIENCE.
YOUR SHOWS HAVE A HUGE POTENTIAL...
IT'S LIKE "GIRLS" MEETS "THE DARK KNIGHT"!

LATER...

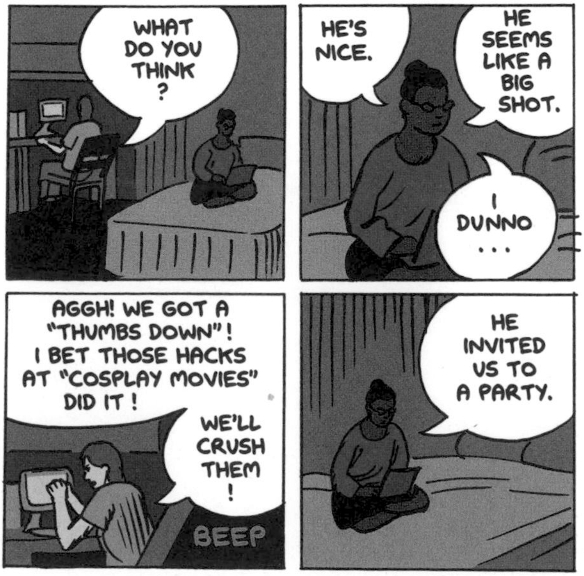
WHAT DO YOU THINK ?
HE'S NICE.
HE SEEMS LIKE A BIG SHOT.
I DUNNO . . .
AGGH! WE GOT A "THUMBS DOWN"! I BET THOSE HACKS AT "COSPLAY MOVIES" DID IT!
WE'LL CRUSH THEM !
BEEP
HE INVITED US TO A PARTY.

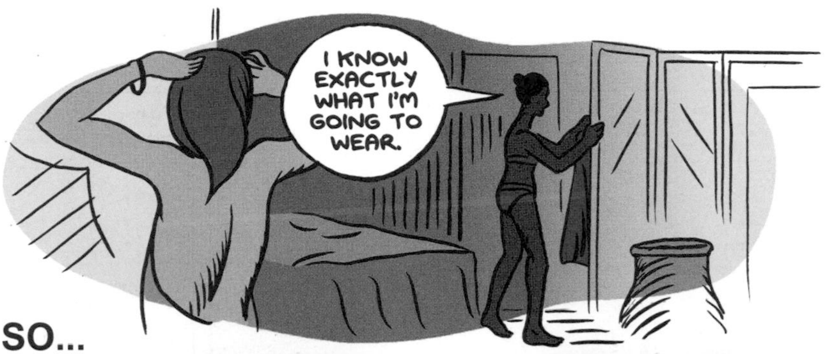
I KNOW EXACTLY WHAT I'M GOING TO WEAR.

AND SO...

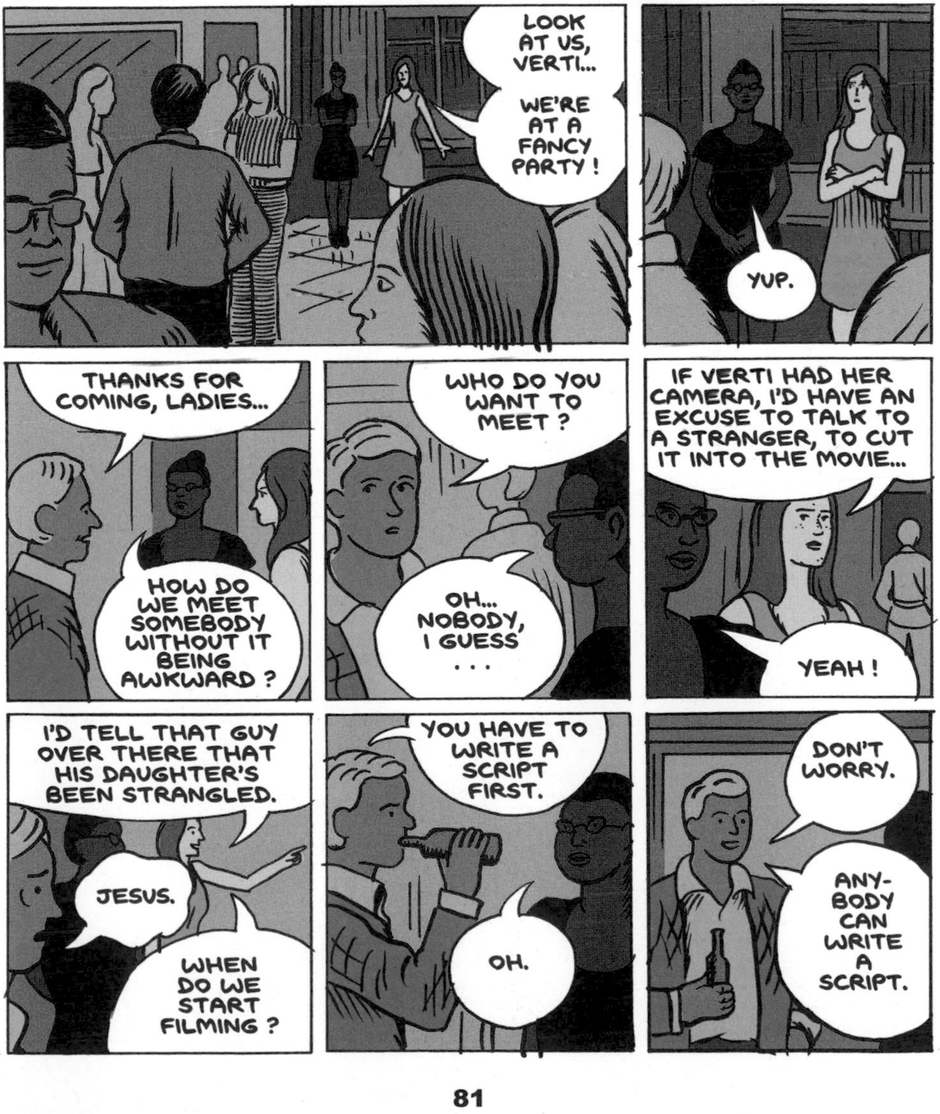
LOOK AT US, VERTI...
WE'RE AT A FANCY PARTY!
YUP.
THANKS FOR COMING, LADIES...
HOW DO WE MEET SOMEBODY WITHOUT IT BEING AWKWARD?
WHO DO YOU WANT TO MEET?
OH... NOBODY, I GUESS . . .
IF VERTI HAD HER CAMERA, I'D HAVE AN EXCUSE TO TALK TO A STRANGER, TO CUT IT INTO THE MOVIE...
YEAH!
I'D TELL THAT GUY OVER THERE THAT HIS DAUGHTER'S BEEN STRANGLED.
JESUS.
WHEN DO WE START FILMING?
YOU HAVE TO WRITE A SCRIPT FIRST.
OH.
DON'T WORRY.
ANY-BODY CAN WRITE A SCRIPT.

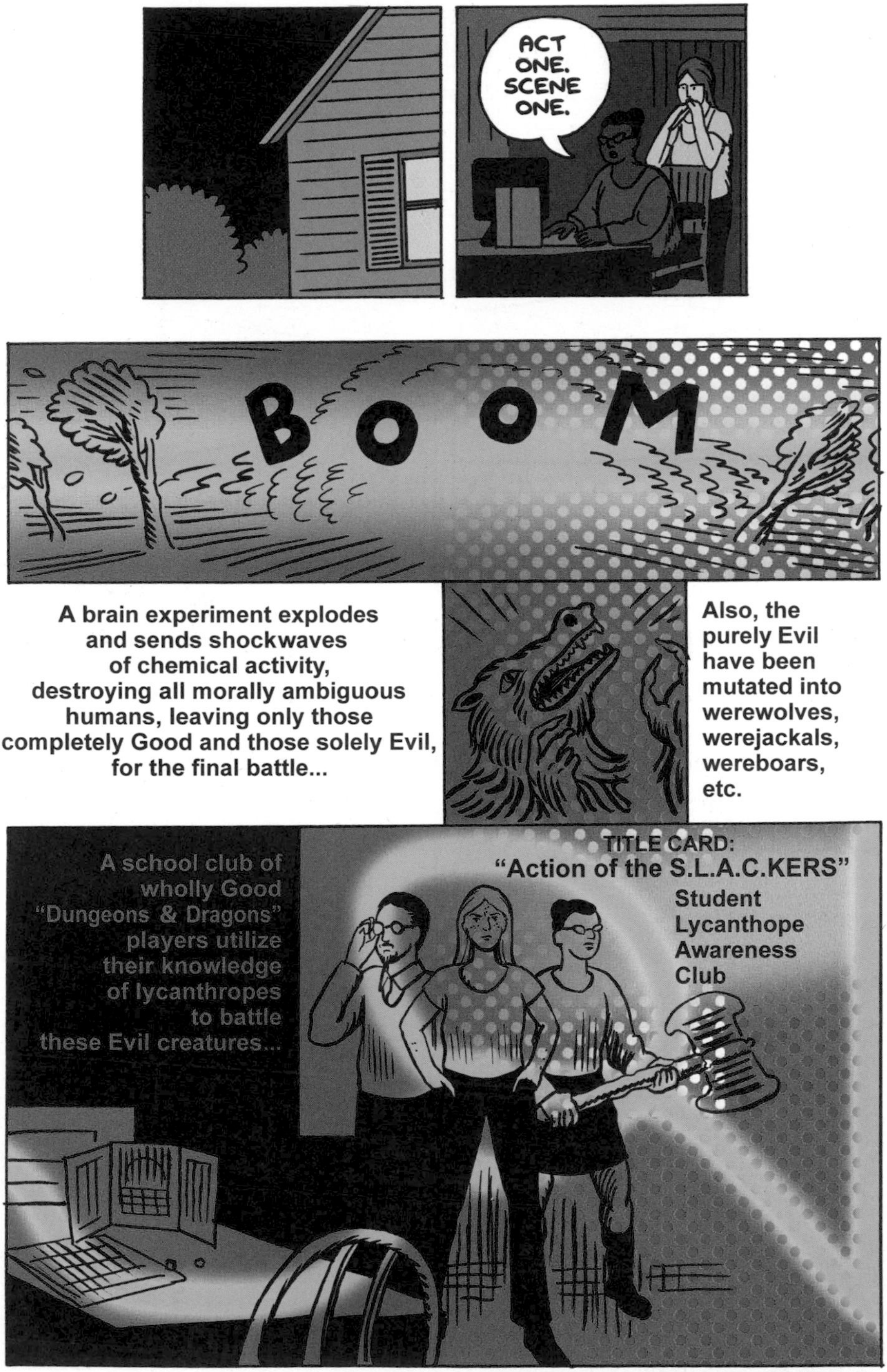
ACT ONE. SCENE ONE.
BOOM
A brain experiment explodes and sends shockwaves of chemical activity, destroying all morally ambiguous humans, leaving only those completely Good and those solely Evil, for the final battle...
Also, the purely Evil have been mutated into werewolves, werejackals, wereboars, etc.
A school club of wholly Good "Dungeons & Dragons" players utilize their knowledge of lycanthropes to battle these Evil creatures...
TITLE CARD:
"Action of the S.L.A.C.KERS"
Student Lycanthope Awareness Club

A "Cosplay Films" Megaproduction

SOON...

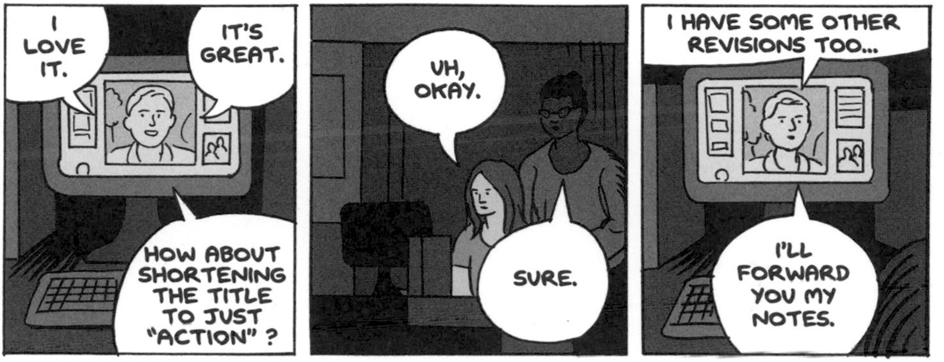
I LOVE IT.
IT'S GREAT.
HOW ABOUT SHORTENING THE TITLE TO JUST "ACTION" ?
UH, OKAY.
SURE.
I HAVE SOME OTHER REVISIONS TOO...
I'LL FORWARD YOU MY NOTES.

A MONTH LATER...

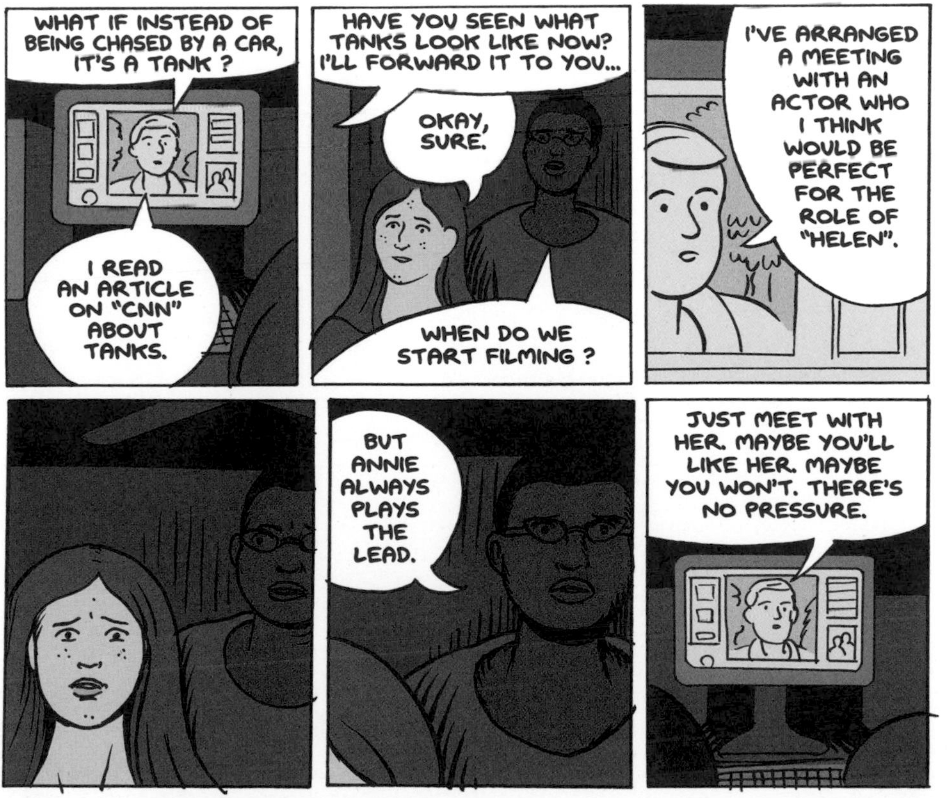
WHAT IF INSTEAD OF BEING CHASED BY A CAR, IT'S A TANK ?
I READ AN ARTICLE ON "CNN" ABOUT TANKS.
HAVE YOU SEEN WHAT TANKS LOOK LIKE NOW? I'LL FORWARD IT TO YOU...
OKAY, SURE.
WHEN DO WE START FILMING ?
I'VE ARRANGED A MEETING WITH AN ACTOR WHO I THINK WOULD BE PERFECT FOR THE ROLE OF "HELEN".
BUT ANNIE ALWAYS PLAYS THE LEAD.
JUST MEET WITH HER. MAYBE YOU'LL LIKE HER. MAYBE YOU WON'T. THERE'S NO PRESSURE.

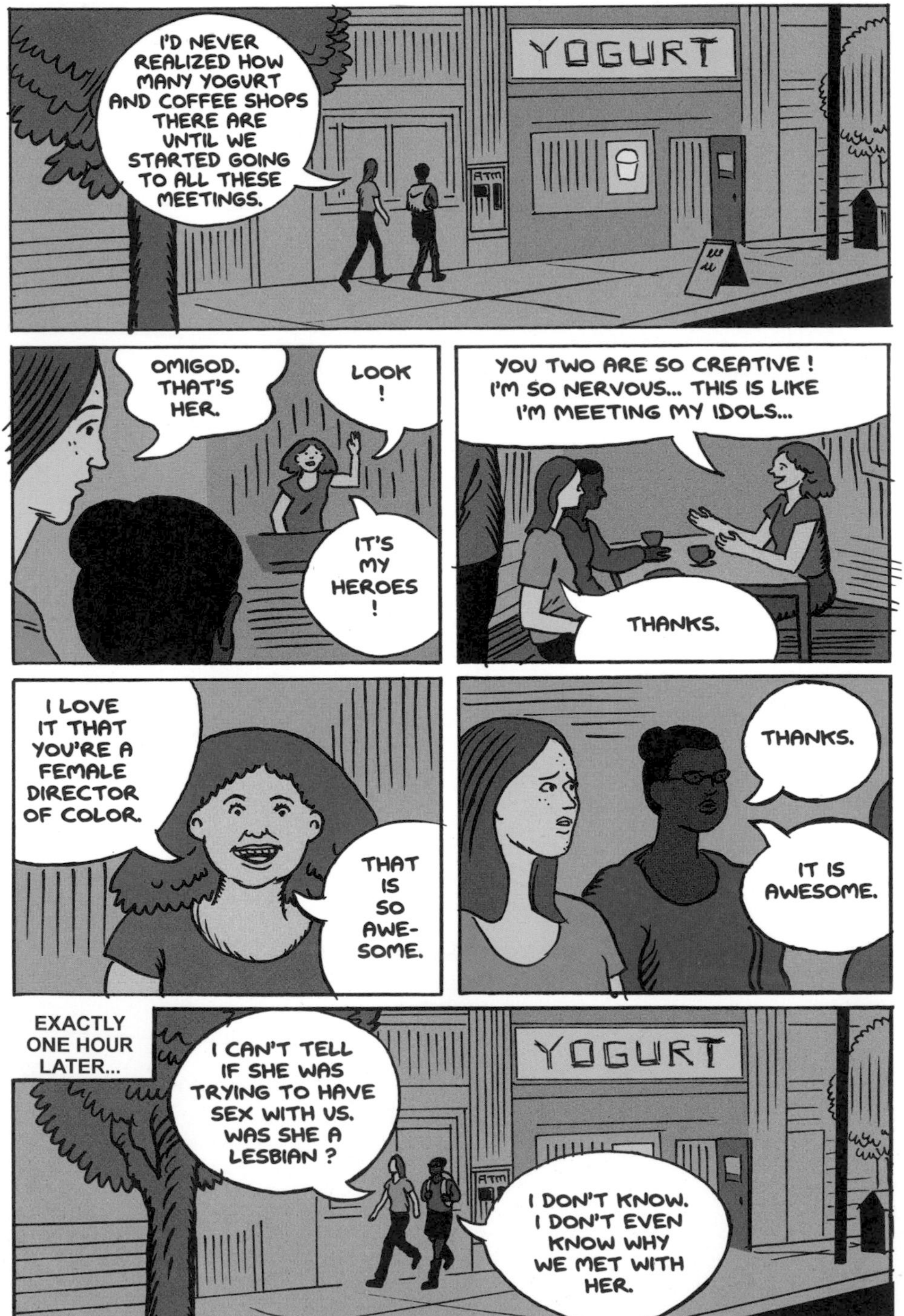
I'D NEVER REALIZED HOW MANY YOGURT AND COFFEE SHOPS THERE ARE UNTIL WE STARTED GOING TO ALL THESE MEETINGS.
YOGURT
ATM
OMIGOD. THAT'S HER.
LOOK !
IT'S MY HEROES !
YOU TWO ARE SO CREATIVE ! I'M SO NERVOUS... THIS IS LIKE I'M MEETING MY IDOLS...
THANKS.
I LOVE IT THAT YOU'RE A FEMALE DIRECTOR OF COLOR.
THAT IS SO AWE-SOME.
THANKS.
IT IS AWESOME.
EXACTLY ONE HOUR LATER...
YOGURT
I CAN'T TELL IF SHE WAS TRYING TO HAVE SEX WITH US. WAS SHE A LESBIAN ?
ATM
I DON'T KNOW. I DON'T EVEN KNOW WHY WE MET WITH HER.

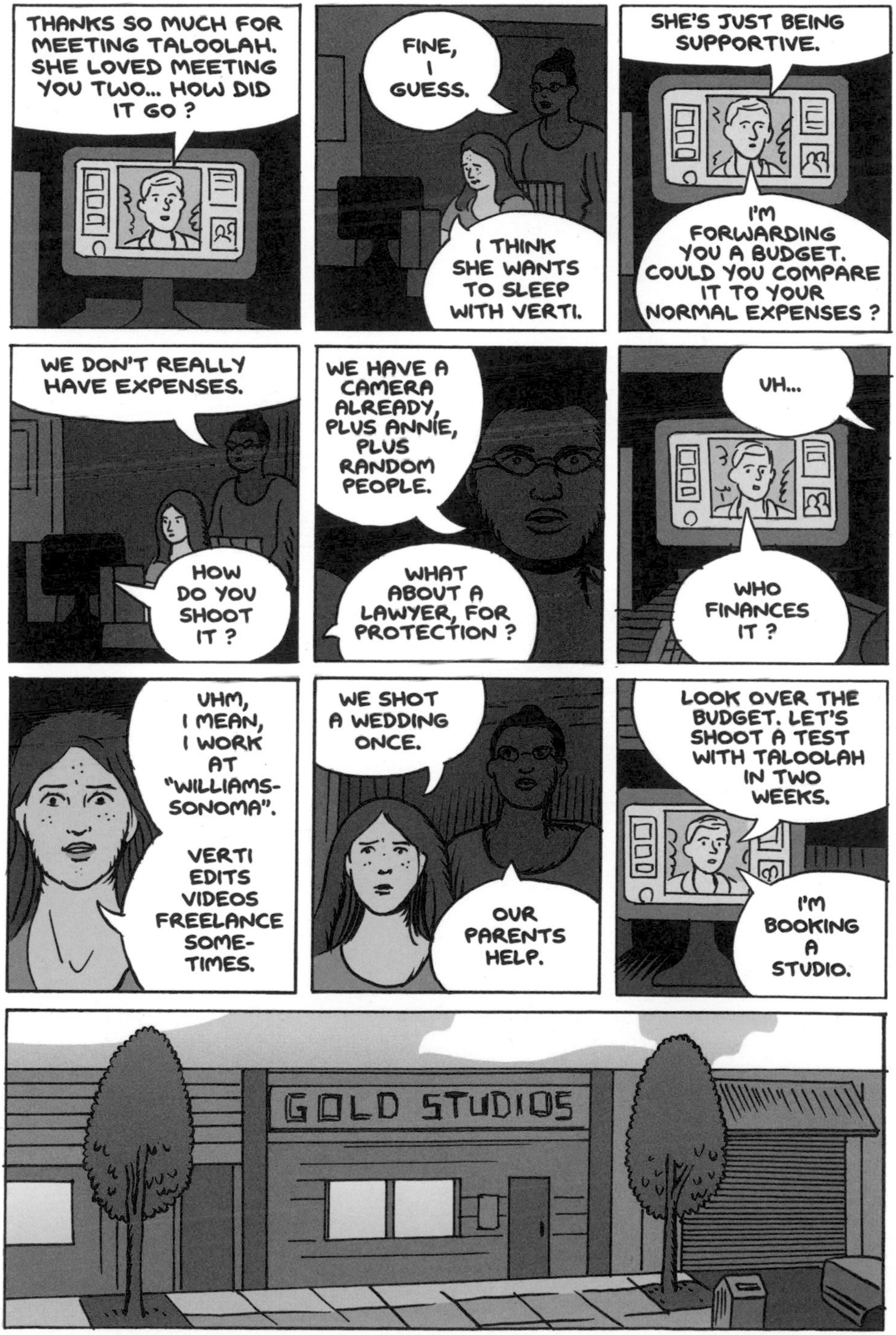
THANKS SO MUCH FOR MEETING TALOOLAH. SHE LOVED MEETING YOU TWO... HOW DID IT GO ?
FINE, I GUESS.
I THINK SHE WANTS TO SLEEP WITH VERTI.
SHE'S JUST BEING SUPPORTIVE.
I'M FORWARDING YOU A BUDGET. COULD YOU COMPARE IT TO YOUR NORMAL EXPENSES ?
WE DON'T REALLY HAVE EXPENSES.
HOW DO YOU SHOOT IT ?
WE HAVE A CAMERA ALREADY, PLUS ANNIE, PLUS RANDOM PEOPLE.
WHAT ABOUT A LAWYER, FOR PROTECTION ?
UH...
WHO FINANCES IT ?
UHM, I MEAN, I WORK AT "WILLIAMS-SONOMA".
VERTI EDITS VIDEOS FREELANCE SOME-TIMES.
WE SHOT A WEDDING ONCE.
OUR PARENTS HELP.
LOOK OVER THE BUDGET. LET'S SHOOT A TEST WITH TALOOLAH IN TWO WEEKS.
I'M BOOKING A STUDIO.
GOLD STUDIOS

INT. UNDERGROUND BUNKER - TIME UNKNOWN

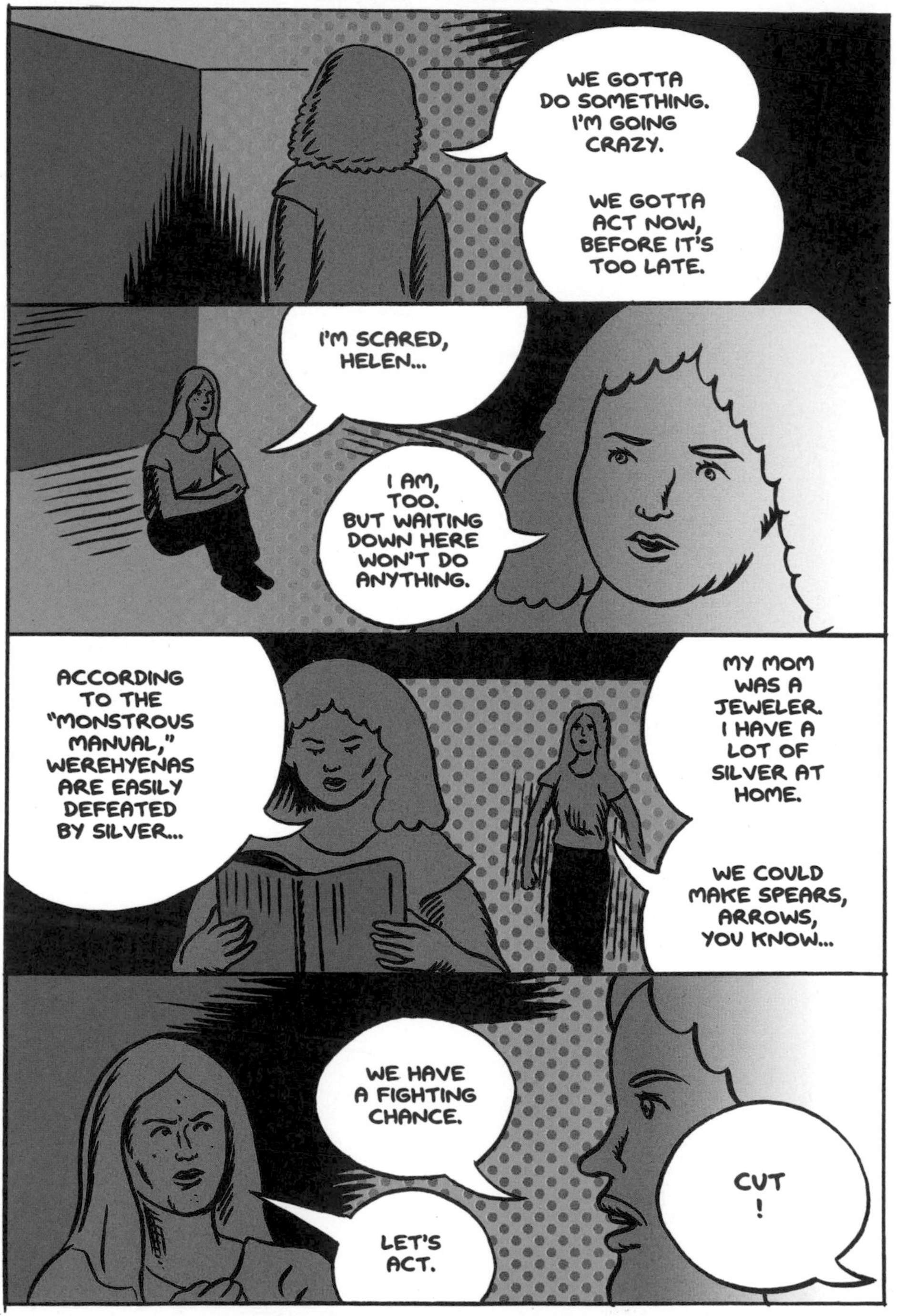
WE GOTTA DO SOMETHING. I'M GOING CRAZY.
WE GOTTA ACT NOW, BEFORE IT'S TOO LATE.
I'M SCARED, HELEN...
I AM, TOO. BUT WAITING DOWN HERE WON'T DO ANYTHING.
ACCORDING TO THE "MONSTROUS MANUAL," WEREHYENAS ARE EASILY DEFEATED BY SILVER...
MY MOM WAS A JEWELER. I HAVE A LOT OF SILVER AT HOME.
WE COULD MAKE SPEARS, ARROWS, YOU KNOW...
WE HAVE A FIGHTING CHANCE.
LET'S ACT.
CUT!

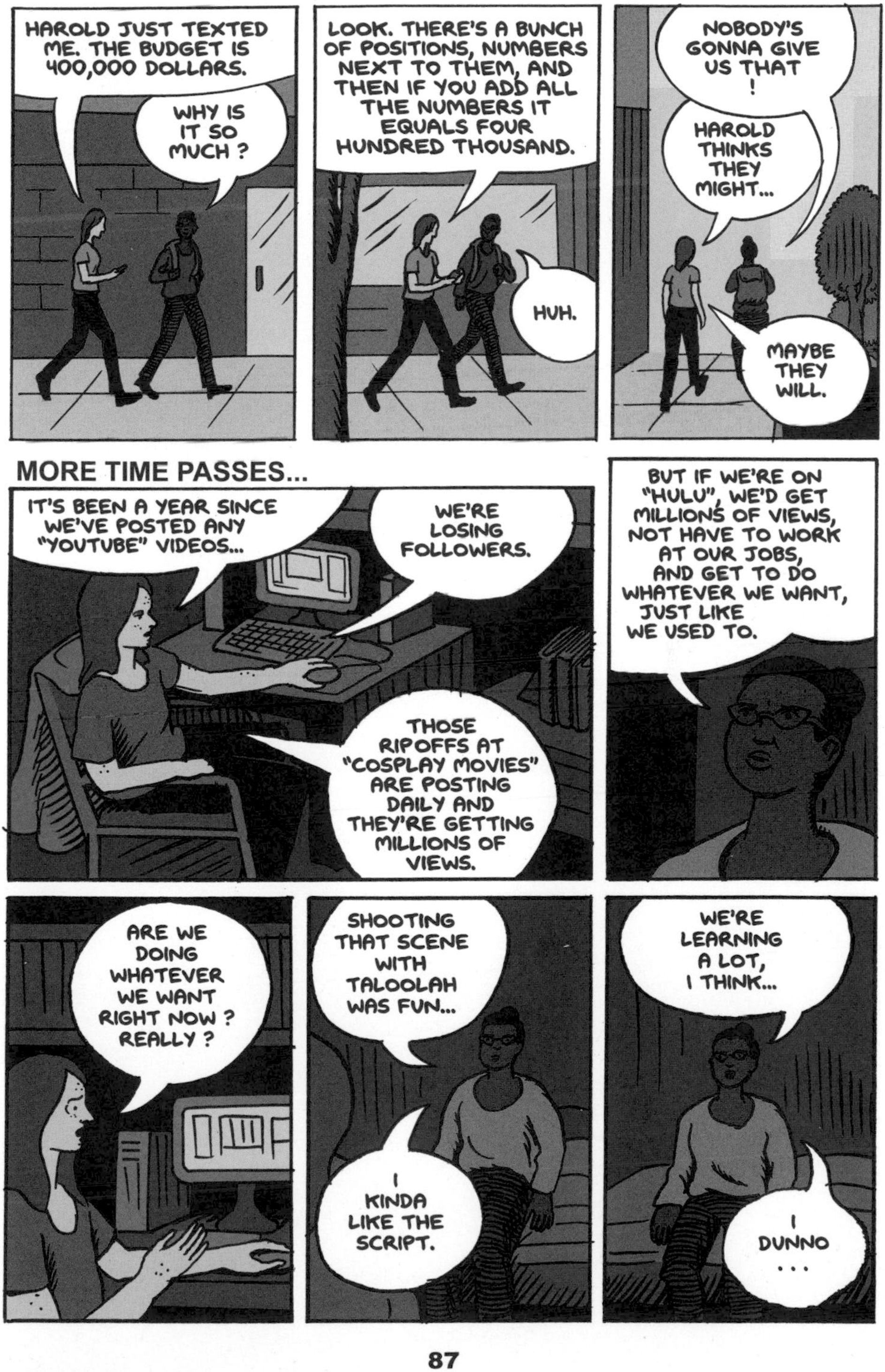
HAROLD JUST TEXTED ME. THE BUDGET IS 400,000 DOLLARS.
WHY IS IT SO MUCH ?
LOOK. THERE'S A BUNCH OF POSITIONS, NUMBERS NEXT TO THEM, AND THEN IF YOU ADD ALL THE NUMBERS IT EQUALS FOUR HUNDRED THOUSAND.
HUH.
NOBODY'S GONNA GIVE US THAT !
HAROLD THINKS THEY MIGHT...
MAYBE THEY WILL.
MORE TIME PASSES...
IT'S BEEN A YEAR SINCE WE'VE POSTED ANY "YOUTUBE" VIDEOS...
WE'RE LOSING FOLLOWERS.
THOSE RIPOFFS AT "COSPLAY MOVIES" ARE POSTING DAILY AND THEY'RE GETTING MILLIONS OF VIEWS.
BUT IF WE'RE ON "HULU", WE'D GET MILLIONS OF VIEWS, NOT HAVE TO WORK AT OUR JOBS, AND GET TO DO WHATEVER WE WANT, JUST LIKE WE USED TO.
ARE WE DOING WHATEVER WE WANT RIGHT NOW ? REALLY ?
SHOOTING THAT SCENE WITH TALOOLAH WAS FUN...
I KINDA LIKE THE SCRIPT.
WE'RE LEARNING A LOT, I THINK...
I DUNNO . . .

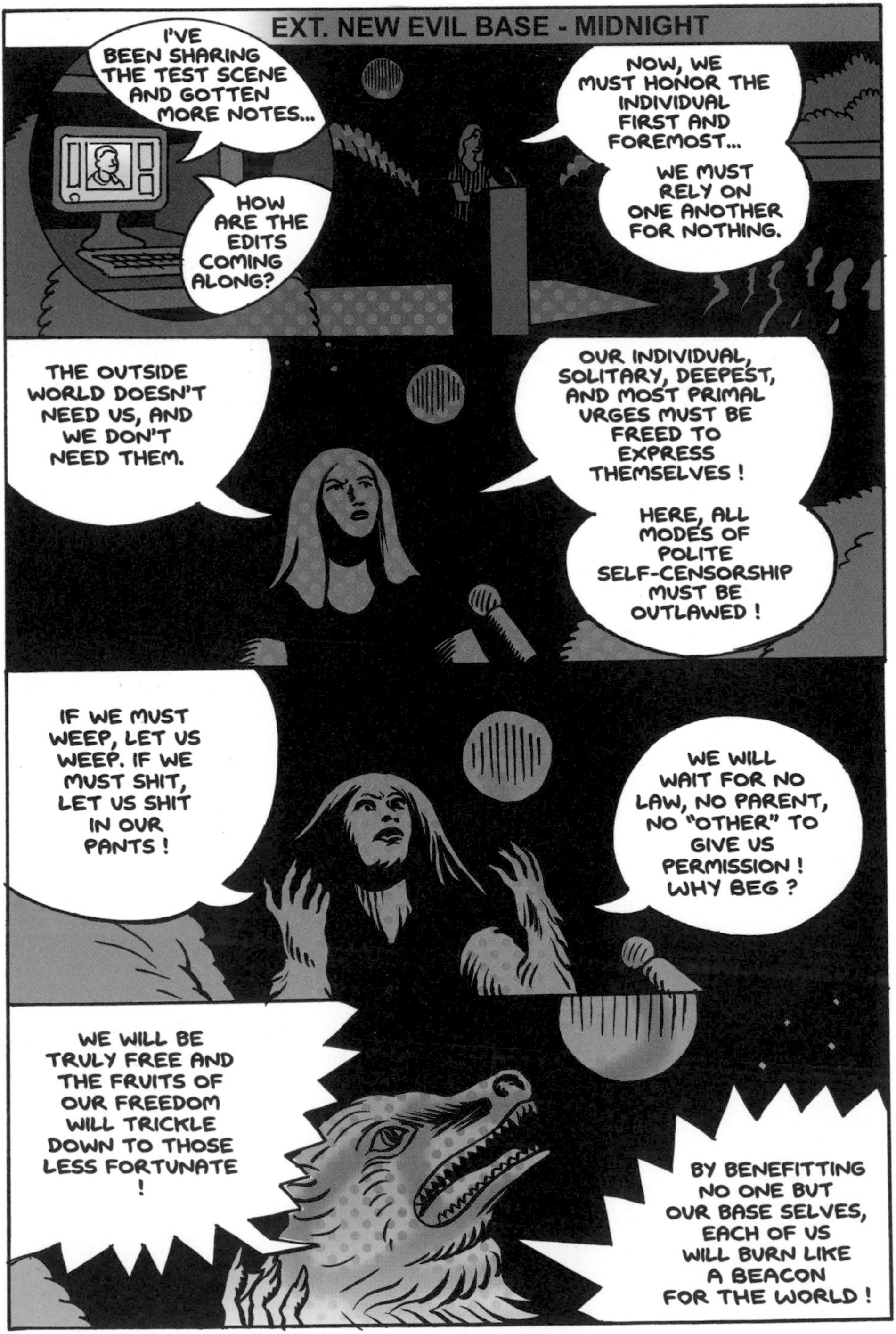
EXT. NEW EVIL BASE - MIDNIGHT
I'VE BEEN SHARING THE TEST SCENE AND GOTTEN MORE NOTES...
HOW ARE THE EDITS COMING ALONG?
NOW, WE MUST HONOR THE INDIVIDUAL FIRST AND FOREMOST...
WE MUST RELY ON ONE ANOTHER FOR NOTHING.
THE OUTSIDE WORLD DOESN'T NEED US, AND WE DON'T NEED THEM.
OUR INDIVIDUAL, SOLITARY, DEEPEST, AND MOST PRIMAL URGES MUST BE FREED TO EXPRESS THEMSELVES !
HERE, ALL MODES OF POLITE SELF-CENSORSHIP MUST BE OUTLAWED !
IF WE MUST WEEP, LET US WEEP. IF WE MUST SHIT, LET US SHIT IN OUR PANTS !
WE WILL WAIT FOR NO LAW, NO PARENT, NO "OTHER" TO GIVE US PERMISSION ! WHY BEG ?
WE WILL BE TRULY FREE AND THE FRUITS OF OUR FREEDOM WILL TRICKLE DOWN TO THOSE LESS FORTUNATE !
BY BENEFITTING NO ONE BUT OUR BASE SELVES, EACH OF US WILL BURN LIKE A BEACON FOR THE WORLD !

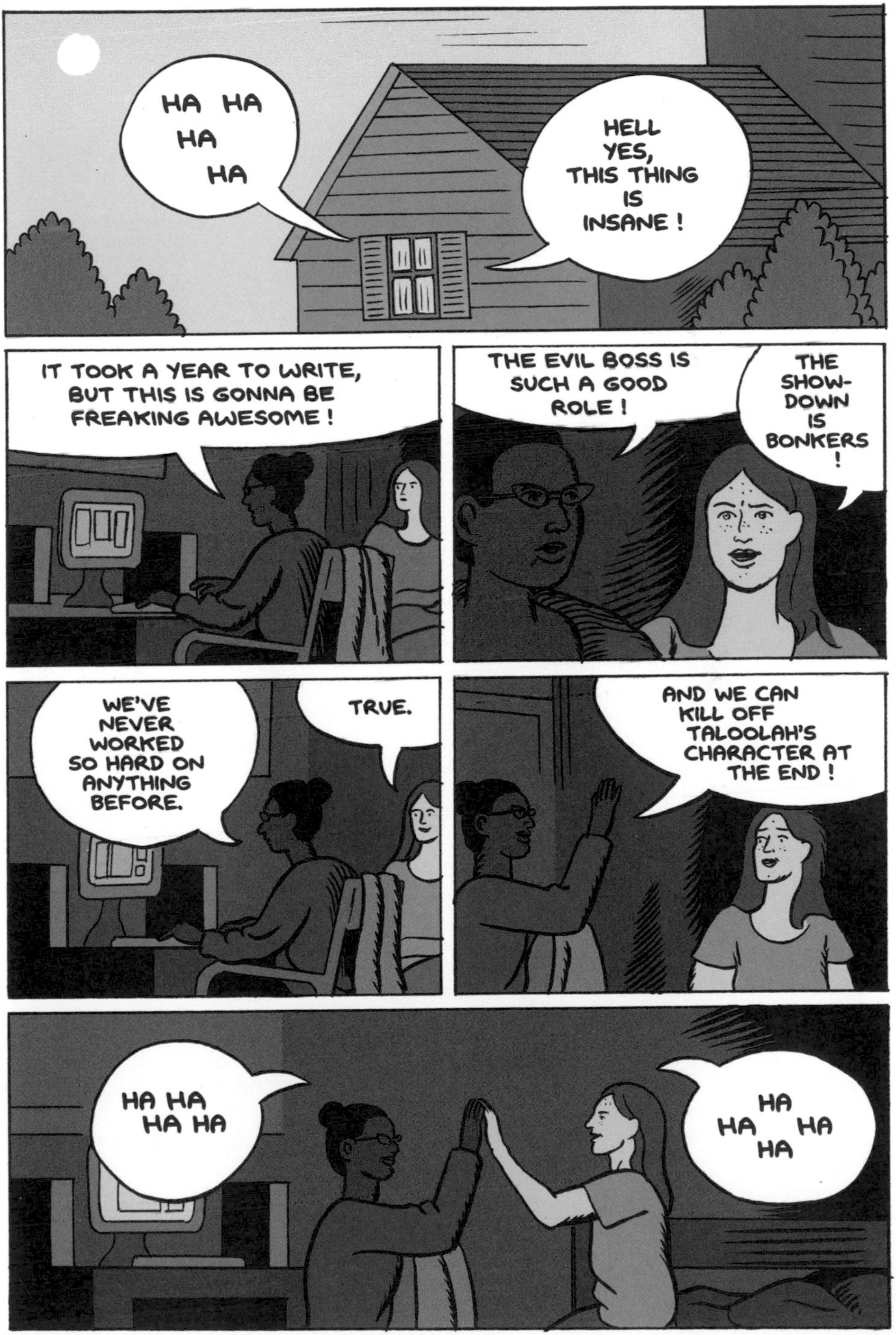
HA HA
HA
HA
HELL YES, THIS THING IS INSANE !
IT TOOK A YEAR TO WRITE, BUT THIS IS GONNA BE FREAKING AWESOME !
THE EVIL BOSS IS SUCH A GOOD ROLE !
THE SHOW-DOWN IS BONKERS !
WE'VE NEVER WORKED SO HARD ON ANYTHING BEFORE.
TRUE.
AND WE CAN KILL OFF TALOOLAH'S CHARACTER AT THE END !
HA HA
HA HA
HA
HA HA
HA

SOON...

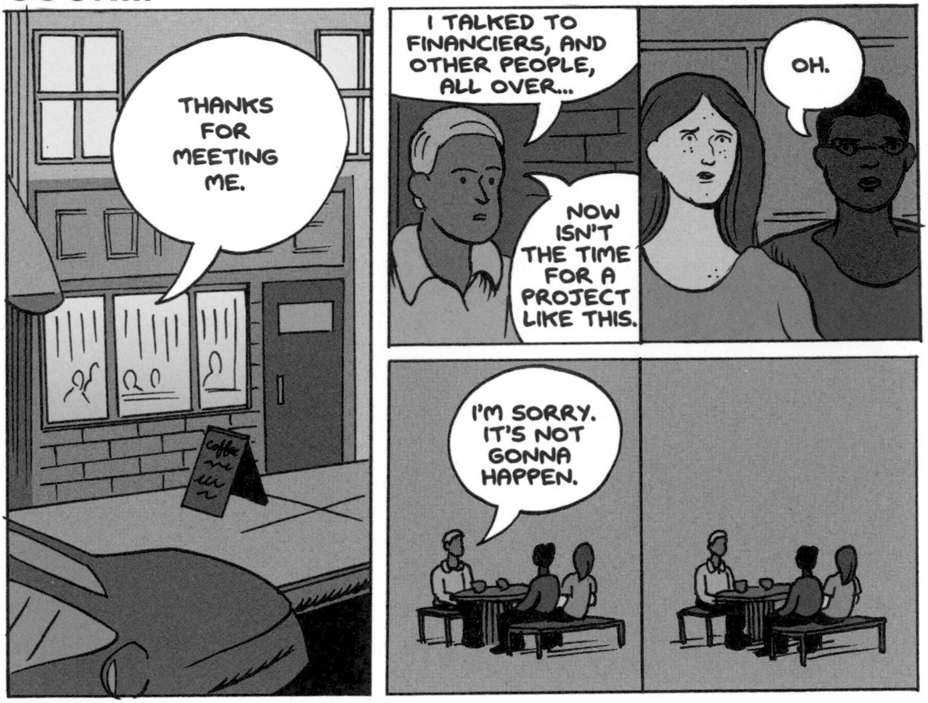

THANKS FOR MEETING ME.
I TALKED TO FINANCIERS, AND OTHER PEOPLE, ALL OVER...
NOW ISN'T THE TIME FOR A PROJECT LIKE THIS.
OH.
I'M SORRY. IT'S NOT GONNA HAPPEN.

THUS...

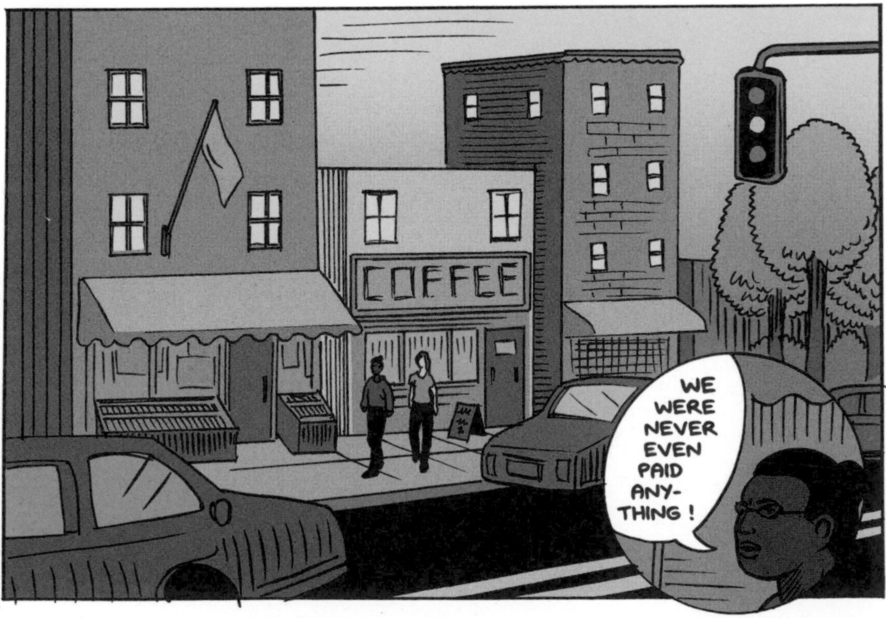

COFFEE
WE WERE NEVER EVEN PAID ANY-THING!

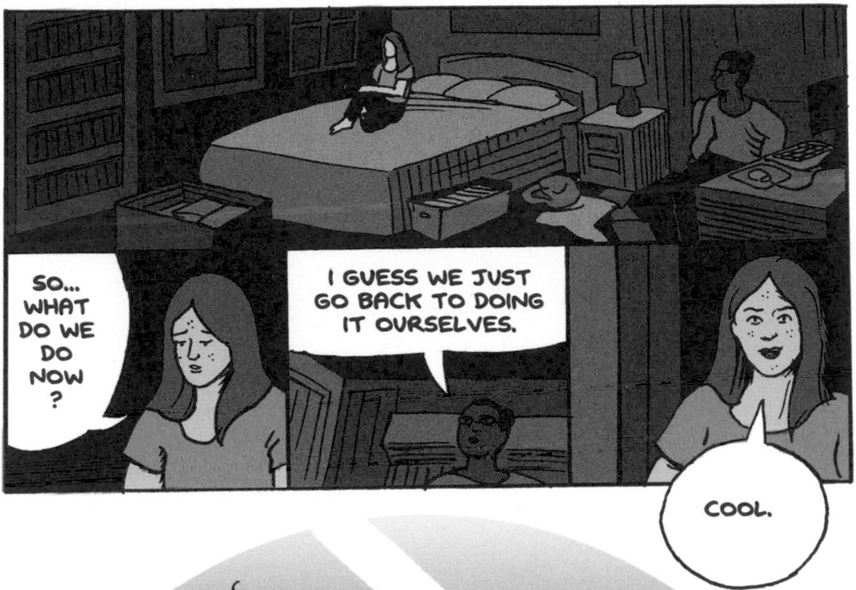
SO... WHAT DO WE DO NOW ?
I GUESS WE JUST GO BACK TO DOING IT OURSELVES.
COOL.

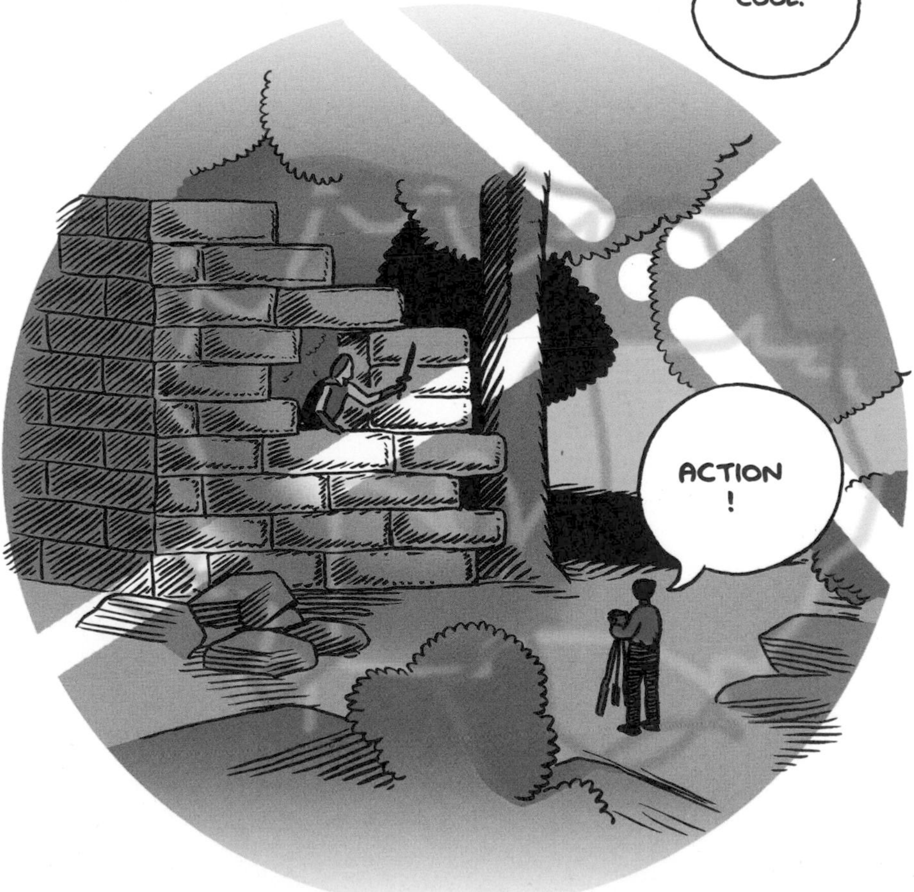
ACTION !

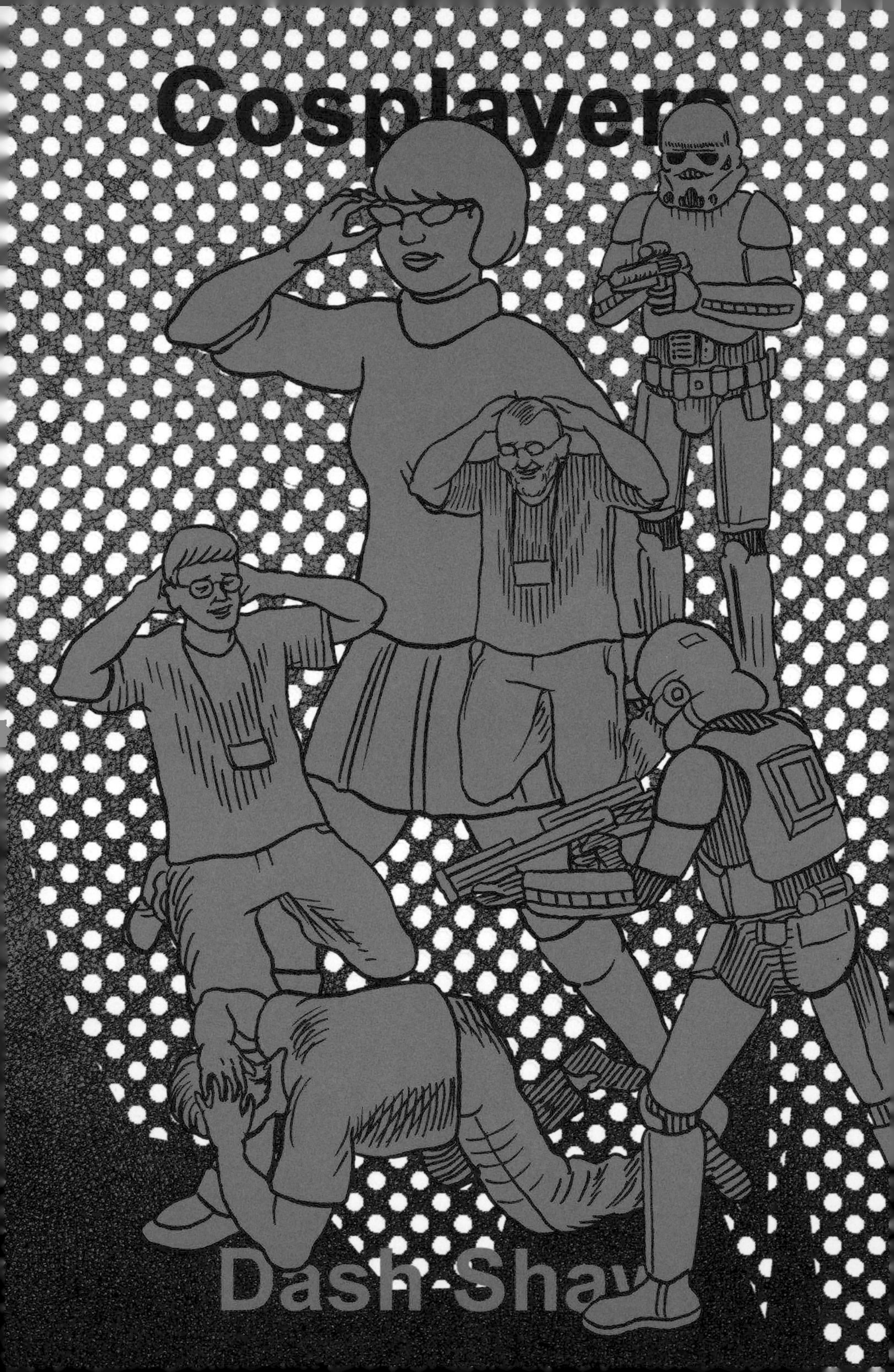
Cosplayers
Dash Shaw

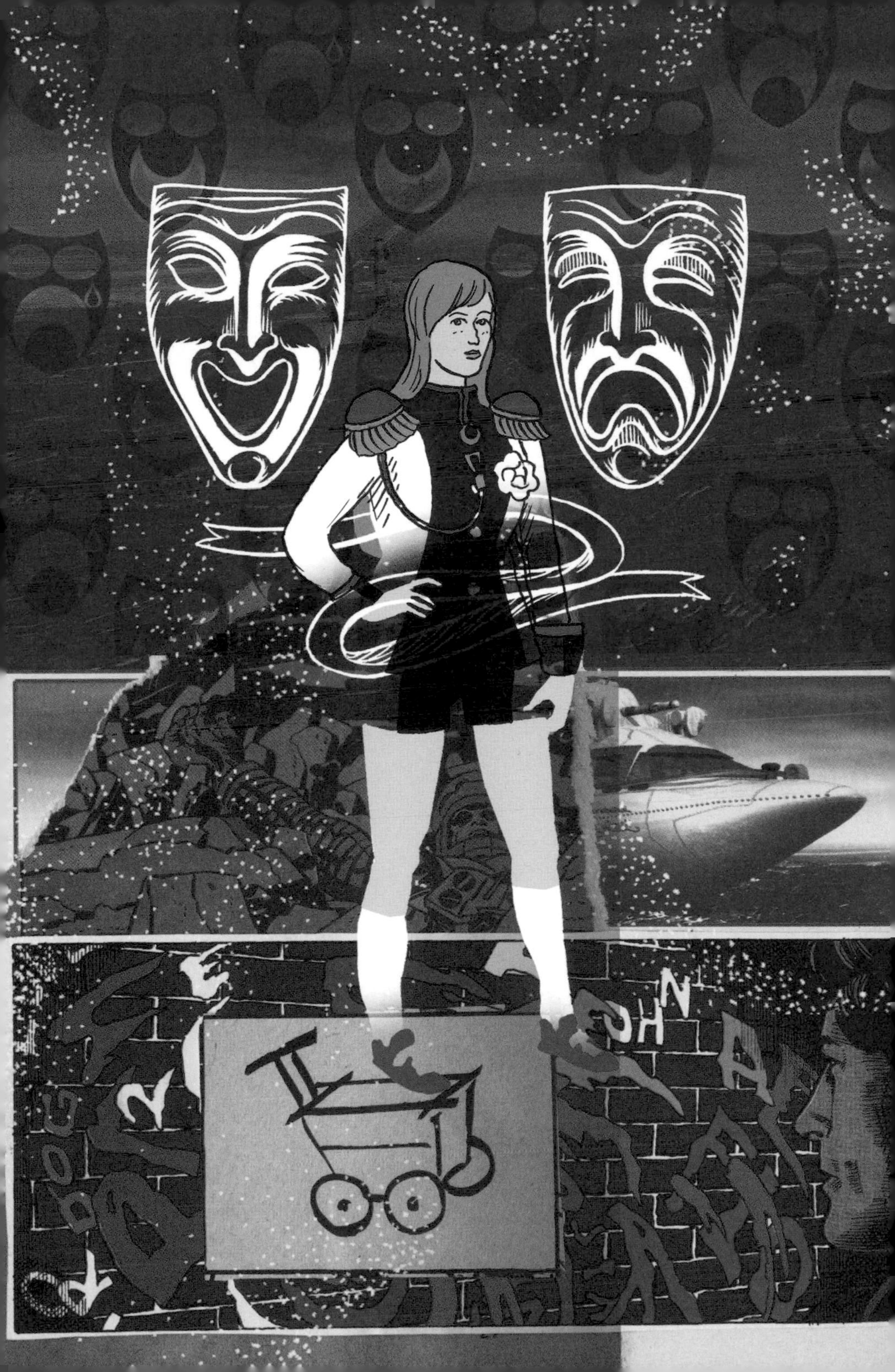

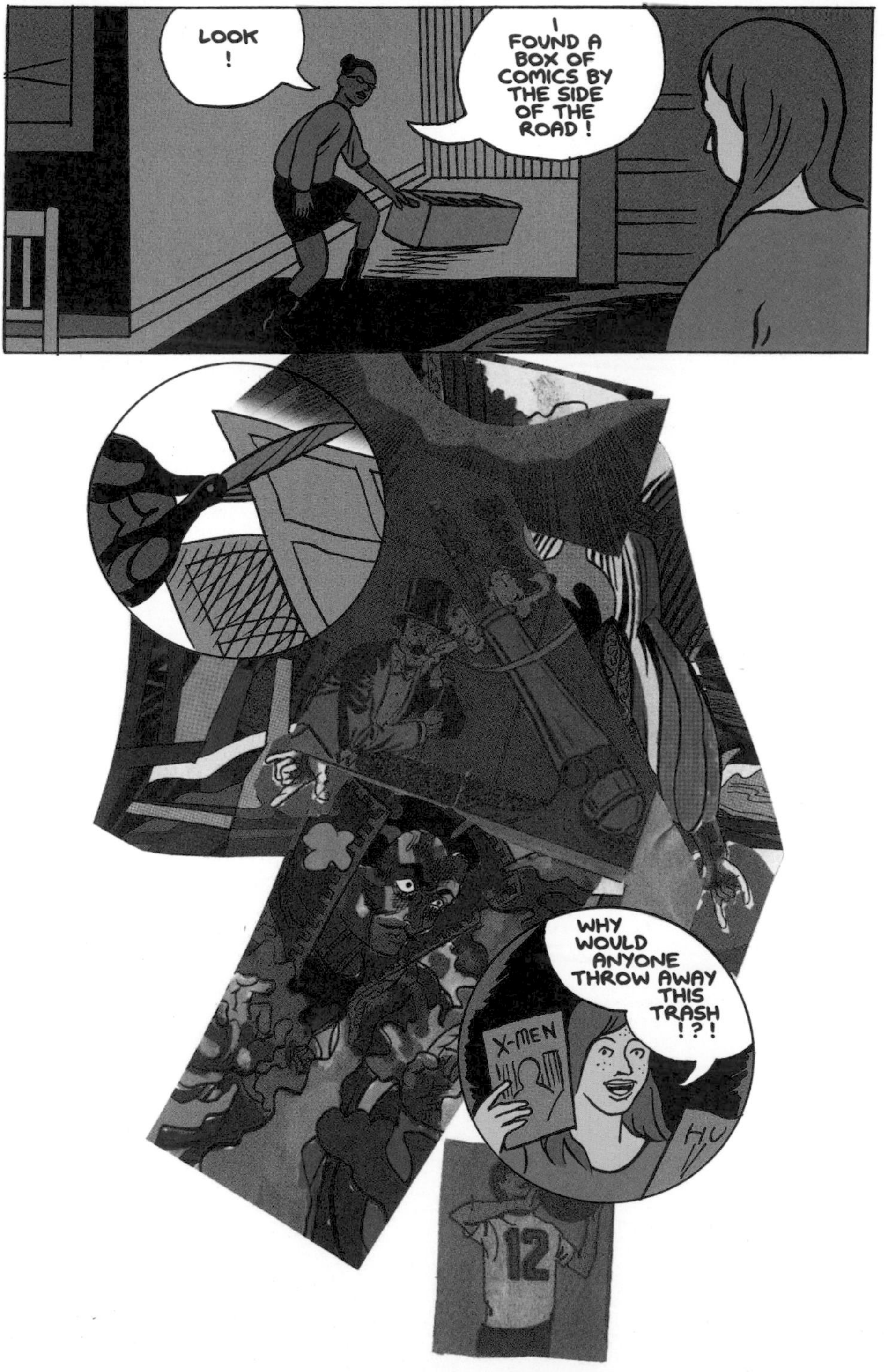
LOOK !
I FOUND A BOX OF COMICS BY THE SIDE OF THE ROAD !
WHY WOULD ANYONE THROW AWAY THIS TRASH !?!
X-MEN
12

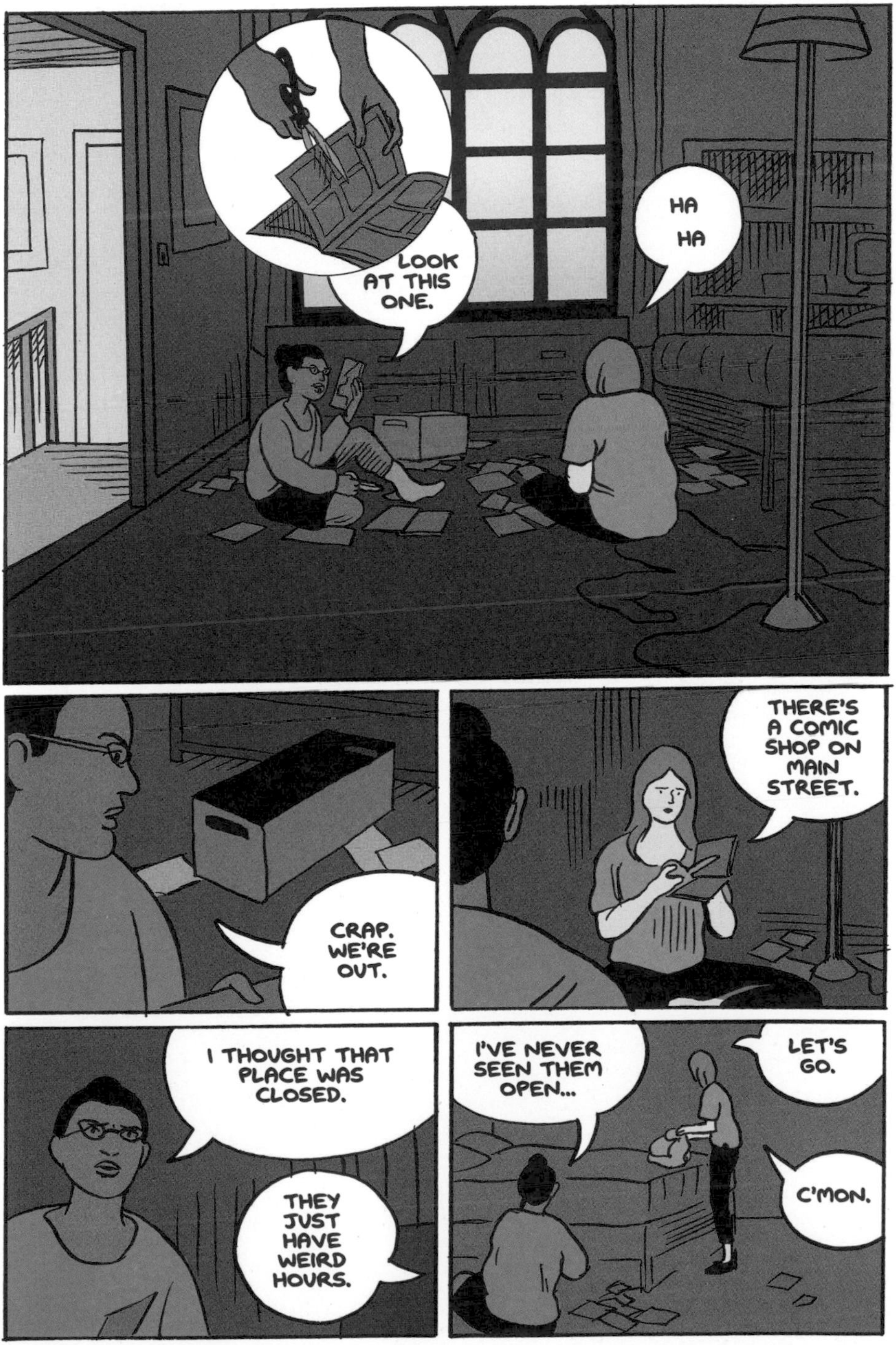
LOOK AT THIS ONE.
HA HA
CRAP. WE'RE OUT.
THERE'S A COMIC SHOP ON MAIN STREET.
I THOUGHT THAT PLACE WAS CLOSED.
THEY JUST HAVE WEIRD HOURS.
I'VE NEVER SEEN THEM OPEN...
LET'S GO.
C'MON.

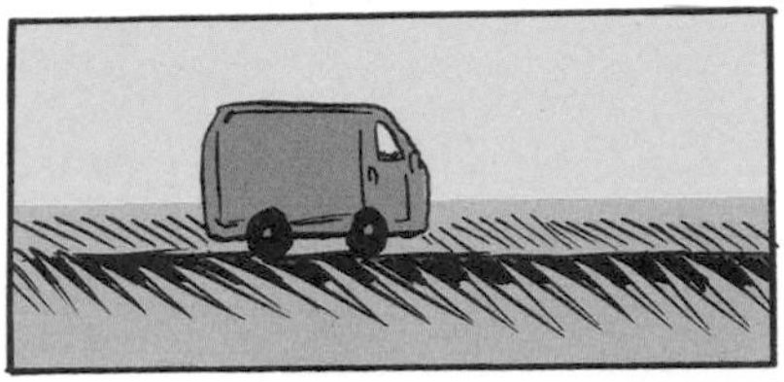

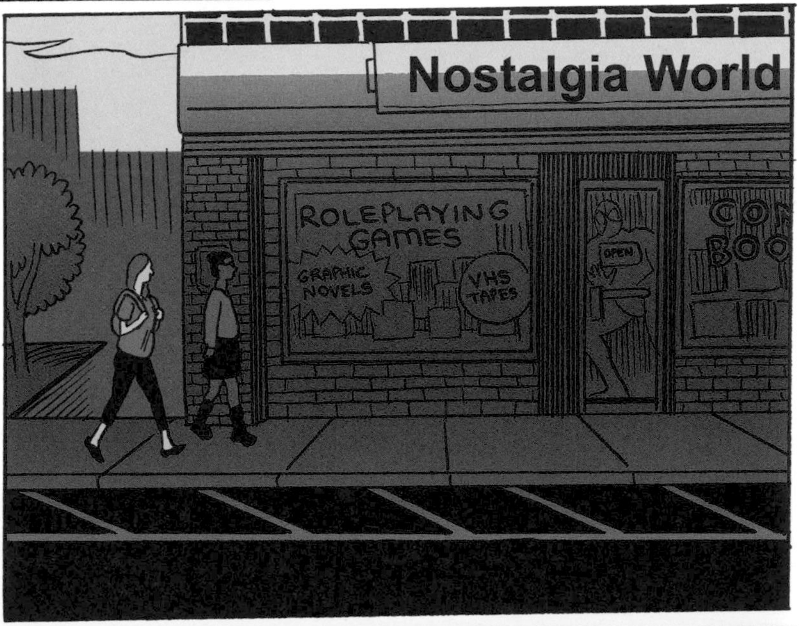
Nostalgia World
ROLEPLAYING GAMES
GRAPHIC NOVELS
VHS TAPES
OPEN

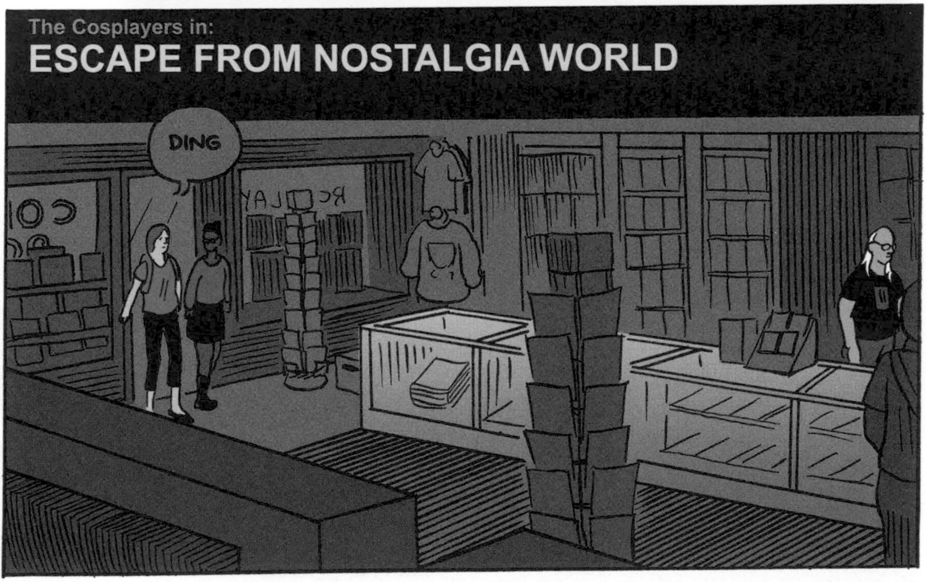
The Cosplayers in:
ESCAPE FROM NOSTALGIA WORLD
DING

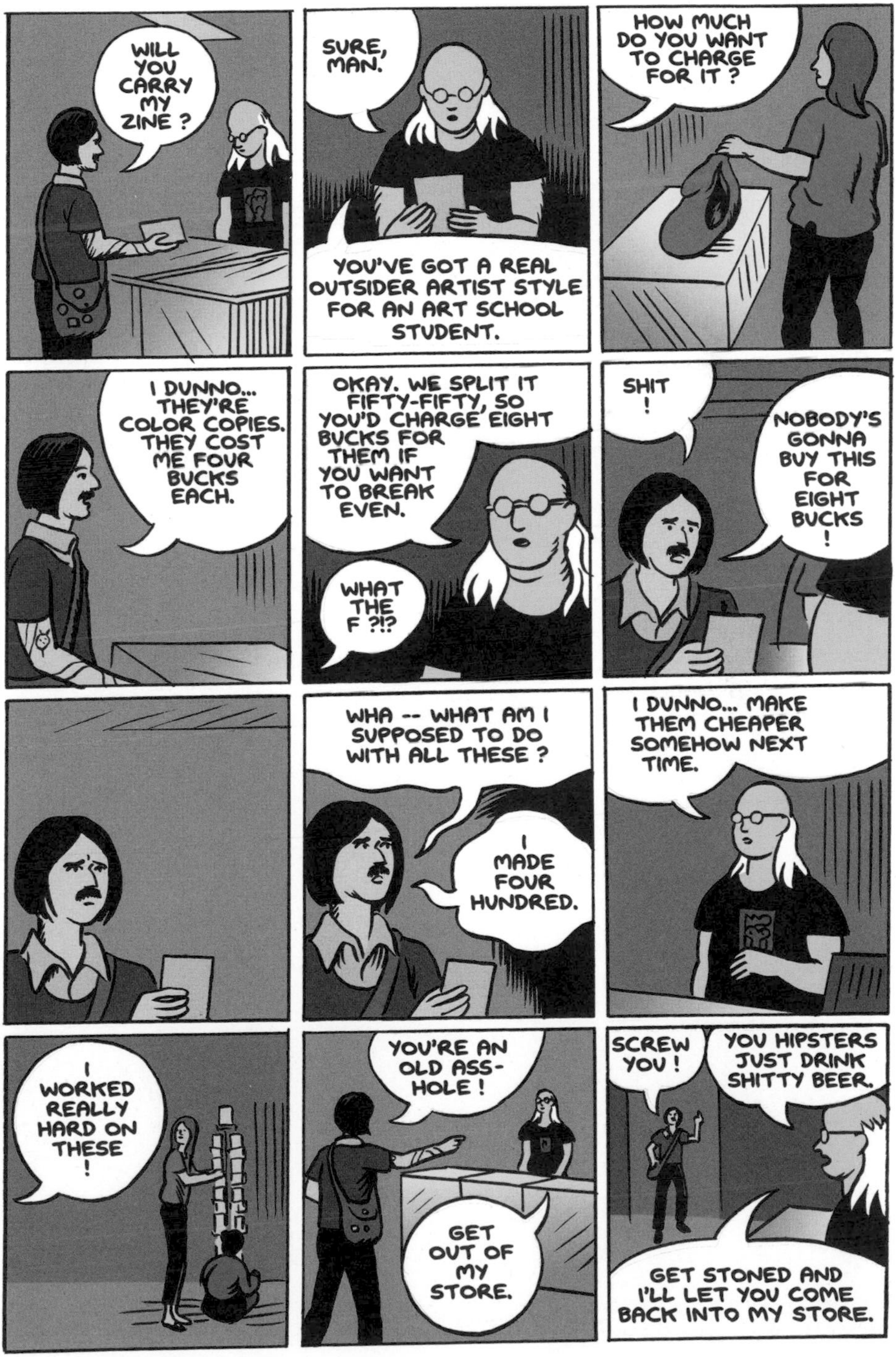
WILL YOU CARRY MY ZINE ?
SURE, MAN.
YOU'VE GOT A REAL OUTSIDER ARTIST STYLE FOR AN ART SCHOOL STUDENT.
HOW MUCH DO YOU WANT TO CHARGE FOR IT ?
I DUNNO... THEY'RE COLOR COPIES. THEY COST ME FOUR BUCKS EACH.
OKAY. WE SPLIT IT FIFTY-FIFTY, SO YOU'D CHARGE EIGHT BUCKS FOR THEM IF YOU WANT TO BREAK EVEN.
WHAT THE F ?!?
SHIT !
NOBODY'S GONNA BUY THIS FOR EIGHT BUCKS !
WHA -- WHAT AM I SUPPOSED TO DO WITH ALL THESE ?
I MADE FOUR HUNDRED.
I DUNNO... MAKE THEM CHEAPER SOMEHOW NEXT TIME.
I WORKED REALLY HARD ON THESE !
YOU'RE AN OLD ASS-HOLE !
GET OUT OF MY STORE.
SCREW YOU !
YOU HIPSTERS JUST DRINK SHITTY BEER.
GET STONED AND I'LL LET YOU COME BACK INTO MY STORE.

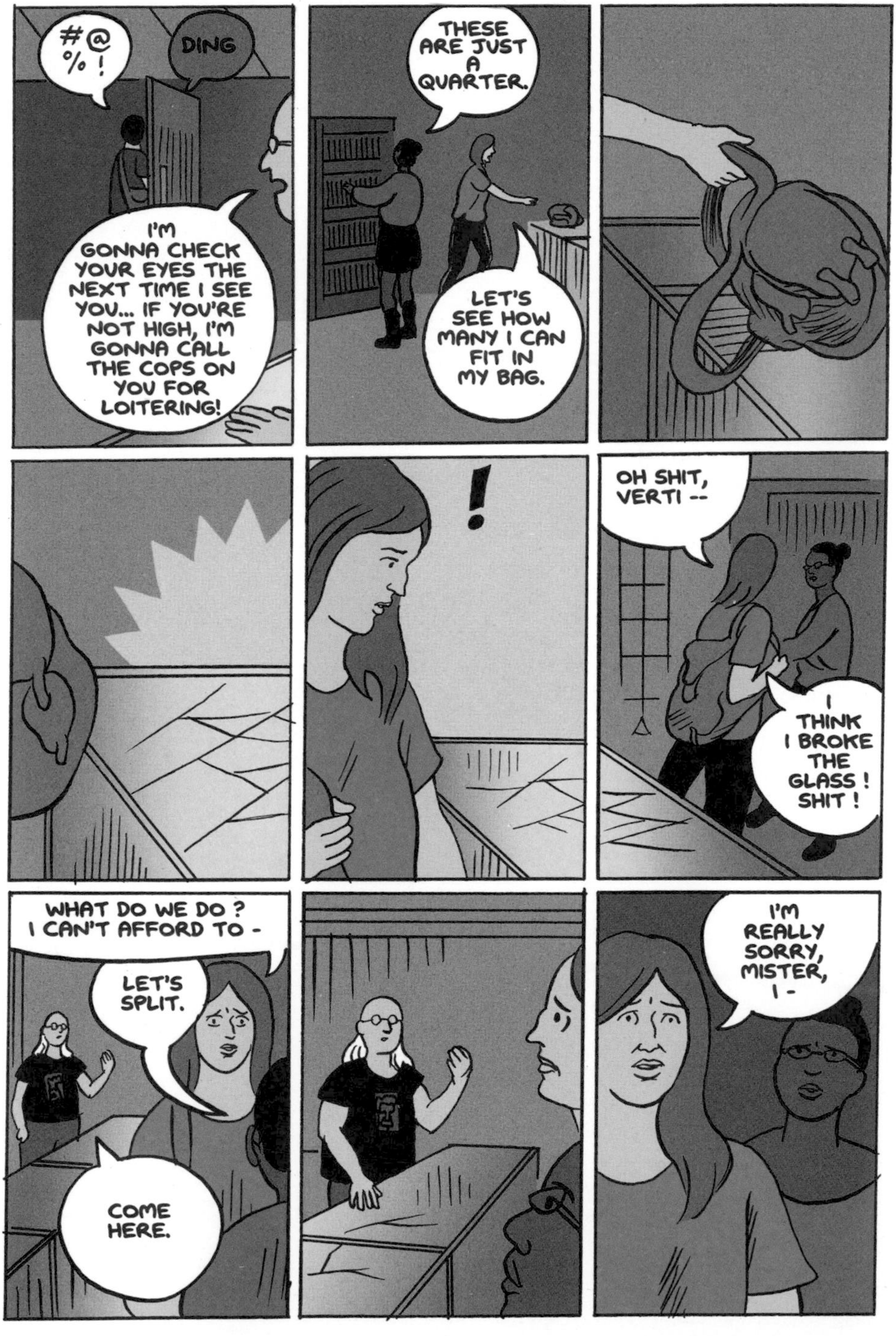
#@%!
DING
I'M GONNA CHECK YOUR EYES THE NEXT TIME I SEE YOU... IF YOU'RE NOT HIGH, I'M GONNA CALL THE COPS ON YOU FOR LOITERING!
THESE ARE JUST A QUARTER.
LET'S SEE HOW MANY I CAN FIT IN MY BAG.
!
OH SHIT, VERTI --
I THINK I BROKE THE GLASS! SHIT!
WHAT DO WE DO? I CAN'T AFFORD TO -
LET'S SPLIT.
COME HERE.
I'M REALLY SORRY, MISTER, I -

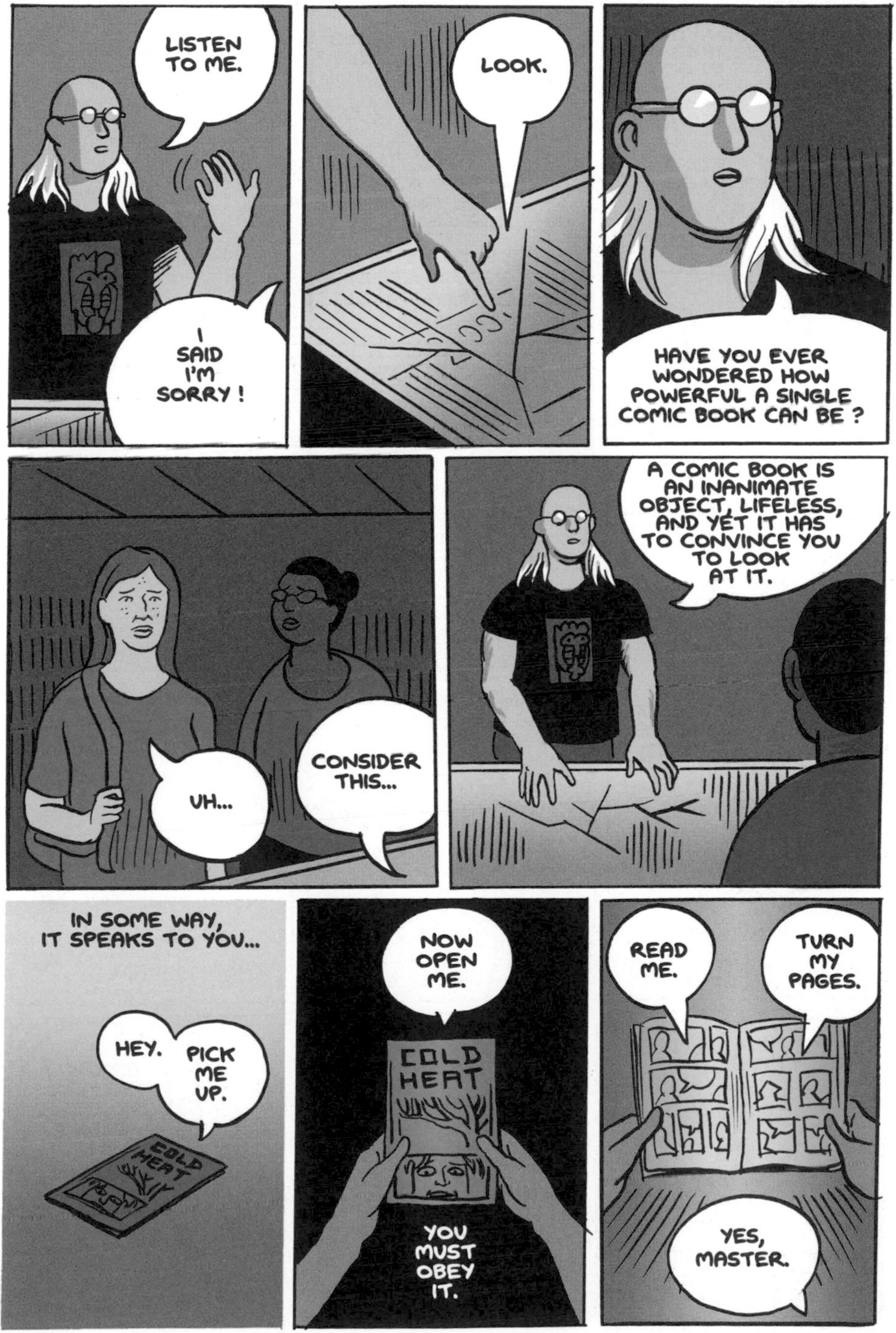
LISTEN TO ME.
I SAID I'M SORRY!
LOOK.
HAVE YOU EVER WONDERED HOW POWERFUL A SINGLE COMIC BOOK CAN BE?
UH...
CONSIDER THIS...
A COMIC BOOK IS AN INANIMATE OBJECT, LIFELESS, AND YET IT HAS TO CONVINCE YOU TO LOOK AT IT.
IN SOME WAY, IT SPEAKS TO YOU...
HEY.
PICK ME UP.
COLD HEAT
NOW OPEN ME.
COLD HEAT
YOU MUST OBEY IT.
READ ME.
TURN MY PAGES.
YES, MASTER.

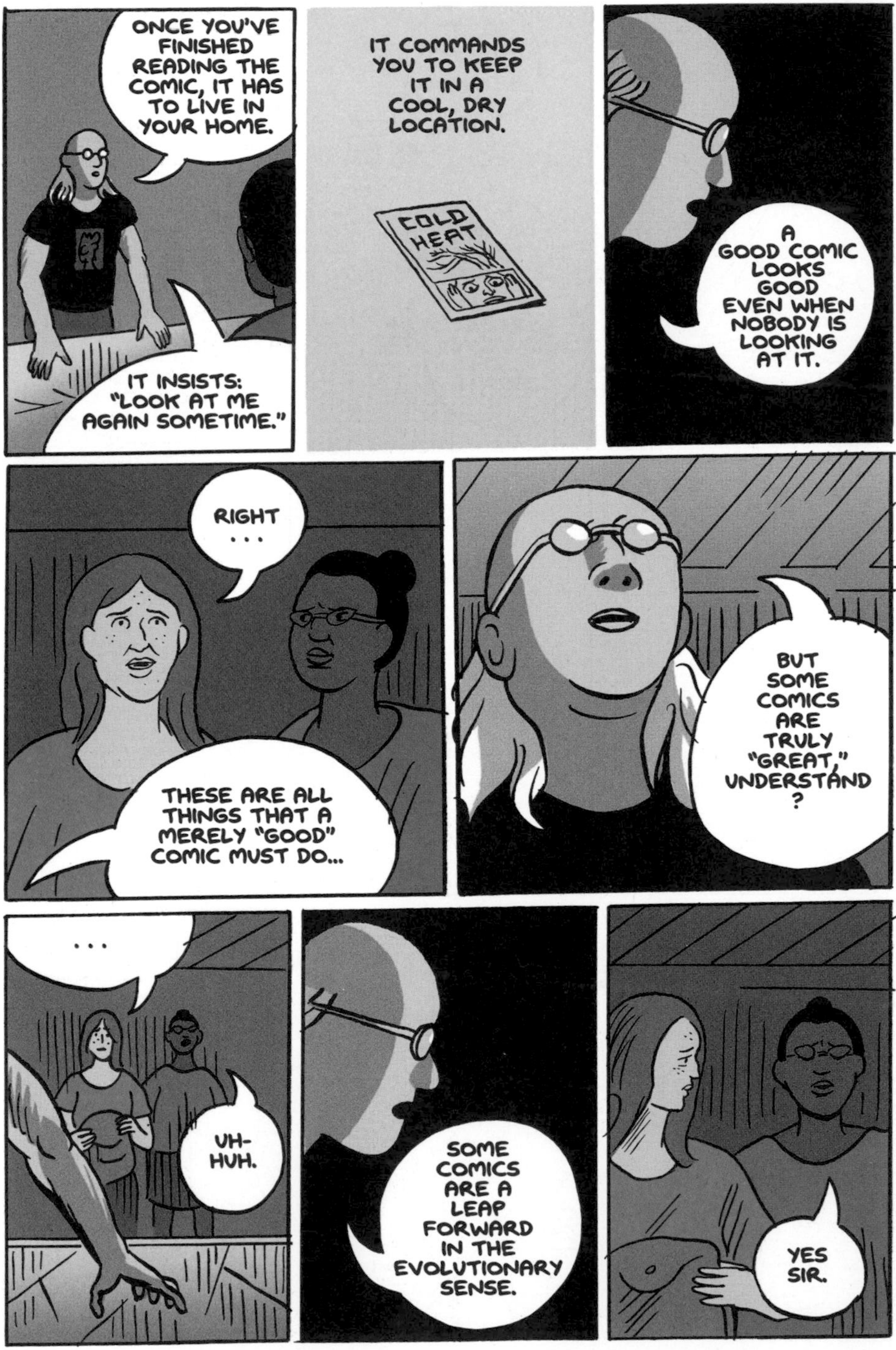
ONCE YOU'VE FINISHED READING THE COMIC, IT HAS TO LIVE IN YOUR HOME.
IT INSISTS: "LOOK AT ME AGAIN SOMETIME."
IT COMMANDS YOU TO KEEP IT IN A COOL, DRY LOCATION.
COLD HEAT
A GOOD COMIC LOOKS GOOD EVEN WHEN NOBODY IS LOOKING AT IT.
RIGHT . . .
THESE ARE ALL THINGS THAT A MERELY "GOOD" COMIC MUST DO...
BUT SOME COMICS ARE TRULY "GREAT," UNDERSTAND ?
. . .
UH-HUH.
SOME COMICS ARE A LEAP FORWARD IN THE EVOLUTIONARY SENSE.
YES SIR.

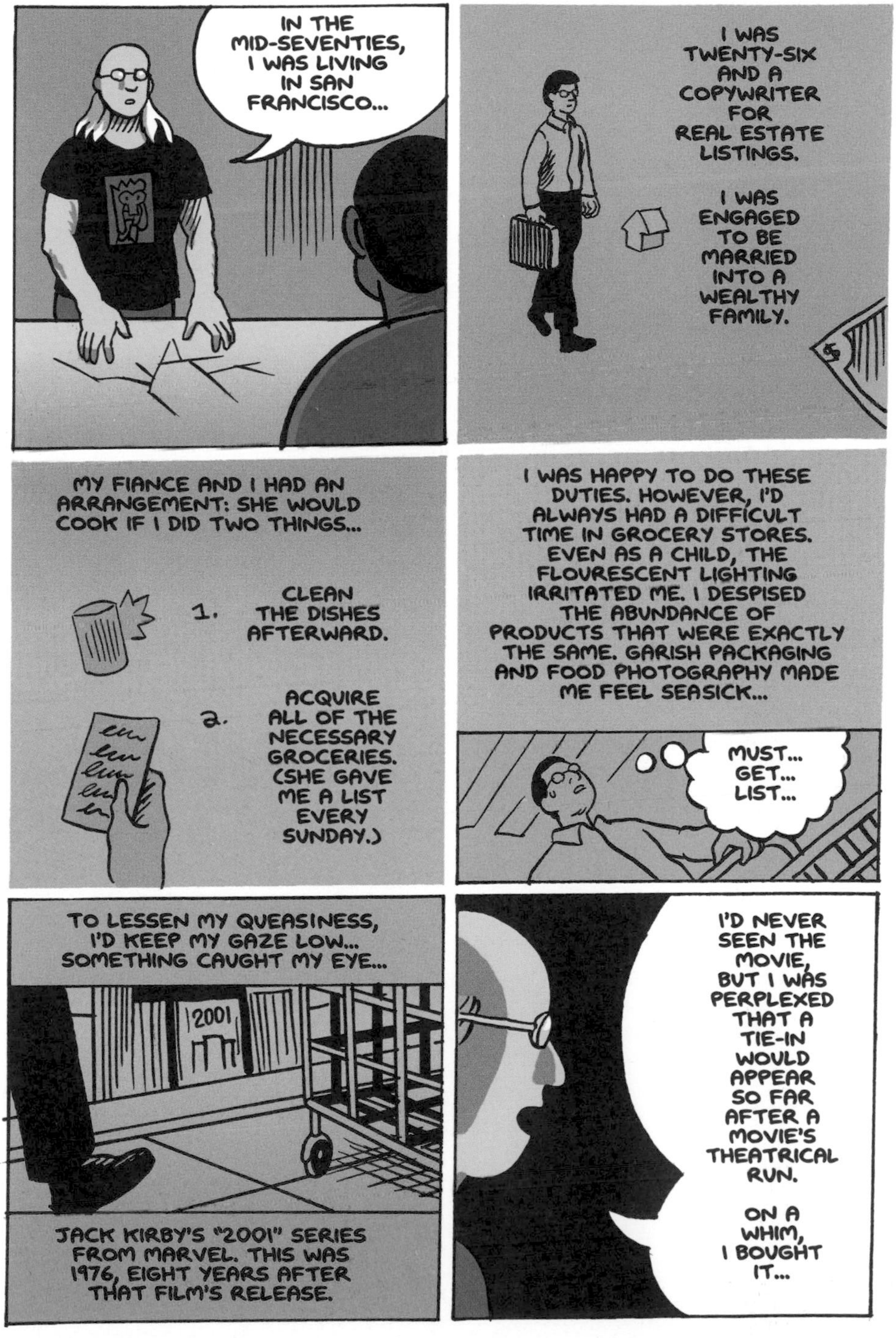
IN THE MID-SEVENTIES, I WAS LIVING IN SAN FRANCISCO...
I WAS TWENTY-SIX AND A COPYWRITER FOR REAL ESTATE LISTINGS.
I WAS ENGAGED TO BE MARRIED INTO A WEALTHY FAMILY.
MY FIANCE AND I HAD AN ARRANGEMENT: SHE WOULD COOK IF I DID TWO THINGS...
1. CLEAN THE DISHES AFTERWARD.
2. ACQUIRE ALL OF THE NECESSARY GROCERIES. (SHE GAVE ME A LIST EVERY SUNDAY.)
I WAS HAPPY TO DO THESE DUTIES. HOWEVER, I'D ALWAYS HAD A DIFFICULT TIME IN GROCERY STORES. EVEN AS A CHILD, THE FLOURESCENT LIGHTING IRRITATED ME. I DESPISED THE ABUNDANCE OF PRODUCTS THAT WERE EXACTLY THE SAME. GARISH PACKAGING AND FOOD PHOTOGRAPHY MADE ME FEEL SEASICK...
MUST... GET... LIST...
TO LESSEN MY QUEASINESS, I'D KEEP MY GAZE LOW... SOMETHING CAUGHT MY EYE...
2001
JACK KIRBY'S "2001" SERIES FROM MARVEL. THIS WAS 1976, EIGHT YEARS AFTER THAT FILM'S RELEASE.
I'D NEVER SEEN THE MOVIE, BUT I WAS PERPLEXED THAT A TIE-IN WOULD APPEAR SO FAR AFTER A MOVIE'S THEATRICAL RUN.
ON A WHIM, I BOUGHT IT...

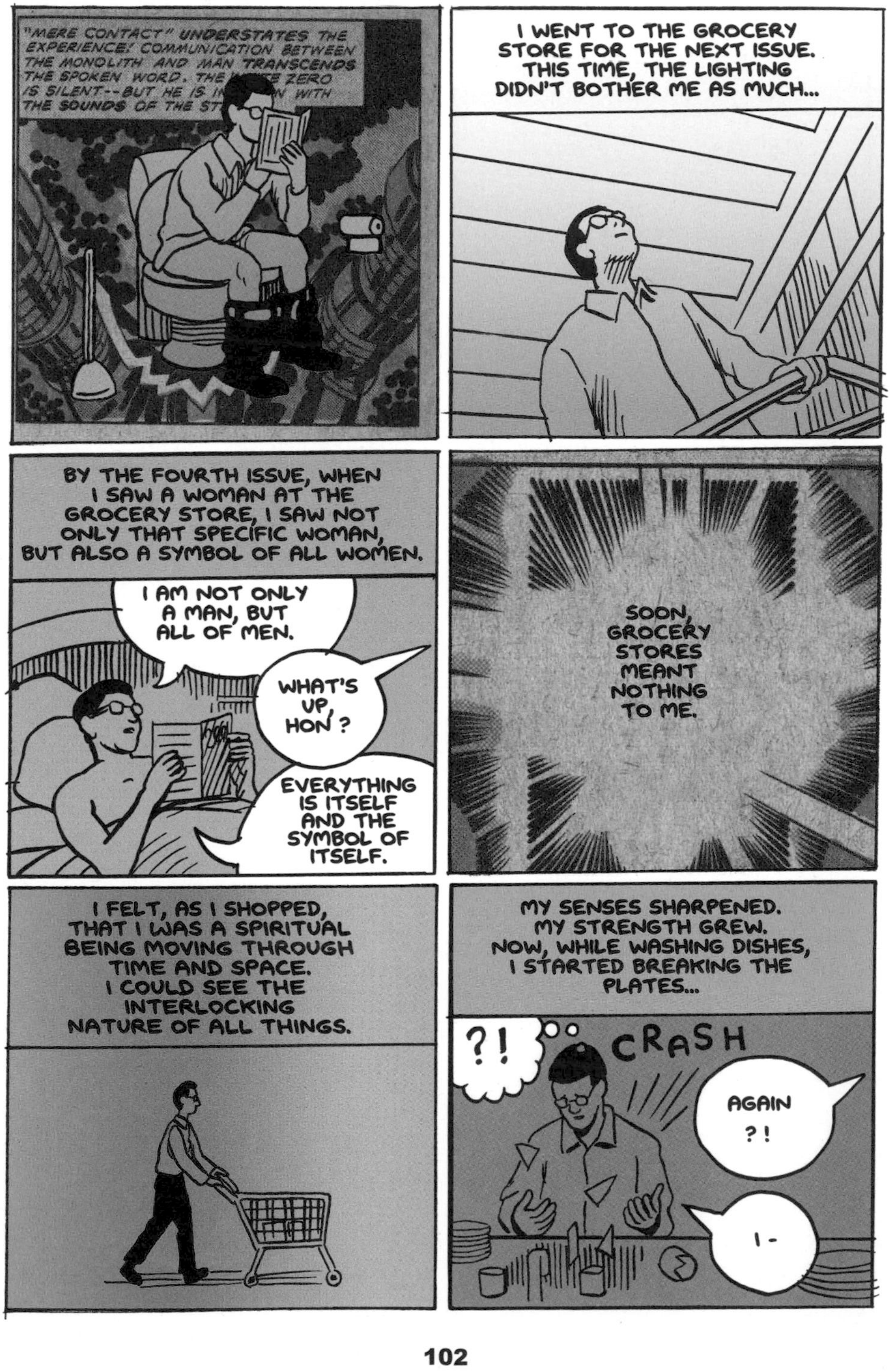
"MERE CONTACT" UNDERSTATES THE EXPERIENCE! COMMUNICATION BETWEEN THE MONOLITH AND MAN TRANSCENDS THE SPOKEN WORD. THE ZERO IS SILENT--BUT HE IS WITH THE SOUNDS OF THE
I WENT TO THE GROCERY STORE FOR THE NEXT ISSUE. THIS TIME, THE LIGHTING DIDN'T BOTHER ME AS MUCH...
BY THE FOURTH ISSUE, WHEN I SAW A WOMAN AT THE GROCERY STORE, I SAW NOT ONLY THAT SPECIFIC WOMAN, BUT ALSO A SYMBOL OF ALL WOMEN.
I AM NOT ONLY A MAN, BUT ALL OF MEN.
WHAT'S UP, HON?
EVERYTHING IS ITSELF AND THE SYMBOL OF ITSELF.
SOON, GROCERY STORES MEANT NOTHING TO ME.
I FELT, AS I SHOPPED, THAT I WAS A SPIRITUAL BEING MOVING THROUGH TIME AND SPACE. I COULD SEE THE INTERLOCKING NATURE OF ALL THINGS.
MY SENSES SHARPENED. MY STRENGTH GREW. NOW, WHILE WASHING DISHES, I STARTED BREAKING THE PLATES...
?!
CRASH
AGAIN ?!
I-

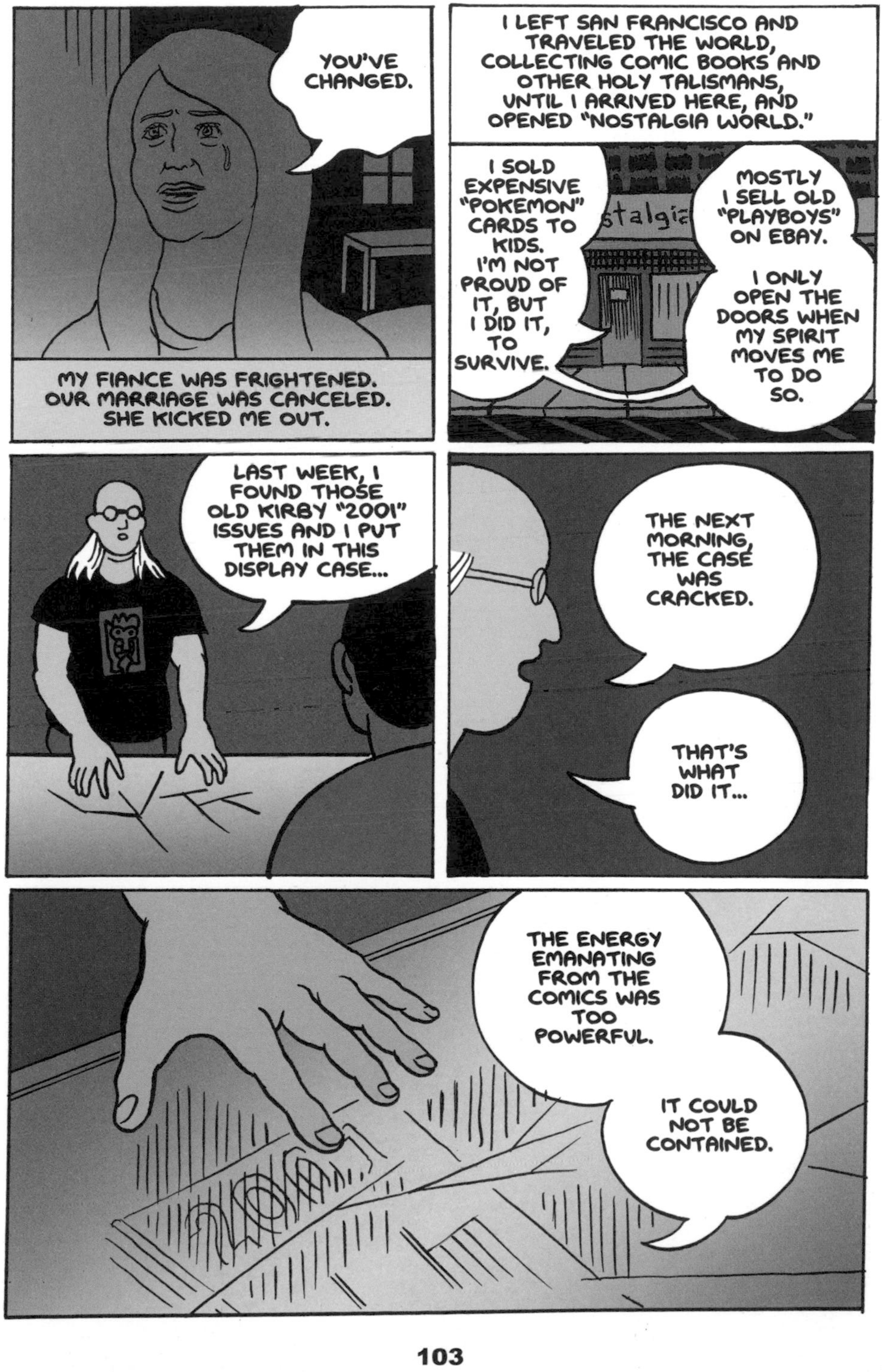
YOU'VE CHANGED.
MY FIANCE WAS FRIGHTENED. OUR MARRIAGE WAS CANCELED. SHE KICKED ME OUT.
I LEFT SAN FRANCISCO AND TRAVELED THE WORLD, COLLECTING COMIC BOOKS AND OTHER HOLY TALISMANS, UNTIL I ARRIVED HERE, AND OPENED "NOSTALGIA WORLD."
I SOLD EXPENSIVE "POKEMON" CARDS TO KIDS. I'M NOT PROUD OF IT, BUT I DID IT, TO SURVIVE.
stalgia
MOSTLY I SELL OLD "PLAYBOYS" ON EBAY.
I ONLY OPEN THE DOORS WHEN MY SPIRIT MOVES ME TO DO SO.
LAST WEEK, I FOUND THOSE OLD KIRBY "2001" ISSUES AND I PUT THEM IN THIS DISPLAY CASE...
THE NEXT MORNING, THE CASE WAS CRACKED.
THAT'S WHAT DID IT...
THE ENERGY EMANATING FROM THE COMICS WAS TOO POWERFUL.
IT COULD NOT BE CONTAINED.

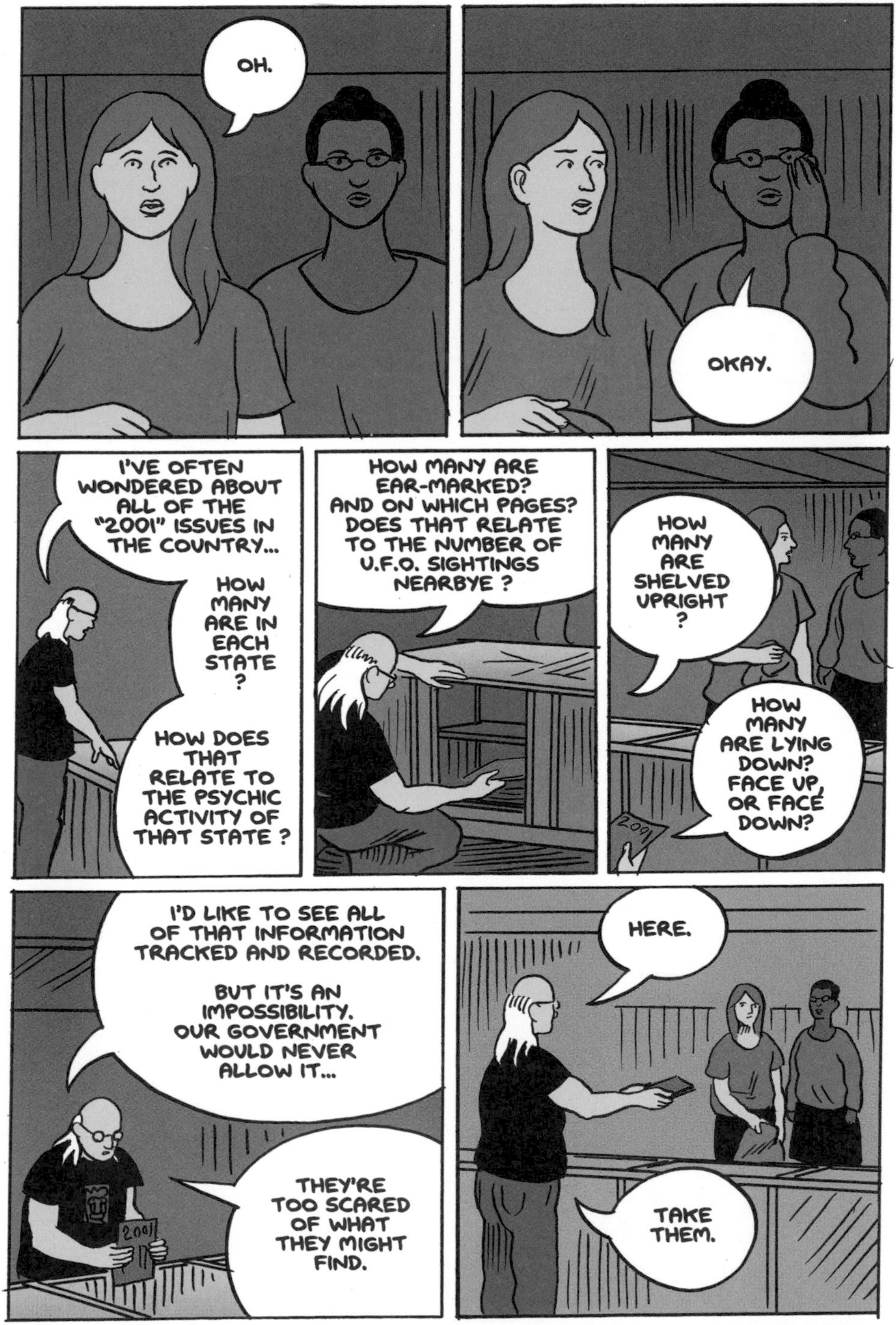
OH.
OKAY.
I'VE OFTEN WONDERED ABOUT ALL OF THE "2001" ISSUES IN THE COUNTRY...
HOW MANY ARE IN EACH STATE ?
HOW DOES THAT RELATE TO THE PSYCHIC ACTIVITY OF THAT STATE ?
HOW MANY ARE EAR-MARKED? AND ON WHICH PAGES? DOES THAT RELATE TO THE NUMBER OF U.F.O. SIGHTINGS NEARBYE ?
HOW MANY ARE SHELVED UPRIGHT ?
HOW MANY ARE LYING DOWN? FACE UP, OR FACE DOWN?
2001
I'D LIKE TO SEE ALL OF THAT INFORMATION TRACKED AND RECORDED.
BUT IT'S AN IMPOSSIBILITY. OUR GOVERNMENT WOULD NEVER ALLOW IT...
2001
THEY'RE TOO SCARED OF WHAT THEY MIGHT FIND.
HERE.
TAKE THEM.

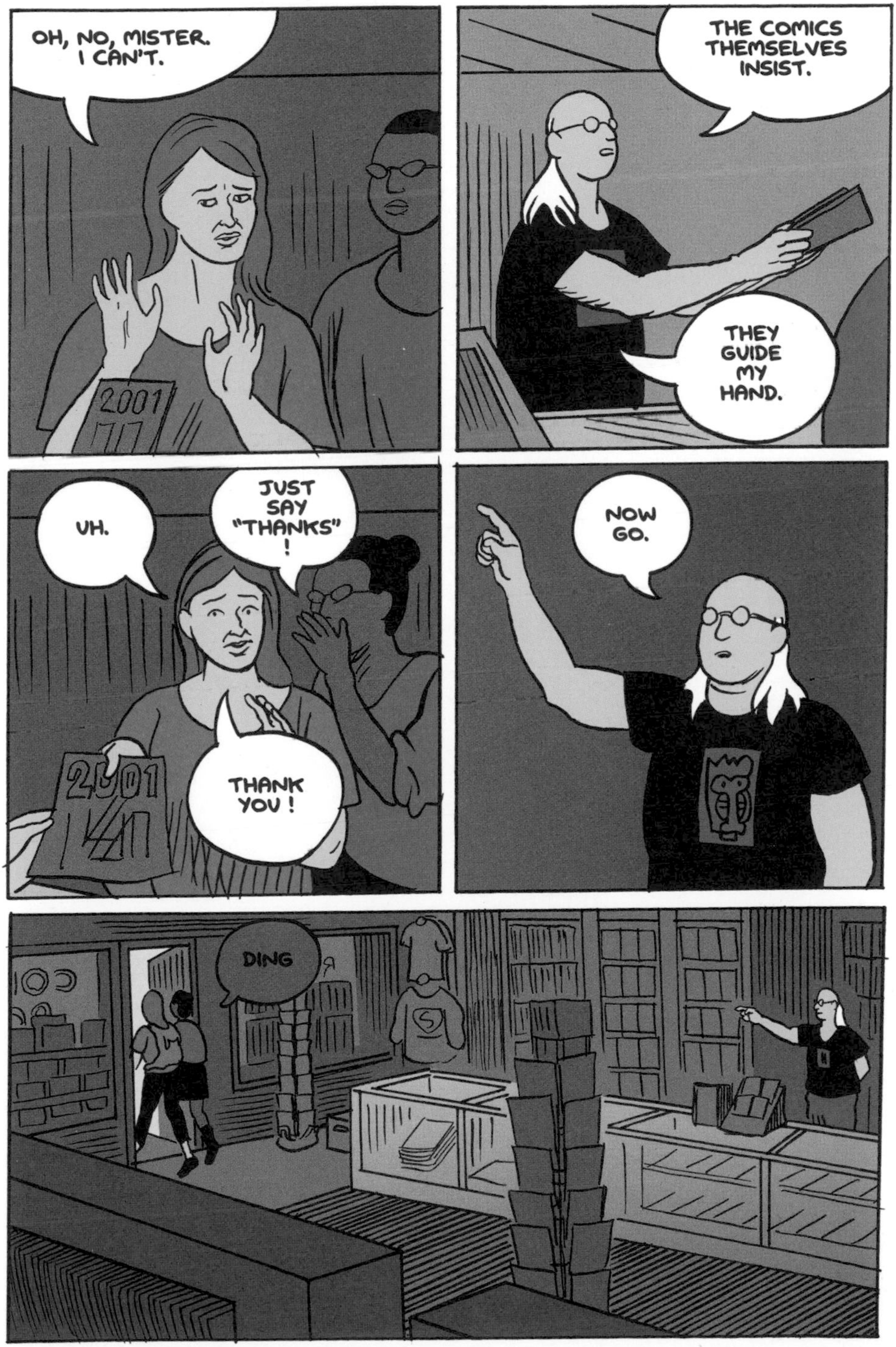
OH, NO, MISTER. I CAN'T.
2001
THE COMICS THEMSELVES INSIST.
THEY GUIDE MY HAND.
UH.
JUST SAY "THANKS" !
2001
THANK YOU !
NOW GO.
DING

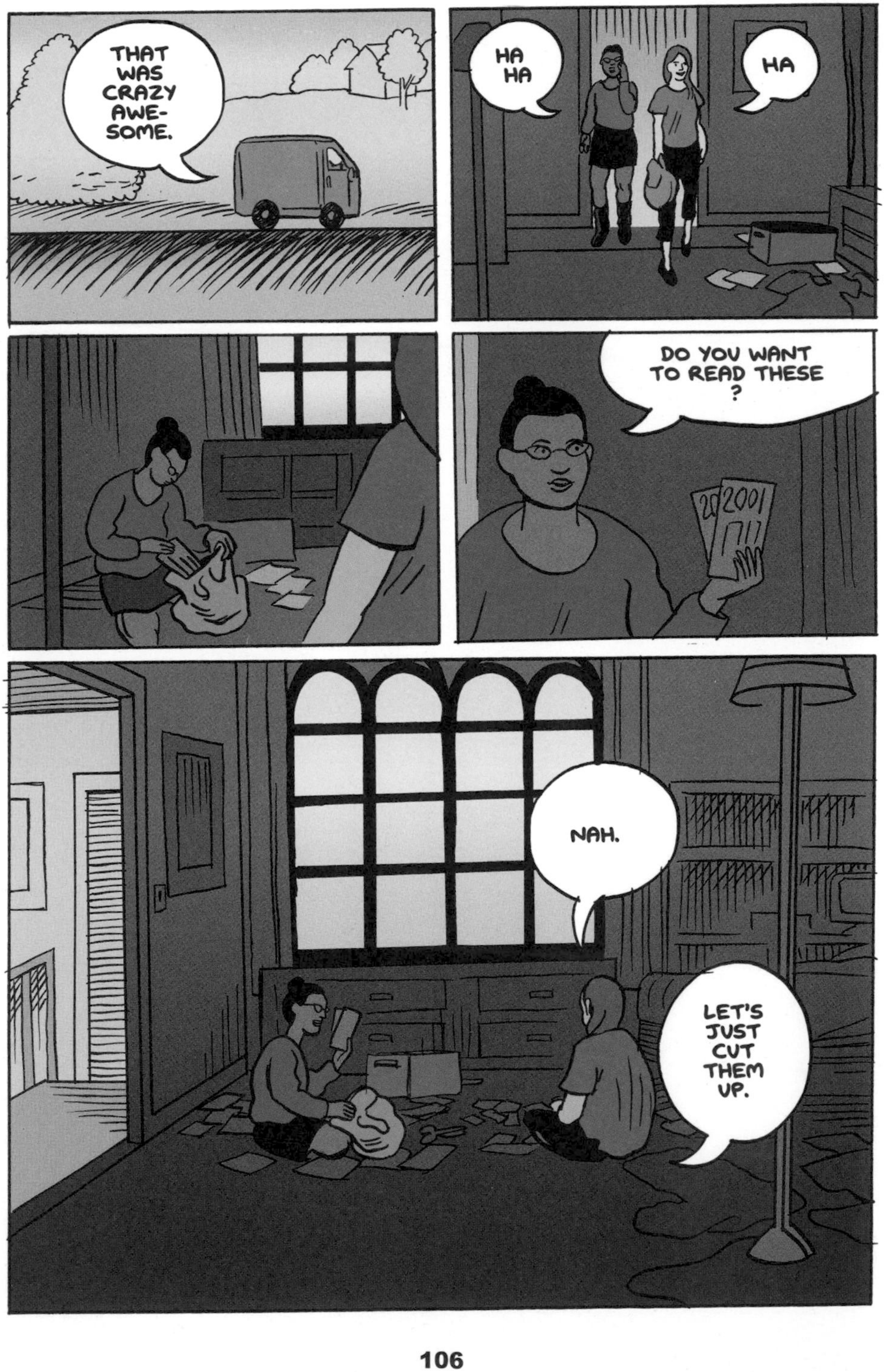
THAT WAS CRAZY AWE-SOME.
HA HA
HA
DO YOU WANT TO READ THESE ?
2001
NAH.
LET'S JUST CUT THEM UP.

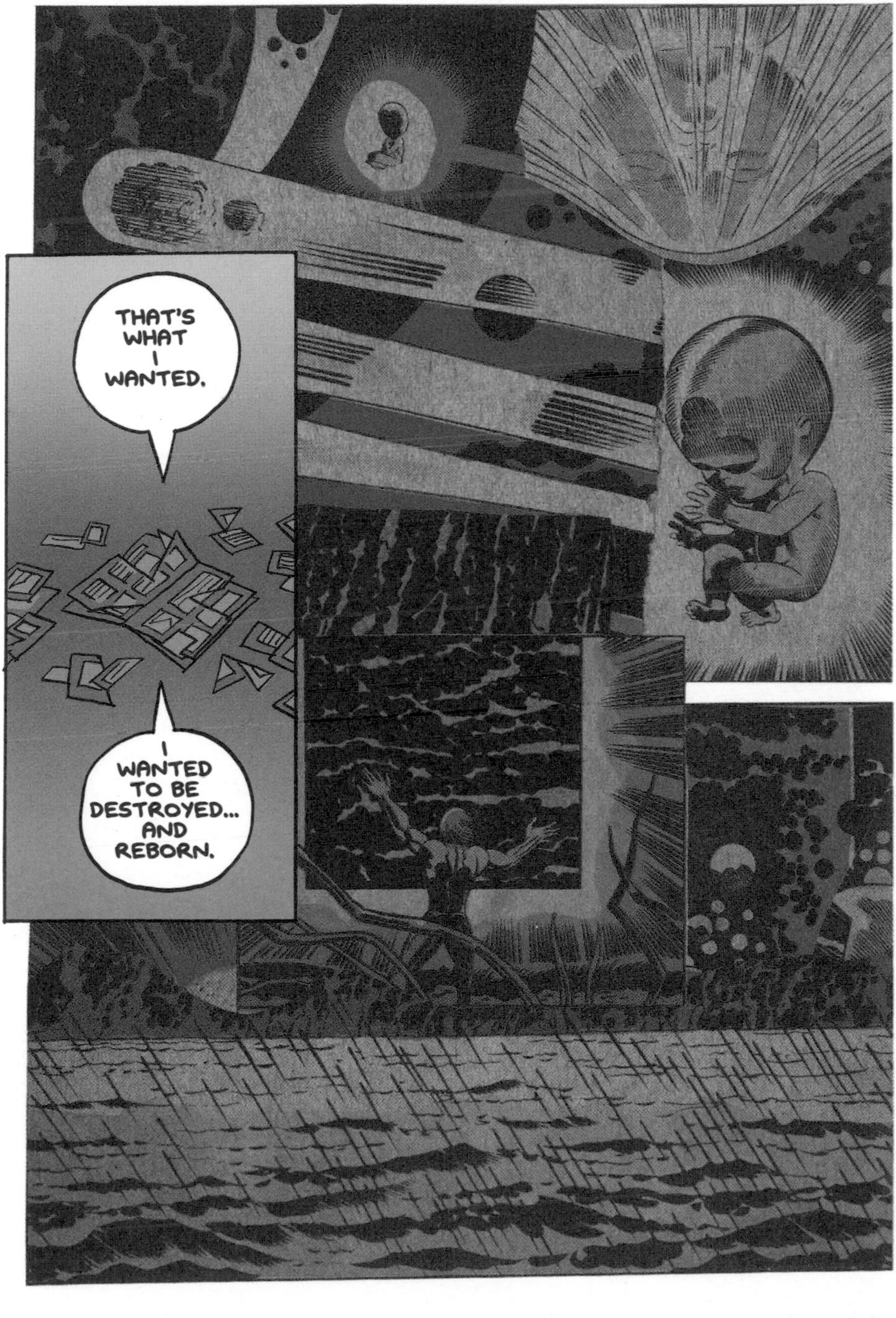
THAT'S WHAT I WANTED.
I WANTED TO BE DESTROYED... AND REBORN.

THE END

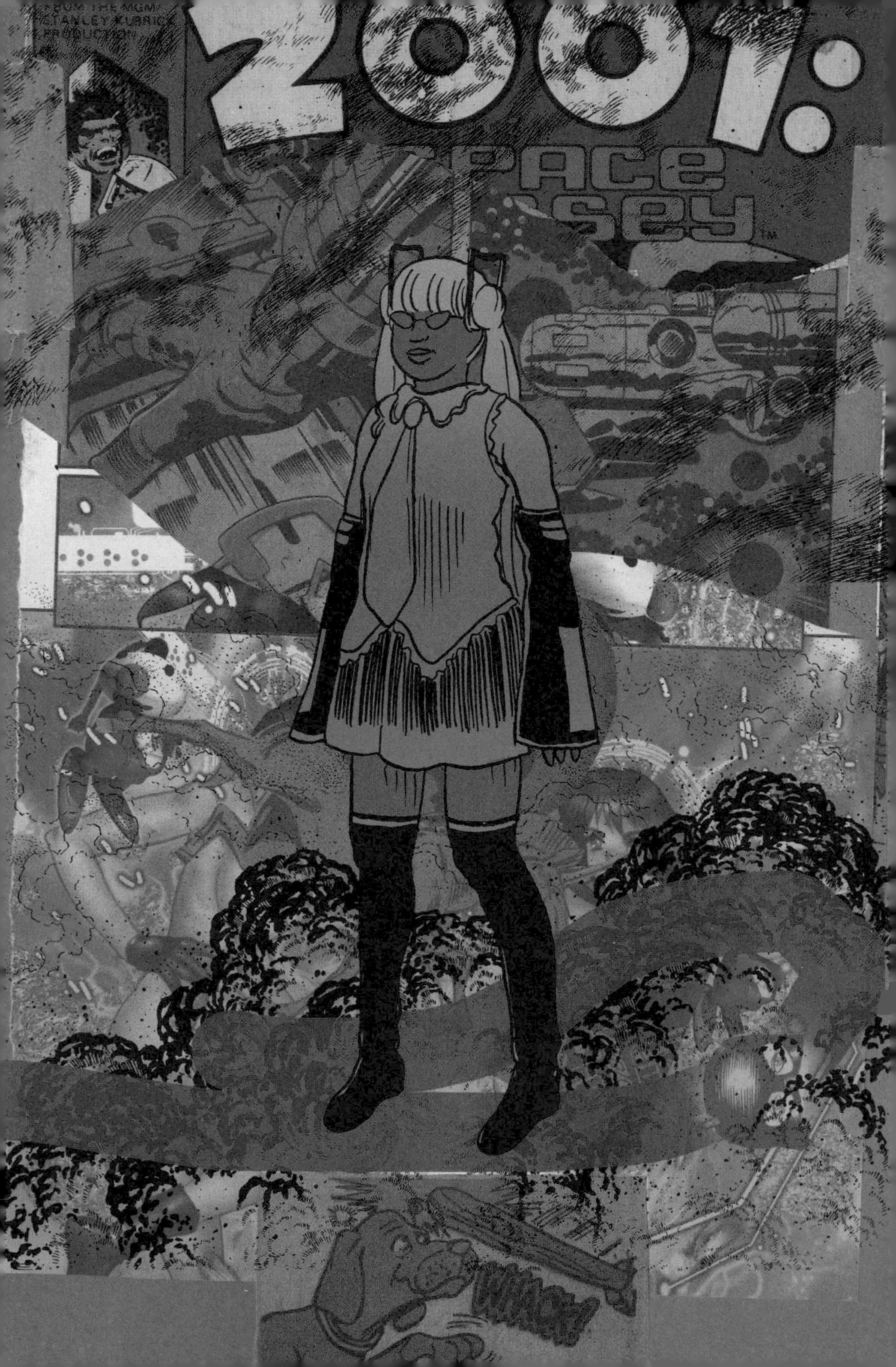
2001:

It's 3am and I'm Wide Awake and Looking at Cosplay Pics Online.

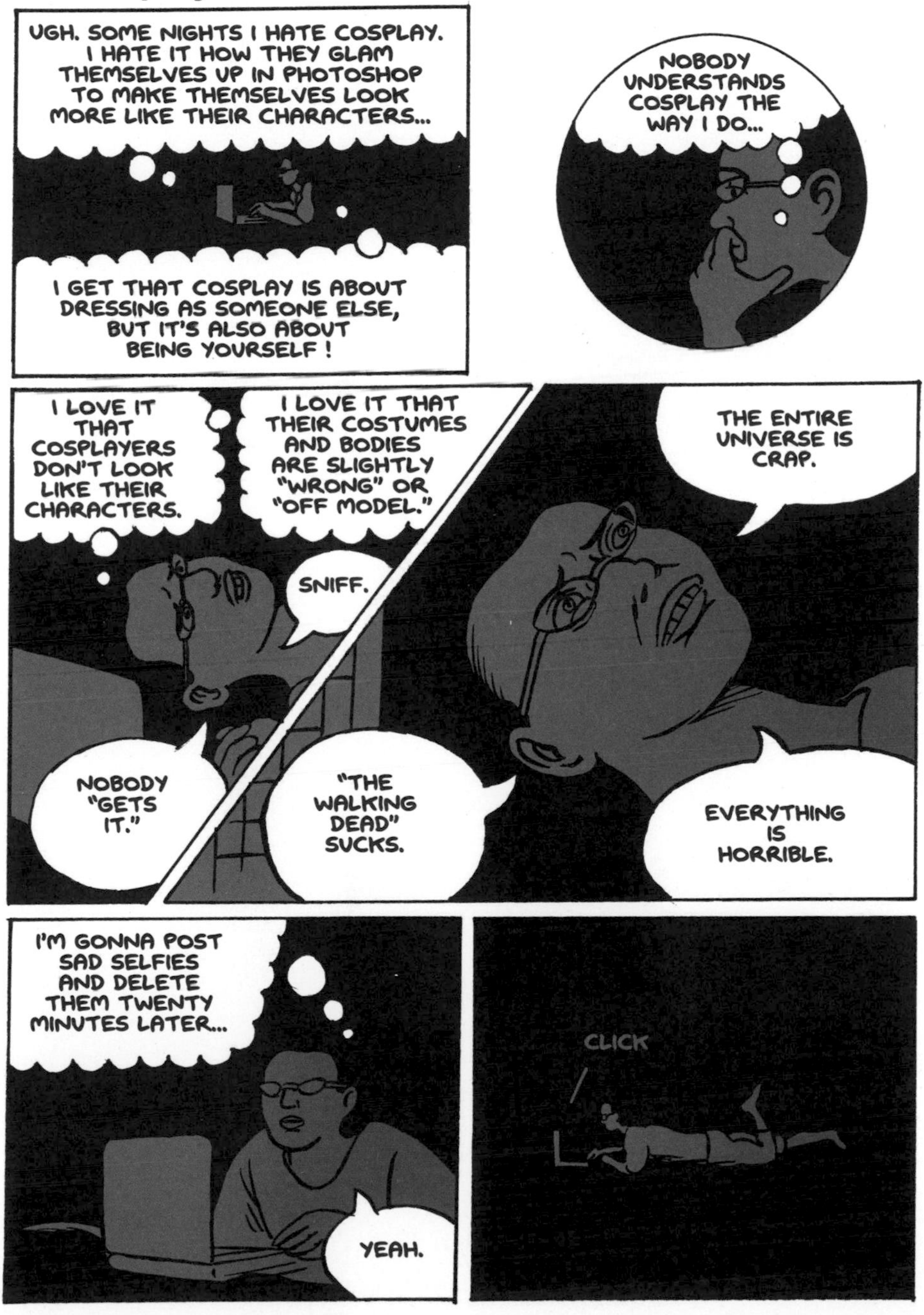

UGH. SOME NIGHTS I HATE COSPLAY. I HATE IT HOW THEY GLAM THEMSELVES UP IN PHOTOSHOP TO MAKE THEMSELVES LOOK MORE LIKE THEIR CHARACTERS...
I GET THAT COSPLAY IS ABOUT DRESSING AS SOMEONE ELSE, BUT IT'S ALSO ABOUT BEING YOURSELF!
NOBODY UNDERSTANDS COSPLAY THE WAY I DO...
I LOVE IT THAT COSPLAYERS DON'T LOOK LIKE THEIR CHARACTERS.
I LOVE IT THAT THEIR COSTUMES AND BODIES ARE SLIGHTLY "WRONG" OR "OFF MODEL."
SNIFF.
NOBODY "GETS IT."
"THE WALKING DEAD" SUCKS.
THE ENTIRE UNIVERSE IS CRAP.
EVERYTHING IS HORRIBLE.
I'M GONNA POST SAD SELFIES AND DELETE THEM TWENTY MINUTES LATER...
YEAH.
CLICK

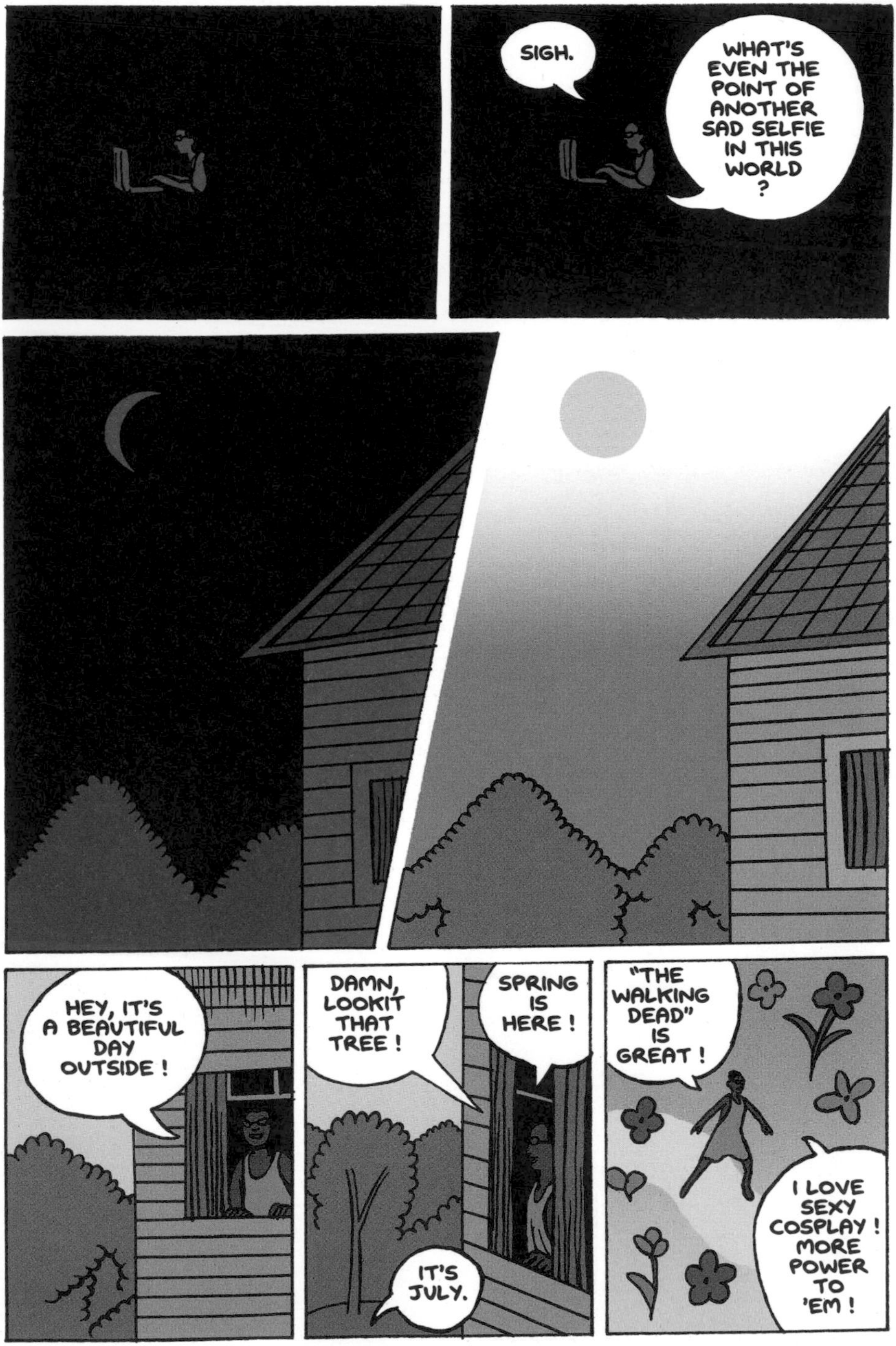
SIGH.
WHAT'S EVEN THE POINT OF ANOTHER SAD SELFIE IN THIS WORLD ?
HEY, IT'S A BEAUTIFUL DAY OUTSIDE !
DAMN, LOOKIT THAT TREE !
SPRING IS HERE !
IT'S JULY.
"THE WALKING DEAD" IS GREAT !
I LOVE SEXY COSPLAY ! MORE POWER TO 'EM !

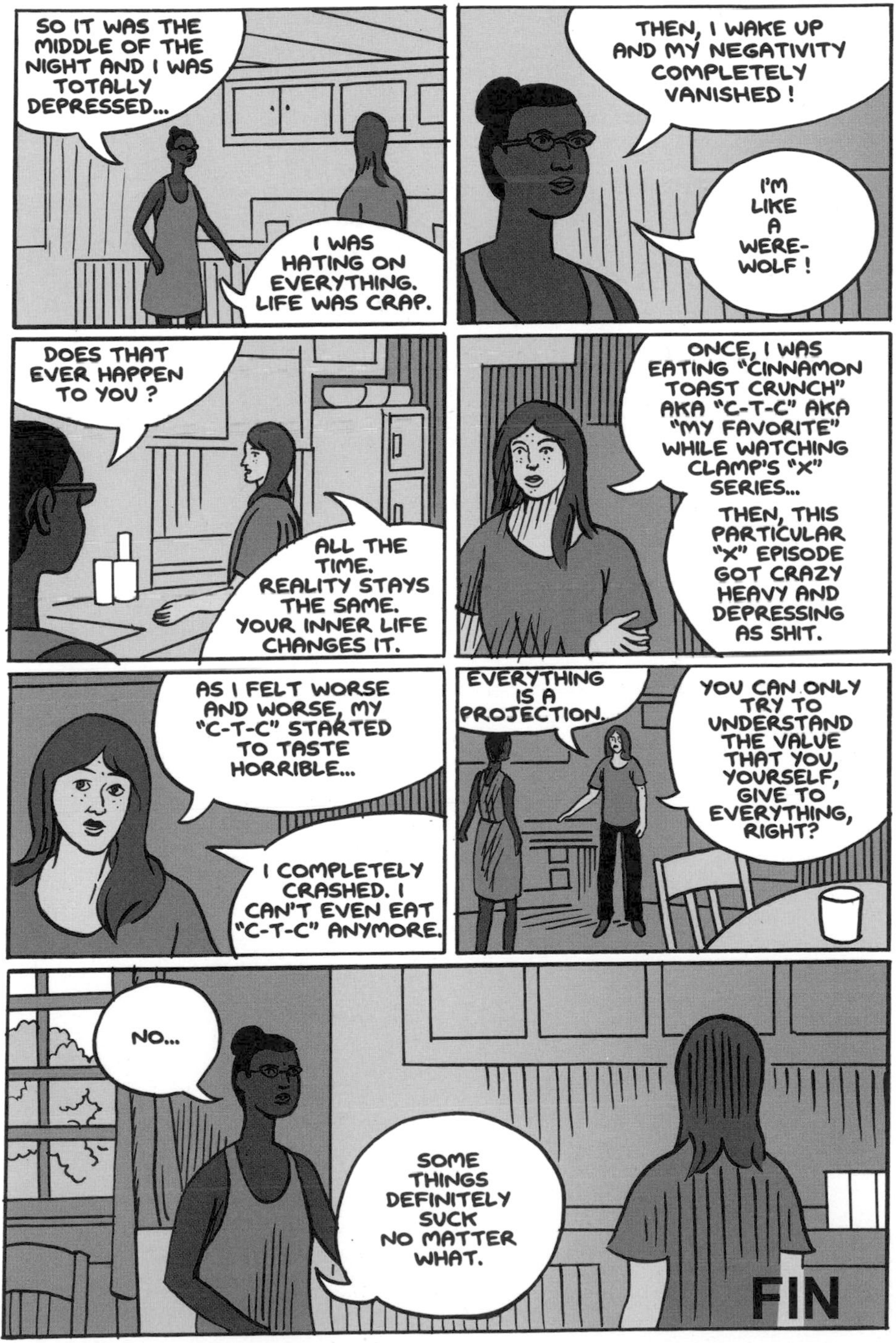
SO IT WAS THE MIDDLE OF THE NIGHT AND I WAS TOTALLY DEPRESSED...
I WAS HATING ON EVERYTHING. LIFE WAS CRAP.
THEN, I WAKE UP AND MY NEGATIVITY COMPLETELY VANISHED !
I'M LIKE A WERE-WOLF !
DOES THAT EVER HAPPEN TO YOU ?
ALL THE TIME. REALITY STAYS THE SAME. YOUR INNER LIFE CHANGES IT.
ONCE, I WAS EATING "CINNAMON TOAST CRUNCH" AKA "C-T-C" AKA "MY FAVORITE" WHILE WATCHING CLAMP'S "X" SERIES...
THEN, THIS PARTICULAR "X" EPISODE GOT CRAZY HEAVY AND DEPRESSING AS SHIT.
AS I FELT WORSE AND WORSE, MY "C-T-C" STARTED TO TASTE HORRIBLE...
I COMPLETELY CRASHED. I CAN'T EVEN EAT "C-T-C" ANYMORE.
EVERYTHING IS A PROJECTION.
YOU CAN ONLY TRY TO UNDERSTAND THE VALUE THAT YOU, YOURSELF, GIVE TO EVERYTHING, RIGHT?
NO...
SOME THINGS DEFINITELY SUCK NO MATTER WHAT.
FIN

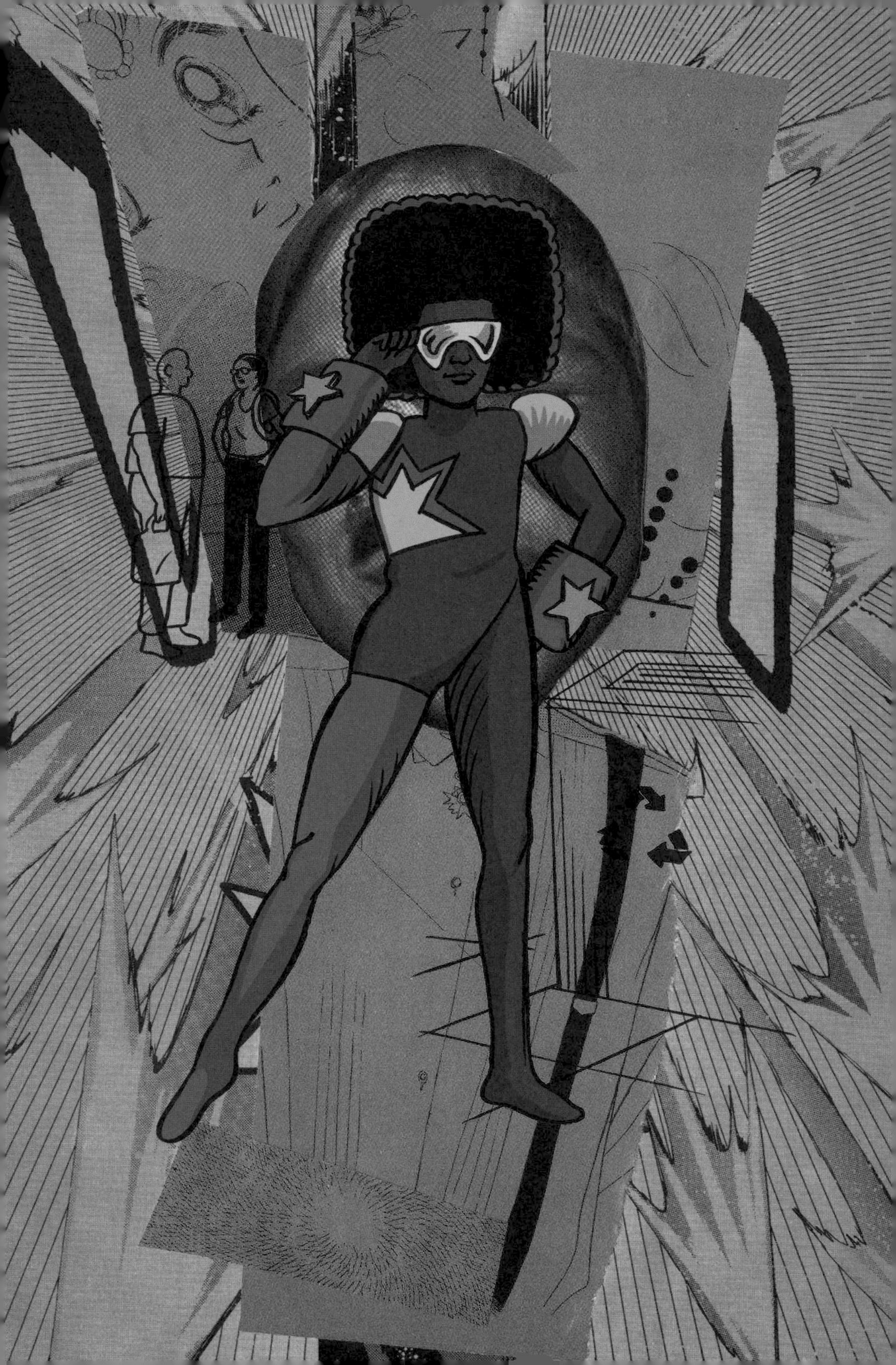

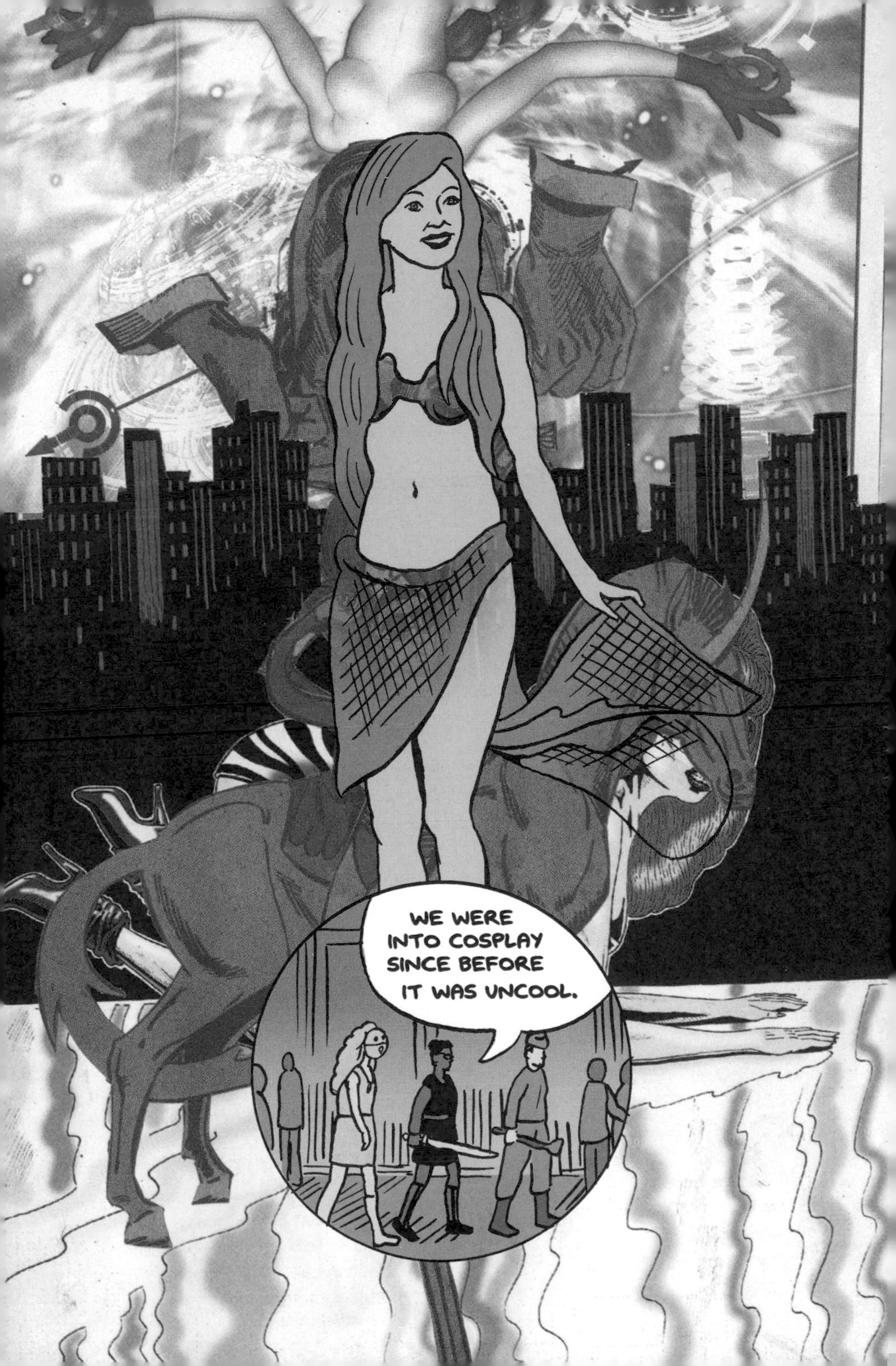
WE WERE INTO COSPLAY SINCE BEFORE IT WAS UNCOOL.

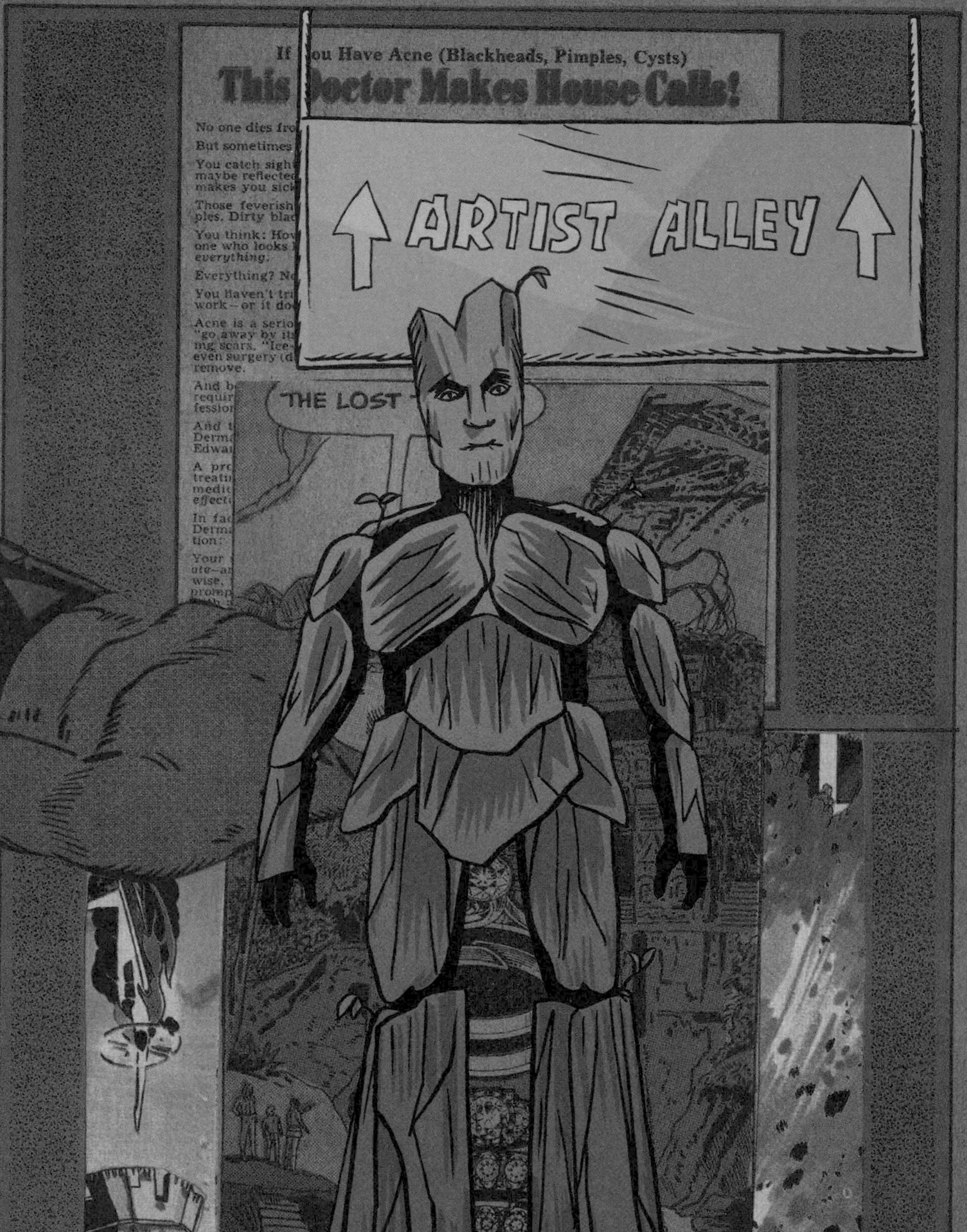

ou Have Acne (Blackheads, Pimples, Cysts)
Makes House Calls!
ARTIST ALLEY
THE LOST

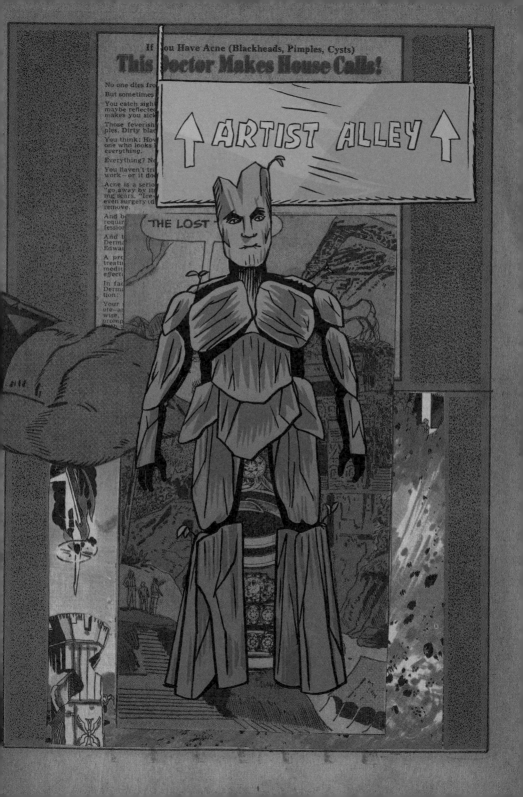

THANKS

The majority of these stories originally appeared as pamphlet comics published by Fantagraphics in 2014. Thanks, Fanta, for publishing them.

Thanks also are due to the friends who would go to comic and anime conventions with me when I was a teenager, in the late '90s.

"Escape from Nostalgia World" was originally a "Free Comic Book Day" comic, so thousands of people went to their local comic shops and received this free comic about the cosplayers going to a store and getting a free comic! It was packaged with an issue of Ed Piskor's *Hip Hop Family Tree*. Huge thanks to Ed and Fantagraphics for arranging for that to happen. Thank you, Ed.

I must also thank: my parents, my brother, Lily Benson, Hal Foster, Curtis Godino, Alex Jacobs, David Karp, Laura Knetzger, Andrew Lorenzi, Kyle Martin, David Mazzucchelli, Bjorn Miner, Jesse Moynihan, Dan Nadel, Gary Panter, Frank Santoro, Rani Sharone, Art Spiegelman, Jean Strouse, Chris Ware, Craig Zobel, and the *HSS* voice actors. Plus some apologies to Daniel Clowes.

This book is dedicated to Jane Samborski.

Thanks for reading.

Dash Shaw, 2016

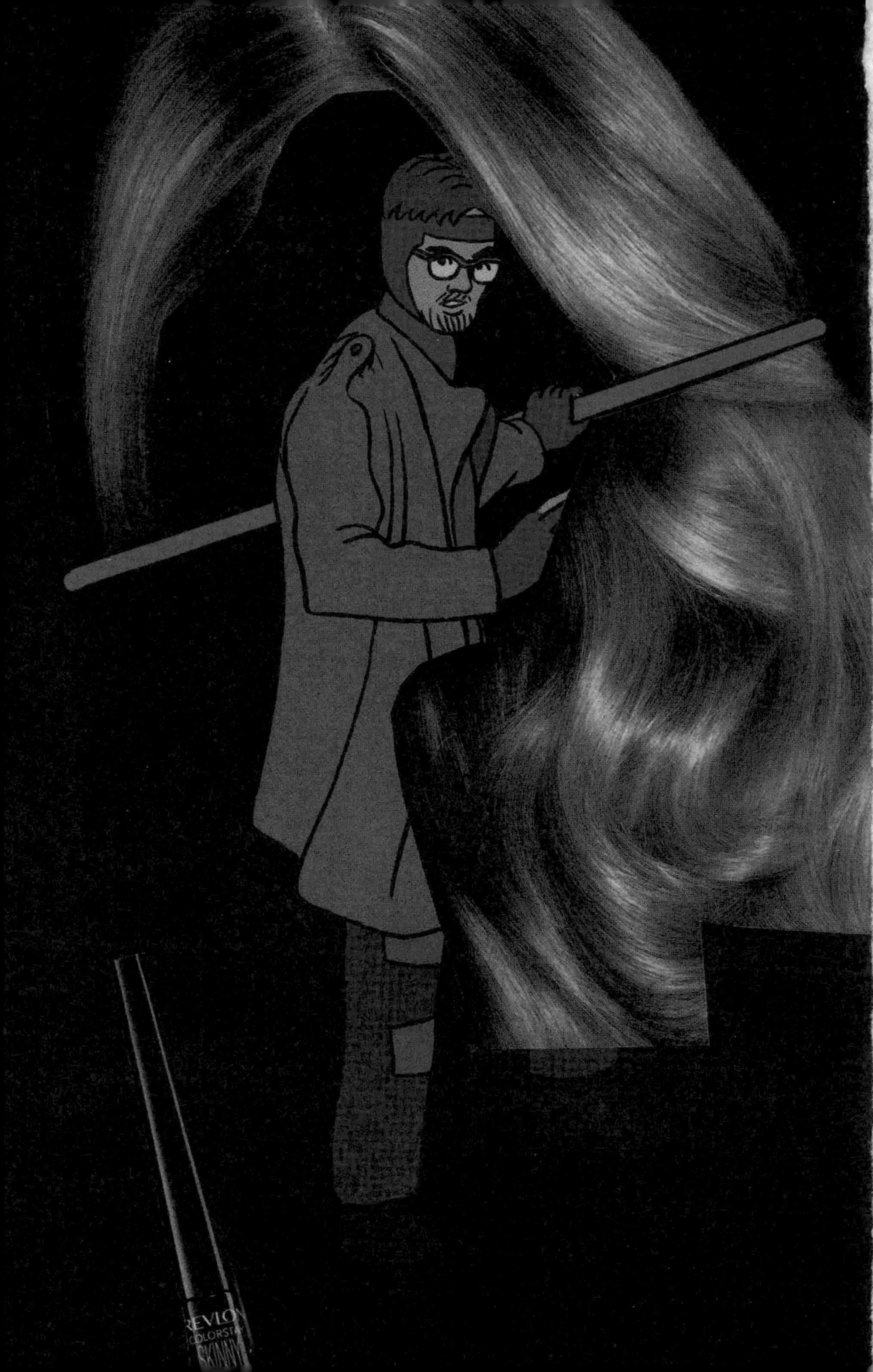
REVLON

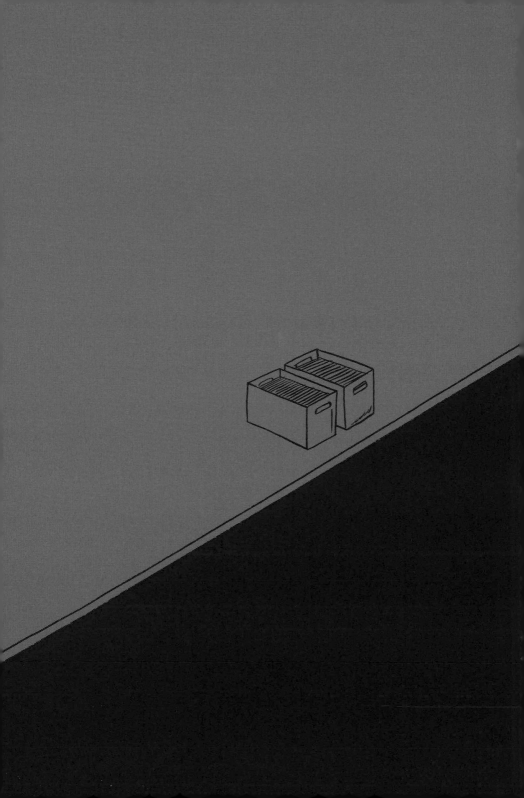